Exploring Cape Hatteras and Cape Lookout National Seashores

Help Us Keep This Guide Up to Date

Every effort has been made by the authors and editors to make this guide as accurate and useful as possible. However, many things can change after a guide is published—trails are rerouted, regulations change, techniques evolve, facilities come under new management, etc.

We would love to hear from you concerning your experiences with this guide and how you feel it could be improved and kept up to date. While we may not be able to respond to all comments and suggestions, we'll take them to heart and we'll also make certain to share them with the author. Please send your comments and suggestions to the following address:

The Globe Pequot Press
Reader Response/Editorial Department
P.O. Box 480
Guilford, CT 06437

Or you may e-mail us at:
editorial@GlobePequot.com

Thanks for your input, and happy travels!

A FALCON GUIDE®

Exploring Cape Hatteras and Cape Lookout National Seashores

Molly Perkins Harrison

FALCON®

GUILFORD, CONNECTICUT
HELENA, MONTANA

AN IMPRINT OF THE GLOBE PEQUOT PRESS

A FALCON GUIDE®

Text design: Nancy Freeborn
Photo credits: All photos are by the author unless otherwise noted.
Maps by Rusty Nelson © The Globe Pequot Press

Library of Congress Cataloging-in-Publication Data

Harrison, Molly Perkins
Exploring Cape Hatteras and Cape Lookout National Seashores/Molly Perkins Harrison.–1st ed.
p. cm–(A Falcon Guide)
Includes bibliographical references and index.
ISBN 0-7627-2609-1
1. Cape Hatteras National Seashore (N.C.)–Guidebooks. 2. Cape Lookout National Seashore (N. C.)–Guidebooks. I. Title II. Series.

GV191.42.N72H37 2003
796'.09756175–dc21

2003048318

Manufactured in the United States of America
First Edition/First Printing

Contents

Cape Hatteras and Cape Lookout National Seashores

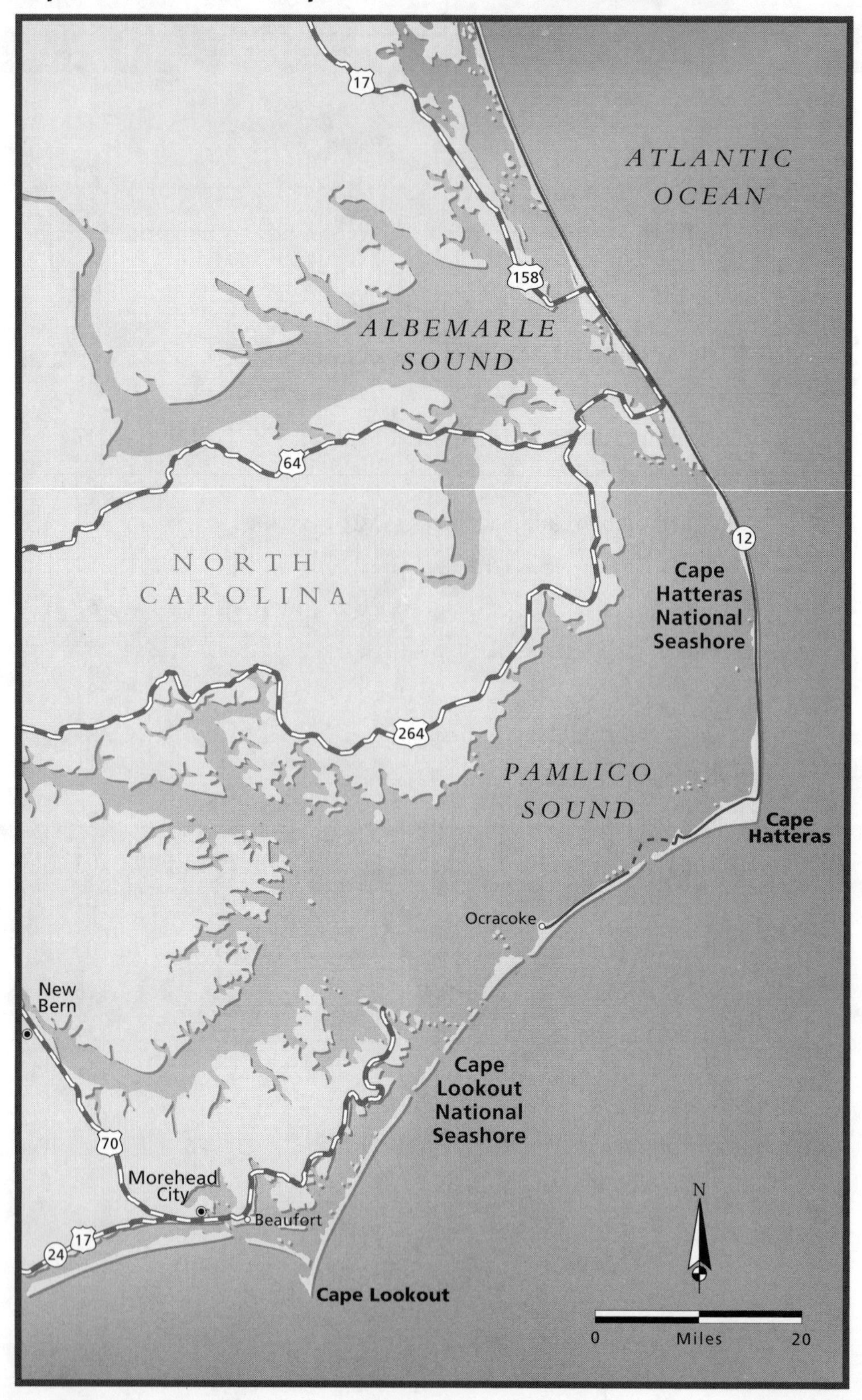

Directory of Maps

Acknowledgments

First and foremost, thanks go to all of the inspired people who worked to establish North Carolina's two national seashores. Without them, 128 miles of our coastline would be a bleak stretch of development instead of open stretches of paradise and there would be no need for this book.

Thanks to editor Erin Turner for thinking of me to write this book and for being such a genuinely supportive and kind person, and to editors Gillian Belnap and Cary Hull for their inexhaustible attention to detail.

So many people helped me gather the information I needed to write this book. Thanks to the National Park Service rangers at Cape Hatteras National Seashore, namely Toni Dufficy and Marcia Lyons. Thanks also to the National Park Service rangers at Cape Lookout National Seashore, including Wouter Ketel, Karen Duggan, and Jeff Cordes. Cape Lookout Ranger Sue Stuska and Carolyn Mason of the Foundation for the Shackleford Banks Horses deserve great thanks for being my tour guides of Shackleford Banks and introducing me to the ways of wild horses. Thanks also to the Outer Banks History Center staff, Brian Patteson, Pat Moore, Trip Forman, Bubba Catoe, Mary Jo Friedman, Sarah Gardner, Brian Horsley, Bonnie Strausser, Christian Pruitt, and the countless people who provide information for me.

I am grateful to everyone, many more than are listed here, who shared his or her knowledge with me and who reviewed drafts of various chapters. I can't give enough thanks to Ken DeBarth, Ruth Fordon, Karen Jones, and Kathleen Brehony of Island Path Workshops and Jones/Brehony Seminars for my inspiring mid-book writers' retreat in Ocracoke.

Love and gratitude to my husband, Patrick, for being patient about my affair with the computer, and to my parents, Ed and Nan Perkins, for their unwavering enthusiasm and support.

Preface

"If, then, we would indeed restore mankind . . . let us first be as simple and well as Nature ourselves, dispel the clouds which hang over our own brows, and take up a little life into our pores."

—HENRY DAVID THOREAU

Connecting with nature and the rhythms of the natural world is an essential part of living. Somewhere within ourselves, we all crave freedom from our material possessions and hectic schedules. We crave the silence and the grace of natural surroundings. When we can let go of our everyday duties and worries and focus on the flow of nature, happiness and peace are found in the fluttering of bird wings or the shape of a wave.

For me, this is the appeal of North Carolina's two neighboring national seashores, Cape Hatteras National Seashore and Cape Lookout National Seashore. These two protected areas of the North Carolina coast provide over 100 miles of pure and simple nature, places where it's easy to "take up a little life into our pores."

In many coastal areas, you have to look hard to find nature; it's often tucked away, secondary to the dwellings and businesses that accommodate vacationers, so that if you want to find it, you have to seek it out. Here, at these national seashores, nature steps up to greet you. Nature invites you outdoors to play, and it's hard to turn her down. These are some of the most beautiful, unaffected coastal areas you'll see on the East Coast.

Cape Hatteras National Seashore and Cape Lookout National Seashore are places for people who love the outdoors and have a fire in their hearts for the natural world. The people who love these areas the most are those who love outdoor activity, whether it's as simple as strolling on the beach or as vigorous as paddling a surfboard out beyond the breakers.

The two national seashores are similar in many ways, yet on the whole they are vastly different. Both consist of barrier islands that are havens for wildlife. Both offer miles and miles of undeveloped land, including ocean and sound shores, estuaries, marshlands, and maritime forests. Both offer outdoor recreation opportunities beyond belief. Both are forever protected from development by the National Park Service. But their similarities end there.

Cape Hatteras National Seashore is the more accessible of the two seashore parks. It occupies three islands—Bodie, Hatteras, and Ocracoke—

which are also occupied by humans. Eight quasi-modern villages dot the islands, and the Cape Hatteras National Seashore runs in fits and starts between them. Between the villages are vast stretches of uninhabited coastal property.

More than three million people visit Cape Hatteras National Seashore every year, and the villages offer many goods and services to accommodate them. The seashore, therefore, offers a mix of wild nature and human comforts, like campgrounds with showers and toilets, plus nearby hotels, restaurants, water sports outfitters, and shops. All the necessities are within easy reach, yet you can still have a quality outdoor experience that is vastly different than urban life.

The 55-mile-long Cape Lookout National Seashore, on the other hand, is rugged, wild, and isolated, with hardly any comforts at all. It is difficult to get to, and therein lies its appeal for many people. At this national seashore, nature takes its course with little human intervention. In fact, Cape Lookout National Seashore was created to be the antithesis of Cape Hatteras National Seashore. When it became apparent that human recreation and natural preservation were always going to conflict at Cape Hatteras National Seashore, Cape Lookout National Seashore was created with the main goal of environmental preservation. Human visitation and recreation are secondary to nature. At Cape Lookout National Seashore, nature takes its course with little human intervention. There is no paved road, no campground, not even a drink machine. This is the place to dig your toes deep into nature—bugs, wind, sandspurs and all.

Most everyone who comes to North Carolina's national seashores develops tenderness in his or her heart for these salty places. Leaving the constant winds, expansive waters, and palette of brown and green land is always wistful. Though I live only a couple of miles from the Cape Hatteras National Seashore and visit it often, every day that I return I feel a wave of emotion, a combination of awe and wonder at its soul-stirring beauty, and relief and gratitude for the people who had enough sense to protect it.

This book is an outdoor recreation guide to these two great national seashores. The main focus is on outdoor activities, giving you an overview of what's available so you can get out and explore the shore. In order to fully appreciate your surroundings, it's important to have perspective about the natural and human history of the areas, and the Overview chapters will help you there.

Since the two national seashores are so different, this book is divided into two sections, one for each park. The book covers all the numerous outdoor

What to Do If You Find an Injured Animal

If you encountered an injured bird or a stranded turtle or marine mammal (dolphin, porpoise, whale, seal), would you know what to do? Your first instinct will probably be to help it, and the best way to do that is to not touch the animal. For one thing, touching marine mammals is illegal. You can be fined if you touch, harass, or disturb a marine mammal or sea turtle. Also, it's dangerous. A frightened animal, whether it's a gull or a seal, will try to defend itself from you.

- The most important thing to do is to call the proper authorities. For stranded or dead sea turtles or marine mammals within Cape Hatteras National Seashore, call a ranger at (252) 473–2111 or (252) 995–6968 or tell a ranger at a visitor center. At Cape Lookout National Seashore, the number is (252) 728–2250. For either seashore, you can call the Marine Mammal Stranding Network at (252) 728–8762. For birds or small wildlife, also call a park ranger. For injured birds or wildlife on Ocracoke Island only, call wildlife rehabilitator Elizabeth Hanrahan at (252) 928–7132. At Cape Lookout National Seashore, you can call the Outer Banks Wildlife Shelter at (252) 240–1200.
- If a marine mammal or turtle has orange paint on it anywhere, it has already been attended to by the proper authorities.
- Don't ignore it. Data collected from these animals helps researchers determine factors of the animal's life and death. Researchers can also learn a lot about the animal's migration patterns and habits.

activities—swimming, paddling, diving, catching wind and waves, hiking, bird- and wildlife-watching, biking, horseback riding, fishing, and more—plus everything you will need to make those activities possible. You'll also find information on camping, finding a hotel, food, or medical care; and attractions to visit.

Enjoy the national seashores, respect nature, and leave as little trace as possible. May you feel the peace of wild things and be blown by winds of every direction while you're here.

Don't Feed the Wildlife

Feeding wildlife is harmful to the animals and can cause them to become a nuisance. Once animals learn that people are a source of food, they will forever be begging.

The animals people most often feed are seagulls, but this can lead to annoying behavior. Greedy gulls have been known to raid many a picnic, taking food right out of human hands. Raccoons have been known to raid coolers and tents. The Shackleford horses are used to a very natural diet; giving them treats, even apples, can make them sick.

There are several reasons not to feed wildlife:

- Feeding animals causes them to lose their fear of humans. When this happens the animals feel free to raid tents, backpacks, and food and trash bags.
- Feeding wild animals encourages them to beg and hang around humans, leaving their waste in human living areas.
- Wild animals are dangerous. They may bite or scratch humans to get food or when food is not available.
- Animals, including seagulls, that become dependent on humans for food may lose their desire to find their own food. In the off-season when visitation is down, they may starve to death.
- Once an animal has learned that it can get food from humans, it will never again behave in its natural way. It will always look to humans for easy food.
- Wild animals and birds have dietary requirements that human foods cannot meet. For example, gulls require high-protein diets, not white bread and processed snack foods.

Never intentionally feed wild animals. Secure all food in a cooler or tightly sealed bag and keep it out of sight. At night, put food and coolers in a vehicle or under a locked lid. (Raccoons can open just about anything.) Dispose of all trash, food scraps, wrappers, napkins, or anything with a food smell in a tightly sealed bag and keep it out of reach of raccoons. Take all trash with you when you leave the islands. Throw all unused bait into the ocean and take any leftover chunks of bait off of fish hooks.

The Basics

While Cape Hatteras and Cape Lookout are two very different national seashores, they do have some things in common. Here are some things to keep in mind while you're at either one.

Weather

Weather-watching is a veritable Outer Banks pastime, popular here because the weather really is fascinating when you're floating on an island. The wind picks up, stops, and changes directions on a whim, stirring up the water or flattening it out like a pond. You can see the dark clouds of storms coming from miles away over the water, hearing their rumbles of thunder long before you feel the first drop of rain. The flat, unobstructed landscape allows you to see it raining a mile away while you stand dry. Spiraling waterspouts can be seen dancing over the water. Lightning crackles in the wide-open sky. Fog settles in on winter mornings. Skies full of clouds paint artistic sunrises and sunsets. And on bright sunny days, the sky and sea merge into one at the horizon.

There can't possibly be as many armchair meteorologists anywhere else as there are on the Outer Banks. This is partly because so many people here make their living outside—commercial fishing, house construction, ferry operating, boat building, landscaping, water—sports instruction, etc.—and because so many people play outside—swimming, surfing, kiting, fishing, etc. Many an Outer Banks surfer or construction worker can carry on a lengthy discourse on isobars and low-pressure systems.

Outer Banks weather is mild, to say the least. Summers are hot but not unbearable, averaging around 84˚F. in July and August, with a constant wind averaging 12 miles per hour to cool things off. Fall temperatures are the most delicious—averaging 71˚F. in October and 63˚F. in November. Winter temperatures (38˚F. to 52˚F. from December through March) are mild compared to other places at this same latitude, mainly because the Gulf Stream waters warm the island air. Those constant winds, which pick up speed a little in the winter, bring an unwelcome chill factor, however. Snow is extremely rare on the Outer Banks. Spring warms up quickly, getting up to 66˚F. in April and 74˚F. in May.

OUTER BANKS AVERAGES

Month	Temperature Range	Average Water Temperature
January	38–52°F.	49°F.
February	38–53	46
March	43–58	46
April	51–66	58–60
May	60–74	68
June	68–80	72–75
July	72–84	76–79
August	72–83	76–79
September	68–79	75–78
October	58–71	68–72
November	49–63	58
December	40–55	55

As you can see, the water is warmest from June through October. The water temperatures listed here are for the Cape Hatteras National Seashore area; the water at Cape Lookout National Seashore will be a few degrees warmer than the temperatures listed here.

Thunderstorms brew up quickly on the banks in the summer months. Always check weather reports when you plan on being outdoors for a long period of time, especially if you are boating or kayaking offshore. Check the Weather Channel or listen to a local radio station, all of which broadcast the weather report often. You can also use a NOAA weather radio tuned to 162.475 mhz.

At Cape Lookout National Seashore, it's a good idea to always have a battery-powered weather radio or cell phone with you and check weather forecasts regularly. There is little shelter on the islands and because of the narrow and flat nature of the land, overwash and flooding are common. If you know bad weather is approaching, don't wait until the last minute to leave the islands. Call your ferry service as soon as possible, because ferries may not be able to run as weather conditions worsen. If you're in a private boat, make a decision whether it is safe to cross. Do not attempt to cross the sound during a thunderstorm or heavy winds and seas. Listen to marine forecasts for small-craft advisories.

When you're outdoors, always watch the skies closely for any change in cloud coverage and look for change in wind direction or a drop in temperature, which can indicate an oncoming storm. Lightning strikes do happen on the Outer Banks every year, sometimes just because humans are the tallest things on the beach. Boaters should be especially cautious about lightning and sudden winds, which can change the mood of the water in a hurry. Get to shore as quickly as you can if you see a storm coming.

Nor'easters are notoriously nasty storms that pummel the coast with chilly northeast winds for days and days in a row. Nor'easters most often occur in fall, winter, and spring. By the way, winds from the northeast are typically cooler and make the air cooler, while winds from the southwest are warm and balmy. The average winds on the Outer Banks range from 11 to 15 miles per hour. Northeast and southwest are the predominant winds. Northeast winds tend to be stronger in the morning and die out as the day goes on, while southwest winds tend to build over the course of the day. Occasional gale force winds blow steadily up to 35 miles per hour, and in storms gusts can blow harder than that. When winds are that strong, gale warnings are announced and small craft are advised to stay off the water.

The beaches of the Outer Banks are affected differently by winds because they face different directions. On the northern end of Cape Hatteras National Seashore, the beaches run north-south, so they are affected mostly by northeast winds. South of Cape Hatteras the beaches run northeast-southwest, so the predominant winds blow parallel to the beaches. South of Cape Lookout, at Shackleford, the beaches face due south and are affected more by southwest winds.

Hurricanes

Hurricanes are the most talked-about weather system on the East Coast, and for good reason. Thanks to the wonders of the Weather Channel, everyone with a TV has seen the incredible property damage and erosion that these storms can leave in their wakes.

The Atlantic hurricane season runs from June 1 to November 30, which just so happens to coincide with prime vacation and fishing season. If you're planning to come to either national seashore during this time, be aware that your vacation could be cut short at any time. Many house-rental companies in the Cape Hatteras area now offer hurricane insurance so that renters will not lose any money should a hurricane cancel their vacations. If you're making any reservations for activities or accommodations in advance, always be sure to ask about the hurricane cancellation policy beforehand.

A hurricane is a type of tropical cyclone—a general term for all circulating weather systems over tropical waters—which spins counterclockwise in the Northern Hemisphere. The storm starts as a tropical disturbance. As winds intensify, it becomes a tropical depression, an organized system of clouds and thunderstorms with a defined circulation and maximum sustained winds of 38 mph or less. From there it may form into a tropical storm, with maximum sustained winds of 39 to 73 mph. If winds reach 74 mph or higher, the storm becomes a hurricane.

The greatest threat to coastal life and property associated with a hurricane is storm surge, a wall of water that can sweep across the coast when the hurricane makes landfall. Hurricane winds cause damage to structures and hurl debris like flying missiles. Heavy rains and floods are also a threat with hurricanes, especially the slow-moving ones that sit over an area for an extended amount of time. Tornadoes are often spawned by hurricanes as they approach land. Hurricanes are classified in categories from 1 to 5, with 5 being the worst. Category 1 storms have winds ranging from 74 to 85 mph and a storm surge of 4 to 5 feet. Category 5 storms have winds over 156 mph and a storm surge of 19 or more feet.

If a hurricane is seriously threatening either national seashore or Dare, Hyde, and Carteret counties officials will announce mandatory evacuations. Cape Lookout National Seashore and Ocracoke Island are evacuated earlier than other areas because of the logistics of getting everyone off the islands via ferries. When weather conditions worsen, ferries will not be able to operate. Mandatory evacuations mean that everyone must leave the islands.

If the National Weather Service issues a Hurricane Watch, it means that hurricane conditions are a real possibility in the area. When a watch is issued, fill your car with gas, review evacuation plans, listen to the radio, stock up on water and food, and make sure you have some cash. If it issues a Hurricane Warning, it means that a hurricane is expected within 24 hours and it's time to start precautionary measures (like getting the heck out of Dodge). Don't wait until the last minute to evacuate. Head inland and stay with friends or relatives or at a motel or a shelter. Always notify an out-of-the-area family member of your evacuation plans.

All watch, warning, and evacuation information will be repeatedly broadcast on local radio stations.

Evacuation routes off Hatteras Island are marked with blue signs. Really, there is just one way out—N.C. Highway 12. Then it's U.S. Highway 64 or U.S. Highway 158 to the mainland. To get off Ocracoke Island, leave as early as possible on one of the ferries. It takes many hours for an organized evacuation; expect traffic jams.

During an evacuation at Cape Lookout National Seashore, rangers will search the islands for any visitors and help them with their ferry accommodations. They start the evacuation process during Hurricane Watches. People are given evacuation priority over vehicles, but the ferry operators work to get as many vehicles off the islands as they can. During a Hurricane Warning, rangers go home and ferry operations cease, unless it is an absolute emergency.

More information about emergency procedures can be obtained at Dare County Emergency Management at (252) 473–3355 or www.co.dare.nc.us; Hyde County Offices at (252) 928–1071; or Carteret County Emergency Management at (252) 728–8470.

Staying Safe

Heat and Sun: Here in the South, you have to think about not only air temperature but also humidity. The combination of high temperatures and high humidity can be dangerous. Too much time outdoors on these overly hot days can lead to heat cramps, heat exhaustion, and heat stroke. Try to limit your time outdoors in the hottest part of the day (10:00 A.M. to 2:00 P.M.) on days of high heat and humidity, and be sure to drink plenty of water and wear sunscreen. Sunscreen is needed even on cloudy days because of the reflection of the sun's rays. You'll always want to have flip-flops or sandals to wear in the summer because the pavement and sand can get dangerously hot in the sun.

Keeping Pets Safe: Dogs don't have sweat glands, so they don't have an efficient way to cool themselves. This makes it really important to keep them off the beach in the hottest part of the day. Never leave a dog in a hot car, even with the windows open. Signs of heat exhaustion/heat stroke in dogs are: excessive panting, purple gums, vomiting, diarrhea, lack of urine production, weakness, disorientation, or collapse. If your dog has any of these symptoms, hose it down with cool water, especially on the belly, and seek veterinary attention.

On the beach or sound, keep your dog from drinking salt water by providing it with lots of cool fresh water. Saltwater ingestion can result in vomiting, severe diarrhea, and dehydration. Also watch what your dog eats on the beach. Rotten fish, fish bones, dead seagulls, fish hooks with a little scrap of bait attached—all of these things are dangerous when ingested. A dog's pads are very sensitive to hot pavement and sand. Carry your dog across very hot surfaces, if possible. If the pads get burned, clean them and apply antibiotic cream or aloe. Another bane to dog pads is sandspurs and cactuses. If your dog suddenly starts limping, it probably has a sandspur that you'll need to get out.

Bugs: The pesky bugs you might encounter in the national seashores include mosquitoes, ticks, biting flies, and bees. Always bring insect repellent with you. Mosquitoes are notorious on the islands in summer and fall. The most mosquitoes I have ever seen in my life—an actual black cloud of them—were at Portsmouth Village on a cool October day. I think I heard the faint sound of mosquitoes laughing as I applied Avon's Skin So Soft. Luckily,

Help Protect Endangered Sea Turtles

Loggerhead, Atlantic leatherback, Atlantic green, Kemp's ridley, and Atlantic hawksbill sea turtles are found in the waters off Cape Hatteras and Cape Lookout National Seashores. All of these are designated as endangered or threatened under the U.S. Endangered Species Act. These turtles, which are among the largest living reptiles, are cold-blooded, breathe air, and lay their eggs on land. As adults, female sea turtles return to the same beaches where they hatched to lay their eggs.

The number of sea turtles worldwide has declined. North Carolina has the second-highest rate of sea turtle mortality (Texas is first) of all U.S. coastal states. In 2000, 332 turtles were stranded on Cape Hatteras National Seashore, due in part to such natural causes as disease and cold stunning, which is caused by prolonged cold weather and low sea water temperatures. But human interaction accounts for more than a third of turtle deaths in North Carolina. Human activities affect sea turtles from the time they are only eggs buried in the sand throughout their whole lives as grown adults swimming in the ocean. Scientists estimate that only one out of 1,000 hatchlings makes it to adulthood. This is because their nesting areas—beaches—are highly used by humans in nesting season, and because human impacts in the ocean—dredging, commercial fishing, boating, and littering—affect the turtles.

- Stay out of posted turtle nest enclosures. All known sea turtle nest sites are posted for the protection of the eggs.
- Obey leash laws. Dogs are attracted to nesting sites and can possibly dig up a buried nest.
- Minimize beachfront lighting by turning off, shielding, or redirecting lights away from the beach. Close blinds and drapes in oceanfront rooms at night to keep the light from reaching the beach. Adult females and hatchlings are disturbed and disoriented by artificial light.
- Remove recreational equipment, umbrellas, chairs, etc. from the beach at night. These can deter turtles' nesting attempts and prevent hatchlings from reaching the ocean.
- Do not build beach bonfires during nesting season. Sea turtles are attracted to the light.
- If you dig a hole in the sand, fill it back up before you leave the beach so a turtle won't fall into it.
- If you encounter a sea turtle on the beach at night, remain quiet, still, and at a distance.

- Leave the tracks left by turtles undisturbed. Researchers use tracks to identify species and nesting sites and to mark the sites for protection.
- Do not litter. Turtles mistake plastic bags, balloons, and styrofoam for jellyfish, their favorite food. Ingested trash blocks their intestines.
- When boating, stay alert and avoid sea turtles if you see them. Propeller and collision impacts result in injury and death of many turtles.

a kind visitor shared some of her powerful DEET-based spray. Mosquitoes, which are also pretty bad at the Hatteras campgrounds, are worse after a rain or flooding and at dawn and dusk. Ticks are found in the seashores as well, only in wooded or thick scrub areas. Be sure to check yourself and pets daily for ticks. Remove them and disinfect the bite area.

Biting flies can be the most annoying of island pests. Greenheads, deerflies, blackflies, and sand flies are common on the seashores from June through August, usually when the wind is mild, and their bites are painful. Biting flies are active only during daylight hours. To repel mosquitoes, ticks, and biting flies, use a DEET- or citronella-based repellent. Spray it on hats and clothes as well. If possible, wear long pants, shoes, and socks. Light-colored clothes seem to attract fewer bugs than dark colors. Use a tent with mosquito netting. And, as Mama always said, don't scratch those bites!

Poison Ivy: Always look out for poison ivy when hiking or walking in thickly vegetated areas. If you don't know what the plant looks like, keep this old adage in mind: Leaves of Three, Let it Be.

Snakes: Many snakes are found around Cape Hatteras National Seashore and Pea Island National Wildlife Refuge: corn snake, black racer, rat snake, eastern hognose snake, eastern king snake, Carolina salt marsh snake, rough green snake, brown snake, and others. Only two are poisonous, the eastern cottonmouth (aka water moccasin) and the canebrake rattlesnake. There are no poisonous snakes on Ocracoke Island or at Cape Lookout National Seashore.

The eastern cottonmouth is found around freshwater wetlands, so the only places you'll encounter it are around Buxton Woods in Buxton and Frisco and in Pea Island National Wildlife Refuge. The canebrake rattlesnake is found around Buxton and Frisco and on Bodie Island, though it is very rare. Both of these poisonous snakes are heavy-bodied with triangular-shaped heads and elliptical eye slits. Their colors are dark. The cottonmouth is olive to pine-straw colored with black banding, but it can get very dark when molting. The rattlesnake is sandy colored with dark bands, a rust color stripe down the back and, of course, rattles.

Always be aware of your surroundings. Stay on paths and always be where you can see your feet. Don't try to kill snakes; ironically, this is the leading cause of snakebites. It is illegal to kill snakes in the national seashore, and besides, there are many more harmless snakes than poisonous snakes. If you see a snake, slowly back away. In the unlikely event that you are bitten by a snake, stay calm and seek medical attention. Try to remember what the snake looked like so you can describe it to someone.

Wildlife: Do not feed, disturb, or harass wildlife. It is illegal to touch, feed, take anything, or cause a change in a wild animal's behavior. Feeding wildlife, including wild horses, upsets the natural balance of the ecosystem and exposes you to potentially dangerous animals. Disturbing and harassing wildlife includes letting your dog chase birds or dig up turtle nests, which is why the leash law is enforced. Remember, the national seashores were provided as much for the rest and relaxation of wildlife as for the humans.

Swimming Safety

Swimming in the Atlantic Ocean is much different than swimming in a lake or a pool, especially on barrier islands like the Outer Banks. The waves are incredibly strong due to nearshore drop-offs and troughs that make them break with more power and force. There also is the danger of riptides and undertows. Unsure swimmers should wear flotation vests, even if they're just wading in the surf. Waves can sweep you off your feet in an instant. Boogie boards or rafts, unless they are leashed to your ankle, are not dependable flotation devices if you can't swim. In 2002 a nonswimmer drowned at Hatteras Island when his Boogie board washed away with a wave.

Swimming Safety Tips:

- Don't swim near inlets where the currents are dangerous.
- Don't swim alone and never swim at night.
- Supervise children at all times. Never look away even for a minute.
- Don't swim during thunderstorms due to lightning.
- Wear a flotation device if you're not a strong swimmer.
- Don't swim near surfers or fishermen.

Rip Currents: Rip currents form due to underwater sandbars that make a trough between the bar and the beach. When the sandbar breaks, trapped water funnels out to sea through the break, forming a sweeping river of water that flows out to sea. People can get caught in these strong currents and be swept rapidly away from the shore. If this happens to you, the most important thing to do is to stay calm and *do not try to swim against the current.* It will only wear you down. Instead, swim parallel to the shore, across the current. Then, work your way back to shore at an angle.

Undertow: When a wave breaks and the water runs back out to sea, an undertow is created. The undertow is usually just a gentle feeling of water moving away from the shore, but sometimes it can be strong enough to wash you off your feet and away from shore. If you're carried out, don't resist or panic. The undertow will subside after a few yards. The next wave will push you back toward shore. Don't swim if the undertow is excessive.

Sharks: Shark attacks are very rare. There have been fewer than twenty shark attacks in North Carolina waters in the last 300 years. But they do occur from time to time, so to lessen your chances of attack, keep these tips in mind: Do not swim alone; avoid being in the water at dawn or during twilight when sharks are most active; don't wear bright clothing or reflective jewelry; avoid swimming if you're bleeding or menstruating; don't thrash about wildly; and don't swim near fishermen, piers, or inlets.

Jellyfish: Jellyfish float on the surface of the water in both the sound and the ocean. Some sting only slightly, but others cause severe pain. Clear jellyfish typically don't sting, but jellyfish with red or bluish tints should be avoided. If you're stung by a jellyfish, apply vinegar or meat tenderizer to the area. Park rangers and lifeguards can assist with jellyfish stings. Don't rub the area since that can force the toxins deeper into your skin. The Portuguese man-of-war, a clear balloon with long bluish tentacles, inflicts the most serious stings. Seek medical attention for its stings.

Stingrays: Stingrays have a sharp spine on the base of their tails that can inflict wounds if you step on one. Stingray punctures usually happen when people are wading in the surf or trying to remove a stingray from a fishing hook. If you do get injured, wash the area and clean the wound and soak the wound in hot water if possible. Seek medical attention.

NPS Beach Driving Rules

Just because beach driving is allowed doesn't mean you can take your Camry anywhere you please. Beach driving is for four-wheel-drive vehicles only, including SUVs, trucks, and ATVs, and it's allowed only in some areas of Cape Hatteras National Seashore. Cape Lookout allows beach driving everywhere except bird- and turtle-closure areas. Beach driving is quite tricky because the sand is very soft. Cars get stuck in the sand all the time, and it's not always easy to get them out.

- All vehicles must be street legal, with all plates, tags, and inspection stickers.
- The driver must have a valid driver's license.
- Maximum speed is 25 mph.
- All regulations that apply to streets and highways of the state also apply to the beach. This includes laws against driving under the influence of alcohol. Open alcohol containers are not allowed in vehicles.
- Beach pedestrians always have the right-of-way.
- Driving or parking on the dunes or vegetation is prohibited. Access the beach only from designated numbered ramps. Driving on the dunes elsewhere is extremely destructive.
- Don't drive in areas that are posted with no vehicles signs. These areas are closed to protect sea turtles, shorebirds, and habitat. Do not walk in these areas either.

Beach Driving Tips

- The possibility of getting stuck in the sand is great, even in a four-wheel-drive vehicle. If possible, bring these items on your beach-driving sojourns: shovel, tire pressure gauge, spare tire, tow rope (at least 14 feet long), flashlight, and bumper jack (with sturdy board to support jack). Park rangers might assist you, but they are not permitted to pull or tow other vehicles. They can recommend commercial towing services, which are limited and costly. Oftentimes a friendly beach driver will stop to give you a tow, but you can't always count on this.
- Many people recommend lowering the pressure in all tires to 20–25 pounds; the softer the sand, the lower the pressure needed for better flotation on the sand. Reinflate tires to normal pressure as soon as possible after leaving the beach, because low tire pressure can affect vehicle braking and maneuverability on paved roads.
- Go slow and try to maintain a steady pace. If your wheels start to spin, back up in your tracks for several car lengths. Accelerate slowly as you move forward.
- Allow an extra-wide berth for other cars and people.
- Try to follow in the tracks of cars that were there before you. Areas that don't have tracks have been avoided for good reasons. Try to avoid areas with reddish-colored sand and lots of shell bits, which can indicate soft, mushy areas.

Help Protect the Piping Plover

The piping plover is a threatened bird species that nests and breeds at Cape Hatteras and Cape Lookout National Seashores. The birds are threatened because of lack of suitable habitat (except at Cape Lookout), caused by coastal development and erosion, pollution and human recreation in their nesting areas, nonnative predators (cats, raccoons, mink), and other factors.

Because the tiny, pale-colored piping plover is threatened with extinction, both seashores manage their lands to protect it. Its preferred habitat is beach and sand-flats with little vegetation and dune development, which explains why it is attracted to both national seashores, Cape Lookout especially. Cape Lookout National Seashore is home to two-thirds to three-quarters of the state's piping plover nests. Actually, the birds do not bother with building a nest. Instead, they lay their eggs directly on the sand. The eggs and chicks are sand-colored, which camouflages them from predators but makes them vulnerable to inadvertent disturbances. They are often stepped on or crushed by walkers, vehicles, or dogs. Fledgling chicks have been known to hide in vehicle tracks, obviously susceptible to impending doom.

To protect these birds, as well as other beach-nesting species, the park service closes portions of the beach during nesting season (April through August). The areas are roped off and well marked with signs. Driving, walking, or letting pets into the closed areas is illegal. When the chicks are old enough to fly, the areas are opened.

To help protect the piping plover, stay out of closed areas. Don't leave garbage, food scraps, or leftover bait on the beach, because that attracts predators to the nesting sites to dine on trash as well as plover eggs and chicks. Keep dogs on a leash and out of closed areas.

- Driving through water is not wise. Make sure you know the depth of the water and the firmness of the sand beneath it before you drive through.
- Beach driving is highly corrosive to your vehicle because of all the salt you encounter. Wash your vehicle, including the underside, as soon as possible.

Cape Hatteras National Seashore

Cape Hatteras National Seashore

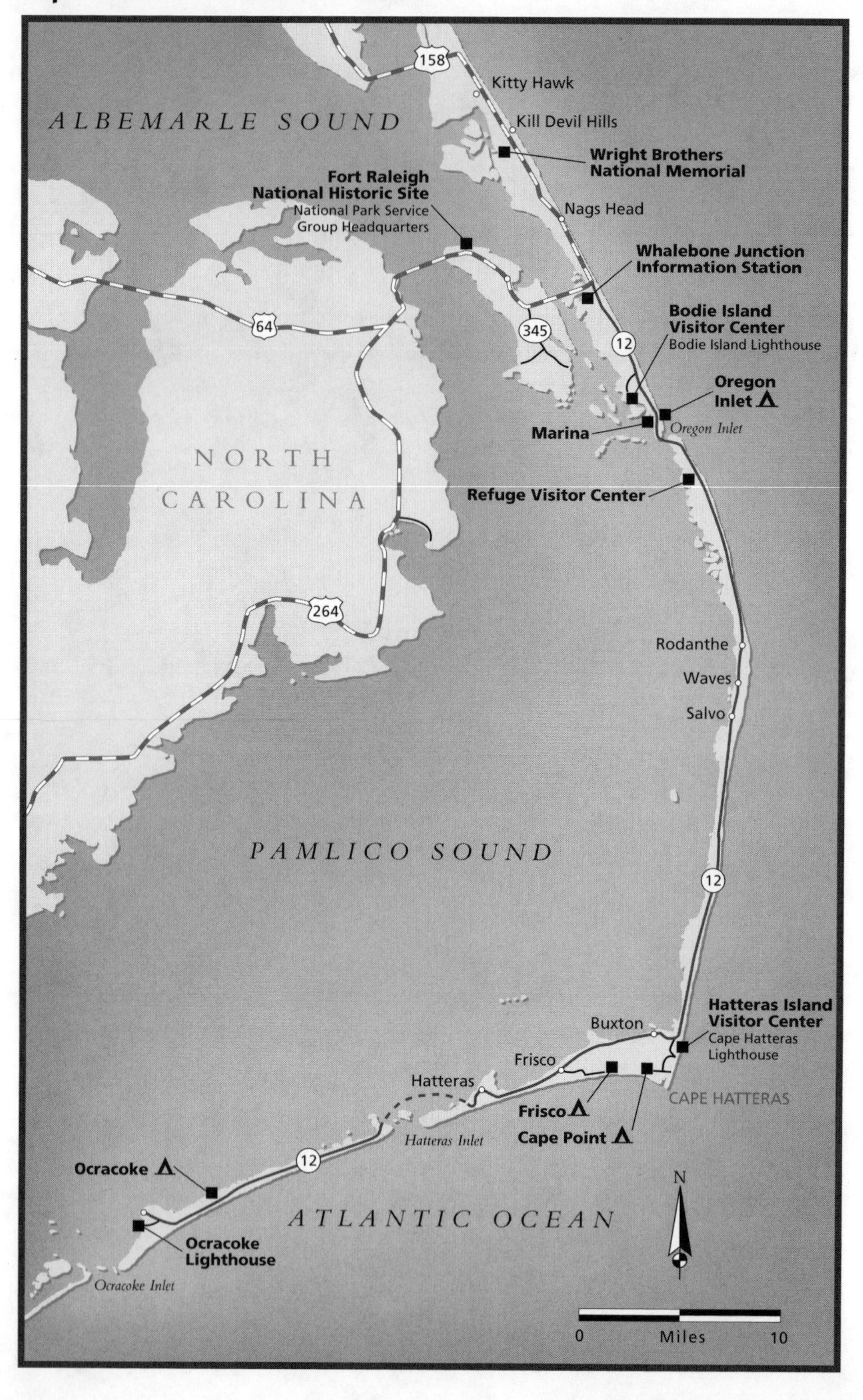

158
Kitty Hawk
ALBEMARLE SOUND
Kill Devil Hills
Wright Brothers
National Memorial
Fort Raleigh
National Historic Site
National Park Service
Group Headquarters
Nags Head
Whalebone Junction
Information Station
64
345
12
Bodie Island
Visitor Center
Bodie Island Lighthouse
Oregon
Inlet
Marina
Oregon Inlet
NORTH
CAROLINA
Refuge Visitor Center
264
Rodanthe
Waves
Salvo
PAMLICO SOUND
12
Hatteras Island
Visitor Center
Cape Hatteras
Lighthouse
Buxton
Frisco
Hatteras
CAPE HATTERAS
Frisco
Cape Point
Hatteras Inlet
Ocracoke
12
N
ATLANTIC OCEAN
Ocracoke
Lighthouse
Ocracoke Inlet
0
Miles
10

Overview

Stretched out on the easternmost edge of the continent, floating out at sea, are the ethereal sand islands of North Carolina's Outer Banks. Here, in the center, on Bodie, Hatteras, and Ocracoke Islands, lies the nation's first coastal preserve and park—Cape Hatteras National Seashore.

With sea and sound lapping at its borders, Cape Hatteras National Seashore is a world amidst water. The Atlantic's blue-green waves curl and crash toward shore, shaping the islands and spraying them with salt. The vast rippling waters of the Pamlico Sound stretch as far as the eye can see, changing color and character daily in response to light and wind. Here, where the waters are exponentially more immense than the land, it's mind-boggling that these tiny sandbars rising up out of the sea are even inhabitable.

Like a 72-mile piece of pulled taffy, Cape Hatteras National Seashore looks tenuous, its long islands stretched lean, almost to the breaking point in places. Their widths vary from about 200 feet to nearly 3 miles at the widest point. The barrier island land is low, averaging only 6 feet above sea level. Its few geographical standouts are flat sandy beach, a rising of man-made dunes, a few tall pockets of maritime forest, and spongy salt marsh. At first the landscape's palette of tans and browns may appear bleak, but the accents of blues, greens, and white, with sprinklings of color from flowers and birds, bring the lowlands to life. The most distinctive quality of the land at Cape Hatteras National Seashore is its openness. The vast, unbroken views are a respite for urban-weary eyes.

This combination of water and open space is what draws all life to these islands. More than three million people visit Cape Hatteras National Seashore every year, all of them enchanted with the idea of having some space of their own or lured by some aspect of the water, whether it's to be in it, on it, or around it.

But outdoor recreation is not the sole raison d'être of Cape Hatteras National Seashore. Waterfowl, shorebirds, sea turtles, marine mammals,

Cape Hatteras National Seashore. NORTH CAROLINA DIVISION OF TOURISM, FILM AND SPORTS DEVELOPMENT

marsh rabbits, amphibians, and many more birds and animals live in or visit these widespread lands and waters as well. The National Park Service, overseers of Cape Hatteras National Seashore, must carefully balance and preserve the fragile environment and its wildlife with the millions of annual visitors and their outdoor activities.

The Lay of the Land

Cape Hatteras National Seashore's northern border is at **Bodie Island,** which hasn't been an island since 1811 when Roanoke Inlet shoaled up. Bodie Island is part of the long barrier spit that contains Corolla, Duck, Southern Shores, Kitty Hawk, Kill Devil Hills, and Nags Head. Cape Hatteras National Seashore borders the town of Nags Head for its first few miles. The seashore's stretch of Bodie Island has no commercial development; its sole structures are the Bodie Island Lighthouse, Coquina Beach Access, Oregon Inlet Campground, Oregon Inlet Fishing Center, and a couple of private homes. The Roanoke Sound borders the island on the west. Bodie Island is nature-oriented, quiet, and peaceful. The nearest towns and villages to Bodie Island are Nags Head and Rodanthe-Waves-Salvo.

Across Oregon Inlet, the first 12 miles of **Hatteras Island** belong to the U.S. Fish and Wildlife Service's 5,915-acre Pea Island National Wildlife Refuge. The Cape Hatteras National Seashore includes all of the oceanfront south of Pea Island and all of the undeveloped land between the island's villages. This open space is what makes this island so captivating. Eighty-five percent of this slender barrier island is undeveloped federal property, where long reaches of rugged dunes, windblown brush, wide beaches, and soundside wetlands are forever protected from development. Rising up out of the island's desolate, unkempt landscape are seven unincorporated communities. From north to south, Rodanthe, Waves, Salvo, Avon, Buxton, Frisco, and Hatteras Village sit along the edges of N.C. Highway 12, the island's main artery. Hatteras Island is activity-oriented and lively, its villages accommodating modern vacations with outfitters, hotels, house rentals, and restaurants. Surfing, kiteboarding, fishing, and scuba diving subcultures thrive on these islands. Hatteras Island is best for vacationers who like an active, outdoorsy vacation.

Rodanthe, Waves, and **Salvo,** sometimes called the TriVillage area, lump together into one community, but the villages do have their distinctions. Rodanthe, legendary in surfing circles, is liveliest of the three, with several restaurants, a pier, a historic lifesaving station and museum, and an enormous amusement park. Waves is residential in character, and Salvo is true to its fishing roots; both have plenty of vacation housing and a couple of restaurants. These villages are definitely places for people who like a simple vacation.

Avon, historically known as Kinnakeet, serves the vacation community with the only chain grocery store, chain restaurant (Subway), and movie theater on the island. Seen from N.C. Highway 12, Avon is active with shopping centers and outfitters and a densely developed oceanfront. But the heart of Avon is the charming, historic residential area tucked back on the soundside.

Buxton is the hub of the island for both residents and visitors. The county schools and offices are located here, so many locals make this village their home. For vacationers, Buxton offers the most hotels of any village on the island, an NPS campground, numerous tackle shops, restaurants, and stores, not to mention the Cape Hatteras Lighthouse. Cape Hatteras, just east of Buxton, is a prime surf fishing location, so this village is often packed with anglers in the spring and fall. At this point, Hatteras Island bends sharply at an elbow-like cape, and the rest of the island faces southeast.

Frisco is mellow and sublime, partially tucked into the trees of Buxton Woods. Frisco is home to numerous vacation homes, some great art galleries, a Native American museum, a pier, a small nine-hole golf course, and a couple of restaurants. Frisco offers the perfect combination of things to do and the sense of private space to do it in. The National Park Service campground here is the most private of them all.

Hatteras Village is a classic fishing village, though the trappings of a tourist economy are slowly taking over. It has five marinas that offer inshore and offshore fishing charters. Hatteras Village is a dichotomous blend of historic homes and fishing culture mixed with a Holiday Inn Express, the fanciest restaurant on the island, oceanfront mega-homes, and a brand-new museum. Located at the southern end of the island, Hatteras Village is the place to catch the ferry to Ocracoke Island.

Across Hatteras Inlet is the 17-mile-long, southeast-facing **Ocracoke Island,** 14 miles of which are undeveloped land belonging to Cape Hatteras National Seashore. Those 14 miles are some of the most isolated beaches you'll see anywhere on the East Coast. The last 3 miles of the island are occupied by tiny **Ocracoke Village,** centered around the snug harbor of Silver Lake. Accessible only by ferry from Hatteras Island or the mainland, Ocracoke Island is remote and magical. It offers everything you need for a peaceful, family-oriented vacation, yet it's a timeless place that relieves visitors of their worries and troubles. Numerous restaurants, motels, bed-and-breakfast inns, campgrounds, quaint shops, and activities beckon travelers to Ocracoke. Like everywhere else on the Outer Banks, Ocracoke is packed with throngs of tourists in the summer and absolutely delightful at any other time.

Creation of Cape Hatteras National Seashore

The story of Cape Hatteras National Seashore's creation is remarkable, considering that it took twenty years for the park to come to fruition, overcoming war, oil booms, political schemes and local opposition.

In 1933 Frank Stick, an Outer Banks artist, real estate developer, and conservationist, made the first proposition for Cape Hatteras National Seashore in a local newspaper article. Stick proposed that the barrier islands from the Virginia border through Beaufort Inlet be preserved as a national park. He saw the park as an opportunity for conservation and at the same time a way to create revenue and employment for the locals in the wake of the Great Depression and a decline in commercial fishing. The public response was instantly favorable.

Stick worked tirelessly to gather support, including that of the National Park Service and numerous congressmen. He convinced two wealthy Pennsylvania brothers to donate their 2,700-acre Hatteras Island hunting lands as the nucleus of the park. In 1935 a state commission was formed to see the project through, and by 1937 the creation of Cape Hatteras National

Surf fishing is fun for all ages. NORTH CAROLINA DIVISION OF TOURISM, FILM AND SPORTS DEVELOPMENT

Seashore was authorized by Congress and enacted into law. But the park was still a long time coming.

For starters, World War II got in the way, and Stick was not available to push the park project. By 1945 the national seashore project was dead in the water, and land condemnation and acquisition was ceased. Landowners and local residents had changed their minds; they wanted a fair opportunity to make money off their land or to hunt on their land, plus there were oil and gas prospects in the area. For two years there was no work on the national seashore project at all, and in 1947 it was proposed that the project be abandoned for at least another two years. That same year, however, David Stick, Frank's son, moved back to the Outer Banks after attending college and working as a reporter. In 1949 both Sticks were stunned when the North Carolina General Assembly proposed to abandon the national seashore project altogether and reinstate the acquired land to the original owners. It was then that David Stick, with the help of his father, decided to try to revive the Cape Hatteras National Seashore because he knew that no one else would.

Though the National Park Service and the federal government were still interested in the park, the local residents had lost interest completely; even the local chambers of commerce came together to oppose the park for various political reasons. The locals were appeased, however, by the government's promise to build N.C. Highway 12, exclude the already established villages from the park, and reduce the proposed park size. First proposed to include all of North Carolina's barrier islands through Beaufort Inlet, the park was now reduced to three of the centrally located islands: a portion of Bodie Island plus Hatteras and Ocracoke Islands through Ocracoke Inlet. In 1952 the park got a major boost when the Mellon Foundation granted $618,000 to help create the first national seashore, with the state matching the grant.

On December 22, 1952, a special ceremony was held in which the state of North Carolina turned over all of its acquired lands to the National Park Service for the creation of the first national seashore in the United States. On January 12, 1953, the dream of Frank Stick—the Cape Hatteras National Seashore—was officially established. The National Park Service did not officially dedicate the Cape Hatteras National Seashore until April 24, 1958.

The Cape Hatteras National Seashore is a 72-mile-long, 30,000-acre park managed by the National Park Service Outer Banks Group. Though the park excludes the eight villages of Hatteras and Ocracoke Islands, it includes a 72-mile-long stretch of oceanfront from Bodie Island through Ocracoke Island. It features three lighthouses, two historic lifesaving stations, a herd of ponies, four campgrounds, beach accesses, nature trails, miles of undeveloped recreation area for humans, and preservation area for wildlife.

Geology and Formation of the Barrier Islands

As a part of the Outer Banks, Cape Hatteras National Seashore is made of sand. Everything on the Outer Banks, from soil and forest trees to homes and lighthouses, is supported only by a foundation of packed sand. There are two types of sand beneath our feet—siliceous, chunks of pulverized rock, and calcareous, flakes of pulverized seashells. The banks of sand take the brunt of the high-energy ocean waves and surges, protecting the coastal mainland.

It is the nature of sand to shift and move, to fly in the wind, and wash to and fro in the water. So what is it that holds these islands in place? Nothing, really. Grass, trees, and structures secure the top layers, but the sands of the Outer Banks are naturally moving and migrating. The Outer Banks are, as John Alexander and James Lazell state in their book *Ribbon of Sand*, "dynamic geological systems capable of moving, as winds and currents and violent storms dictate." Geologist Robert Dolan uncovered this fascinating information in 1959 by digging 140 holes all along the Outer Banks. Prior to that, scientists had varying notions about what kept the Outer Banks in place, with the general idea that barrier islands were supported by fixed coral reefs. The unstable nature of the Outer Banks, however, is an asset. If the barrier islands were fixed, if they did not shift and move with the elements, they would be under water.

Geologists disagree in detail about how the barrier islands of the Outer Banks were formed, but the general consensus is that their formation of the Outer Banks is directly linked to global warming and cooling and the subsequent change in sea levels over the past 100,000 years. During the ice ages, sea level was much lower because all of the water was frozen at the Earth's poles. About 19,000 years ago, the shoreline of what is now North America extended much farther, out beyond the continental shelf edge. North Carolina was a much larger land area with vast forests, marshes, and river valleys extending beyond the continental shelf. When sea level rose in a period of global warming, the shoreline retreated, the forest disappeared, and ridges of sand dunes began to form parallel to the beaches. As sea level continued to rise, the dune ridges breached and the area behind the ridges flooded, creating lagoons (sounds) between the ridges (now islands) and the mainland.

As the sea level rose, one would have expected the islands to submerge into the sea. But a complex system of geologic processes and weather-related forces caused the islands to migrate away from the sea to the west, rolling landward instead of sinking under the sea.

The Outer Banks are moving and will continue to move westward, toward the mainland, and laterally. But in *Ribbon of Sand*, Alexander and Lazell assure us that the Outer Banks will always exist. They will just move inland, naturally migrating as they are meant to do.

Since their formation, the Outer Banks have constantly changed. The islands migrate westward, the front (ocean) side eroding and the back (sound) side growing. They change shape constantly, and no two islands are alike. Inlets open, migrate south, and close, forming new islands or melding old ones together. Ocracoke Inlet was open in 1585 when European explorers visited the area, and it is still open today. Hatteras and Oregon Inlets opened during an 1846 hurricane. At least nine other inlets have opened and closed since maps of the area were first drawn.

Main Habitats of Cape Hatteras National Seashore

Ocean Beach: The Atlantic Ocean laps at the shores of Cape Hatteras National Seashore and commingles with the land in many ways. The forces of the ocean shape the islands, and its constant sprinkling of salt scorches the edges of trees and plants, allowing only the hardiest to survive. The sandy beach is stark and bare, but beneath the surface of the wet sand lives a variety of microscopic plants and animals, including mole crabs (aka sand fleas) and coquina crabs that burrow in the sand.

The rich life of the Atlantic Ocean is often visible on the shores of the seashore. Crab bodies, fish bones, starfish, shells, sand dollars, jellyfish, seaweeds, egg cases, and a variety of odd-looking creatures and objects are often found washed up on the beach—artifacts of the sea. Bottle-nosed dolphin are seen cavorting just offshore, and sea turtles emerge from the ocean to lay their eggs on land. On the dry part of the beach are the holes of ghost crabs, sand-colored goblins that scurry along the beach. You can also find plants here, such as sea rocket and the very rare sea beach amaranth. Birds use the beaches extensively. Such ground-nesting birds as terns, piping plovers, American oystercatchers, and black skimmers set up housekeeping on the beach and sand flats in summer. Shorebirds flit and hop around the tide line, dining on worms and other creatures that live in the sand, while great gulls, pelicans, and other birds fly overhead in search of fish and food.

Dunes and Shrub Zone: At the dune line the first major areas of vegetation appear. Salt-tolerant grasses, such as sea oats, saltmeadow hay, and American beach grass, stabilize the dunes. The sharp dune line along the Cape Hatteras National Seashore is not a natural one. It was built in the 1930s and planted with stabilizing grasses. (See Human Effects on Cape Hatteras National Seashore in this chapter.) Animals that might be found in the dunes include reptiles and snakes, small rodents, cottontail rabbits, possums, raccoons, and red fox. The small red fox is an inhabitant of Bodie and Hatteras Islands only, not Ocracoke. On the wider parts of the islands, between the dunes and the soundside marsh, is the shrub zone, farther from the ocean and therefore more diverse in plants and animals. It is covered with grasses, herbs, shrubs, and salt-stunted trees, including wax myrtle, yaupon, live oak, eastern red cedar, beach elder, prickly pear cactus, and sand spurs. These trees and shrubs are bent toward the southwest, gnarled by northeast winds and salt spray. Small animals roam these lands, including rodents, rabbits, possums, raccoon, snakes, and a variety of songbirds.

Maritime Forest: The area known as Buxton Woods is the oldest of the three remaining maritime forests on the Outer Banks (others are at Nags Head Woods and Shackleford Banks). It is one of the most distinctive regions of Cape Hatteras National Seashore. Buxton Woods spreads at the widest part of the island—from just north of Cape Point to the soundside of the island and down through Frisco, encompassing about 900 acres. The maritime forest may not strike you as odd at first, as it looks similar to forests of the mainland. But think about it: This forest snuggles up next to the ocean, and you can hear the waves rolling in at the shore from the midst of the forest if you stop and listen. The woods are predominantly loblolly pine, live oak, yaupon, bayberry, and red cedar, but there are also unique species tucked in here, like dwarf palmetto (Buxton Woods is the northernmost location of this plant), dogwood, Spanish moss, and ferns. Buxton Woods also houses an incredible freshwater pond known as Jennette's Sedge. A variety of wildlife—including mink, otter, nutria, turtles, squirrels, white-tailed deer, moles, snakes, frogs, skinks, moles, woodpeckers, thrush, and other birds—is drawn to this fresh water and forest. Buxton Woods appears to be a lush, healthy forest, but in actuality it is a stressed ecosystem due to its loose, sandy, nutrient-poor soil; low water table; human clearing; wind; and salt.

Salt Marshes: The salt marsh is the most productive of all the Outer Banks ecosystems. The marsh produces invisible but essential vegetation and adds nutrients to the marine food chain and provides habitat that nurtures young sea animals. The marsh is alive with worms, crustaceans, lichens and algae, and plants such as saltmarsh cordgrass, black needlerush, and salt-meadow hay. The vegetation depends on whether or not the marsh areas are flooded daily or only intermittently. Fiddler crabs burrow in the sulfurous mud; baitfish and minnows flit in the water; oysters, mussels, and clams conglomerate on the bottom; river otters, muskrats, and nutria wander around the shores, while snakes, especially the Carolina salt marsh snake, slither around in the mud. A variety of birds are always seen at the marsh, including herons, ibis, and egrets wading at the shore.

The Sound: Between the barrier islands and the mainland is a lagoon known as the Albemarle-Pamlico Sound system, which includes seven sounds. The Pamlico Sound backs up all of Cape Hatteras National Seashore, except for Bodie Island, which borders the Roanoke Sound. Several rivers, including the Neuse, Chowan, Roanoke, and Pamlico, feed the sound with fresh water, while the inlets from the Atlantic Ocean feed the sound with salt water, creating a brackish blend. The Albemarle-Pamlico system is the second-largest estuary in the United States (Chesapeake Bay is the largest). The sound includes approximately 3,000 square miles of estuary and 30,000 square miles of watershed and is on average only 13 feet deep, with the deepest point being 26 feet. The sound is an important fishery resource for shrimp, oysters, blue crabs, clams, flounder, striped bass, trout, drum, and other finfish. It also provides essential habitat for waterfowl and birds, like snow geese, tundra swan, ducks, herons, egrets, osprey, and pelicans.

Brief History of Bodie, Hatteras, and Ocracoke Islands

The earliest inhabitants of the barrier islands were Hatteras Indians living on Hatteras Island at a village they called Croatoan. Other native tribes used the Outer Banks as their hunting and fishing grounds, but the Hatteras Indians were the only tribe to live here, in the protected area of Buxton Woods. Indians first encountered European explorers in the sixteenth century, and it is believed that the Hatteras Indians had contact with the "Lost Colony" of

English settlers who disappeared from Roanoke Island in 1587. The only thread the English colonists left to their whereabouts was the word CROATOAN carved into a tree.

In the late 1600s settlers from mainland English colonies trickled to the Outer Banks, though the earliest report of an English land grant on Hatteras Island wasn't until 1711. Over the next hundred years, several enclaves of residents sprouted at Chicamacomico (present-day Rodanthe), Kinnakeet (Avon), the Cape Hatteras area, Ocracoke, and Portsmouth. The Hatteras Indians were gone by the early 1700s, due to intertribal warring and poverty. Ocracoke Inlet was becoming a major shipping lane for merchants bringing goods from the Atlantic Ocean and across the Pamlico Sound to the mainland. The merchant shipping brought many jobs for the villagers at Ocracoke and Portsmouth, but it also attracted pirates. Between 1713 and 1718 several notorious pirates roamed the banks. Surprisingly, the most legendary, Blackbeard, only pirated for two years until he was beheaded in 1718 by British Naval Lt. Robert Maynard.

The early residents of the Outer Banks made a living by hunting, farming, building boats, raising livestock, and fishing. Many residents of Ocracoke and Portsmouth were pilots who navigated ships through Ocracoke Inlet. By the late 1700s another occupation arose due to the proliferation of shipwrecks: Vendue masters were hired to take possession of and auction off the salvaged cargo of wrecked ships.

Bodie, Hatteras, and Ocracoke Islands played a role in the Revolutionary War. During the Revolution the trickiness of the Outer Banks inlets proved an asset to the colonists. The British found the inlets too treacherous to blockade and station for any length of time, so the Revolutionaries, who knew how to navigate them, were able to use the inlets to bring supplies to the mainland. Several sea battles ensued off the Outer Banks as the British endeavored to close off these supply routes.

Shipwrecks were so common at the Outer Banks, especially off Cape Hatteras at Diamond Shoals, that the federal government had to do something. In the late 1700s and early 1800s, the government built several rudimentary lighthouses. For various reasons, these lighthouses did not survive. The lighthouses that stand today were built in the mid- to late 1800s: Ocracoke (1823), Cape Hatteras (1870), and Bodie Island (1871). In 1874 the federal government also established the U.S. Life-Saving Service, erecting stations all along the Outer Banks, including three stations on Hatteras Island. In 1878 six additional stations were added on Bodie and Hatteras Islands. Locals were employed as lifesavers to patrol the beaches and rescue the crew if any were discovered. (If you're interested in Outer Banks shipwreck history, read David Stick's *Graveyard of the Atlantic.)*

In the meantime the Civil War played out much of its drama on the Outer Banks. The famous Federal gunboat, *Monitor*, sank off Cape Hatteras and is now a National Marine Sanctuary. Civil War forts were located near Ocracoke, Hatteras, and Oregon Inlets, and the Bodie Island Lighthouse was blown up to keep it from falling into Union hands. Another war that came amazingly close to Hatteras and Ocracoke Islands was World War II. German U-boats lurked off the coast, and Cape Hatteras earned the name Torpedo Junction for the number of torpedoes fired off its shores. At least sixty Allied vessels were lost to German torpedoes, but a fair number of German U-boats also lie on the bottom of the sea.

Tourism was much slower coming to Hatteras and Ocracoke Islands than it was to the northern Outer Banks areas of Nags Head, Kill Devil Hills, and Kitty Hawk. Both islands were accessible only by rudimentary ferry or boat and neither had a paved highway until the 1950s, so anyone who did visit had to drive over the sand. The lack of such amenities tended to keep the number of outsiders down, leaving the Bankers to enjoy quiet, isolated, and self-sufficient lives.

Waterfowl hunters and sportsmen had been coming to Hatteras and Ocracoke Islands since the late 1800s, so the islanders weren't totally immune to visitors. But it wasn't until the 1940s and 1950s that visitation began to pick up. First came the anglers, lured by the tales of fighting fish in the surf and out at sea. Then came the surfers, happy to be able to drive down N.C. Highway 12 to Buxton starting in 1952.

Easier access to the islands brought a flood of visitors eager to explore these isolated places. The Herbert Bonner Bridge spanning Oregon Inlet was constructed in 1963, allowing cars to drive onto the island instead of waiting for the ferry. In turn Ocracoke's visitation peaked because travelers could drive down Hatteras to the Ocracoke ferry, which the state had taken over in 1957, offering easier access from Hatteras.

Today Hatteras Island and Ocracoke Island thrive almost entirely on the tourist industry, but a few locals still make a traditional living by fishing, crabbing, building boats, or working for the modern-day lifesaving service, the Coast Guard. While tourism and development are changing the villages rapidly, the presence of the Cape Hatteras National Seashore ensures that some things about Hatteras Island will never change.

Human Effects on Cape Hatteras National Seashore

Humans have affected the landscape of the Outer Banks in numerous ways, by allowing livestock to graze openly on the islands, planting trees, damming the marsh to attract waterfowl, and dredging inlets to keep them open.

Ever since English-speaking people have occupied these islands, there

Sea oats sway in the wind at the dune line.

has been a battle between man and sea. No matter how hard man tries to stop the shoaling of an inlet or the encroachment of the sea, nature always wins. The best modern example of this is the Cape Hatteras Lighthouse. The ocean encroached on the historic landmark for most of its existence, despite the installation of sandbags and groins to protect it. Finally the National Park Service had to give up on the notion of moving the ocean. It relocated the lighthouse 1,500 feet from the sea during the summer of 1999.

One of the most interesting alterations to the Outer Banks landscape was the construction of a man-made dune line, built to slow down the erosion of the Outer Banks. Left to their own devices, the Outer Banks would be totally flat, as can be seen at Cape Lookout National Seashore. In the mid-1930s, to stop erosion and protect the banks, the Civilian Conservation Corps and Works Project Administration employed 1,500 men to build a dune formation along the Outer Banks from the Virginia border through Hatteras Island (Ocracoke Island was included later).

First, a sand fence was erected to trap blowing sand. As the sand began to collect into small dunes, 142 million square feet of grasses, including sea oats, American beach grass, and cordgrass, were planted as binders. The system worked, and the dunes are still there. One reason is that soon after the dunes were built, open-range grazing of livestock was outlawed in North Carolina. Without that law, all the free-ranging horses, cows, sheep, and pigs would have eaten up all the newly planted vegetation.

No one knew at the time, however, that the formation of the dunes would contribute to beach erosion, not retard it. In the 1970s coastal geologists learned that ocean overwash is essential to a barrier island system and that by eliminating the possibility for overwash (by building dunes) the beaches would get narrower, not wider. To prove their point, the scientists compared the beaches at Cape Lookout, which did not have man-made oceanfront dunes, with the beaches of the northern Outer Banks. The beaches at Cape Lookout had remained the same width, while the northern Outer Banks beaches had receded. Today the National Park Service does not try to affect the beaches of the Cape Hatteras National Seashore by maintaining the dunes or nourishing the beaches.

Another hot issue of man vs. nature on the Outer Banks is the shoaling of inlets and man's constant battle to keep them open. The Outer Banks inlets are regularly dredged to keep them passable, but most geologists say it is a losing battle. Oregon Inlet, an important gateway to the ocean for both recreational and commercial fishermen, is one of the most expensive inlets to maintain because it needs constant dredging to maintain a regular depth. For more than a decade, fishermen and politicians lobbied for the construction of rock jetties that would keep the inlet open. Environmentalists fought them, saying the environmental hazards were too great. After a long, expensive battle, the federal government finally decided, in May 2003, not to build jetties. The struggle to keep this inlet open by dredging will continue indefinitely.

Some Things to Know

How to Get Here

Getting to Cape Hatteras National Seashore requires passage over water—traversing several bridges or boarding a slow-going ferry. Eastern North Carolina is a watery, swampy, marshy place, so the roads don't ever lead in a straight shot to anywhere. The highways and byways bend and twist to avoid swamps and rivers, meld into bridges that span creeks and sounds, and then stop abruptly at land's end.

Distances to the Outer Banks from other cities:

New York City — 430 miles
Washington, D.C. — 270 miles
Atlanta, Georgia — 600 miles
Norfolk, Virginia — 90 miles
Raleigh, North Carolina — 215 miles
Myrtle Beach, South Carolina — 320 miles

From the North: Follow Interstate 95 South to Richmond, Virginia, and then take I–64 East toward the Norfolk/Virginia Beach/Chesapeake area. Stay on I–64 to Chesapeake, Virginia (or take I–64 to 664 South and back to I–64 East). Follow signs to Virginia Highway 168 South, the Chesapeake Expressway. There is a $2.00 toll on this road. To bypass the toll, take 168 South Business. In North Carolina, 168 changes names to U.S. Highway 158 East. This road will lead you all the way to the Outer Banks. Once on the Outer Banks, stay on US 158 for 17 miles. In Nags Head you will come to an intersection that allows you to turn left on N.C. Highway 12. Make the left and you will enter Cape Hatteras National Seashore's north entrance at Bodie Island in less than a mile. The Whalebone Visitor Center will be on your right.

For a less crowded and much more scenic trip into North Carolina, you can opt to take U.S. Highway 17 South from Chesapeake, Virginia. US 17 South will lead you through Dismal Swamp National Wildlife Refuge, right alongside the beautiful Dismal Swamp Canal. US 17 takes you to Elizabeth

City, where you'll then get on US 158 South down to the Outer Banks. It takes a little bit longer this way, but the countryside is worth seeing.

From the West: If coming over land, from Interstate 95 in North Carolina, take U.S. Highway 64 East toward Rocky Mount, North Carolina. If coming from Raleigh or farther west, take I–40 to US 64 East. Follow US 64 East through Williamston, Plymouth, and several small towns, over the Alligator River (drawbridge) to Manns Harbor, where you'll cross the 5.2-mile Virginia Dare Memorial Bridge over the Croatoan Sound. Follow US 64 over two more bridges, one large and one small, and you'll see the turnoff to N.C. Highway 12 South on your right. Take the right and you'll be at the north entrance to Cape Hatteras National Seashore.

The best way to come from the west is to board the Swan Quarter–Ocracoke Ferry and make much of your trip over water. From I–95, take US 264 East. If coming from Raleigh or farther west, take US 64 East to US 264 East. Take N.C. Highway 45 to Swan Quarter off US 264. Follow signs to the Swan Quarter Ferry. The ferry transports vehicles over the Pamlico Sound—a two-and-a-half-hour ride—to Ocracoke Island, the southern entrance to the Cape Hatteras National Seashore. (Don't forget to make ferry reservations. See our Ferry Schedules section in this chapter.)

From the South: For the nonferry version, take Interstate 95 to Wilson, North Carolina, traveling on U.S. Highway 264 East all the way to the Outer Banks. This is a long, scenic drive, but it's beautiful. For a slightly shorter trip, take US 264 East to Greenville, North Carolina, then switch over to US 64 via N.C. Highway 13. Stay on US 64 all the way over the Virginia Dare Memorial Bridge, and then look for signs to N.C. Highway 12 South and Cape Hatteras National Seashore on your right.

The Cedar Island–Ocracoke Ferry is a great way to access Cape Hatteras National Seashore from the south. From I–95, take U.S. Highway 70 East through Goldsboro, Kinston, New Bern, Havelock, and Morehead City. From I–40, take US 17 North to US 70 East. US 70 East gets narrower and quieter as it winds through countless small towns. In the town of Atlantic, US 70 ends, and you'll take Highway 12 North to Cedar Island. The Cedar Island Ferry is a two-and-a-quarter-hour ride across the Pamlico Sound. It ends at Ocracoke Island, the southernmost point of Cape Hatteras National Seashore. (Don't forget to make ferry reservations. See our Ferry Schedules section.)

From the East: If you're boating to Cape Hatteras National Seashore from the open Atlantic Ocean, you'll come in through one of three inlets—Oregon, Hatteras, or Ocracoke, all notoriously tricky to cross. See our Boating chapter for a list of marinas that can accommodate transients and for information about traversing these inlets.

Ferry Schedules

Two toll ferries bring passengers and their vehicles from the mainland, across the Pamlico Sound, to the southern portion of Cape Hatteras National Seashore. These two ferries, which operate between Ocracoke Island and Swan Quarter or Cedar Island, charge a toll and require reservations. You must show up at the ferry terminal thirty minutes before your departure time to claim your reservation. (Seriously. Ferry personnel have been known to give reservations away to a waiting passenger on extremely busy days.)

The Hatteras Inlet–Ocracoke Ferry is a free ferry that connects Ocracoke and Hatteras Islands within the Cape Hatteras National Seashore boundaries. It runs often and does not require reservations.

All types of motor vehicles are welcome on the ferry routes. Snack machines and ADA-accessible rest rooms are onshore at the ferry terminals. The rest rooms on the vessels are not wheelchair accessible. On the longer ferry trips, there are snack and drink machines onboard.

Information can be obtained by calling (800) BY–FERRY (293–3779). Reservations can be made at the individual terminals in person or by phone. For information or to double-check ferry schedules, visit www.ncferry.org.

Crossing times and fares are subject to change, so always call ahead.

Cedar Island–Ocracoke Ferry

2¼-hour crossing

Reservations required

One-Way Fares: $15.00 for one vehicle (more for trailers or long vehicles), $3.00 for cyclist, $1.00 for pedestrian

Cedar Island terminal: N.C. Highway 12, Cedar Island, (800) 856–0343 or (252) 225–3551

Ocracoke Island terminal: N.C. Highway 12, Ocracoke Island, (800) 345–1665 or (252) 928–3841

May 21 to September 30

Leaves Cedar Island	*Leaves Ocracoke*
7:00 A.M.	7:00 A.M.
8:15 A.M.	
9:30 A.M.	9:30 A.M.
	10:00 A.M.
	10:45 A.M.

Noon	Noon
1:00 P.M.	
1:45 P.M.	
3:00 P.M.	3:00 P.M.
	4:30 P.M.
6:00 P.M.	6:00 P.M.
8:30 P.M.	8:30 P.M.

March 26 to May 20; October 1 to November 11

Leaves Cedar Island	*Leaves Ocracoke*
7:00 A.M.	7:00 A.M.
9:30 A.M.	9:30 A.M.
Noon	Noon
3:00 P.M.	3:00 P.M.
6:00 P.M.	6:00 P.M.
8:30 P.M.	8:30 P.M.

November 12 to March 25

Leaves Cedar Island	*Leaves Ocracoke*
7:00 A.M.	7:00 A.M.
10:00 A.M.	10:00 A.M.
1:00 P.M.	1:00 P.M.
4:00 P.M.	4:00 P.M.

Swan Quarter–Ocracoke Ferry

2½-hour crossing

One-Way Fares: $15.00 vehicle (more for trailers or long vehicles), $3.00 for cyclist, $1.00 for pedestrian

Swan Quarter terminal: N.C. Highway 45 (Oyster Creek Road), (800) 773–1094 or (252) 926–1111

Ocracoke Island terminal: N.C. Highway 12, Ocracoke Island, (800) 345–1665 or (252) 928–3841

May 21 to September 2

Leaves Swan Quarter	*Leaves Ocracoke*
6:30 A.M.	7:00 A.M.
12:30 P.M.	9:30 A.M.
4:00 P.M.	4:00 P.M.

September 3 to May 20

Leaves Swan Quarter	*Leaves Ocracoke*
6:30 A.M.	9:30 A.M.
12:30 P.M.	4:00 P.M.

Hatteras Inlet–Ocracoke Ferry

40-minute crossing

Free

Hatteras Island terminal: N.C. Highway 12, Hatteras Village, (800) 368–8949 or (252) 986–2353

May 1 to October 31

Leaves Hatteras	*Leaves Ocracoke*
5:00 A.M.	5:00 A.M.
6:00 A.M.	6:00 A.M.
7:00 A.M.	7:00 A.M.
7:30 A.M.	8:00 A.M.
*Every 30 minutes on both sides from 8:00 A.M. until 7:00 P.M.	
	7:30 P.M.
8:00 P.M.	8:00 P.M.
9:00 P.M.	9:00 P.M.
10:00 P.M.	10:00 P.M.
11:00 P.M.	11:00 P.M.
Midnight	Midnight

November 1 to April 30

Departs both sides every hour from 5:00 A.M. to midnight.

Getting Here by Air

If you want to fly commercial to the Outer Banks, you're out of luck. The nearest commercial airport is in Norfolk, Virginia, more than 90 miles away. If you fly into Norfolk International (ORF), you can rent a car to travel to Cape Hatteras National Seashore. Contact Norfolk International Airport at (757) 857-3351 or www.norfolkairport.com.

Chartered or private planes can fly into Dare County Regional Airport (MQI) in Manteo, about 15 miles from Cape Hatteras National Seashore. This is a full-service regional airport with two lighted runways that measure 3,300 and 4,300 feet. Fuel is available. Car rentals are available at the airport. Call (252) 473-2600.

The National Park Service manages two small airstrips in Cape Hatteras National Seashore. Billy Mitchell Airstrip is in Frisco (252) 995-3646, and Ocracoke Island Airstrip is on Ocracoke Island just east of the village. Both are unlighted, unattended, and without fuel. The runways are about 3,000 feet. A parking lot and pay phone are on each site. If you bring a bicycle, you can bike to nearby Frisco or Ocracoke Village.

Getting Around

Once you've arrived at Cape Hatteras National Seashore, it is extremely difficult to get lost or even lose your bearings. These islands are so narrow—less than a half mile in many places—that they allow room for only one main road, N.C. Highway 12. This two-lane highway is the backbone of the islands. Lots of smaller roads and streets branch off this highway, but no matter where you go, you'll always have to traverse part of Highway 12. Except for on Ocracoke Island, most stores, restaurants, and services are based along this road. Highway 12 abruptly ends at the southern tip of Hatteras Island at the ferry terminal, then picks back up on Ocracoke Island and leads through the village. The highway ends again at the western ferry terminal on Ocracoke Island.

Highway 12 is marked with milepost markers, though they are not widely referenced by locals. They will, though, help you familiarize yourself with how far along the road you are, and some people, especially rental agencies, may refer to them in relation to house rentals. The MP markers start in Kitty Hawk, so the first marker in Cape Hatteras National Seashore is MP 22. Another thing that can help you know where you are is the numbers on the National Park Service beach accesses and ramps. The accesses and ramps are numbered according to their distance from the north entrance to Cape Hatteras National Seashore. Ramp 72 in Ocracoke, therefore, is 72 miles from the north entrance, while Ramp 4 at Oregon Inlet is only 4 miles from the northern entrance. You get the picture.

The narrowness of the islands allows for almost constant sight of the water as well. This makes it possible to determine which direction you're heading at all times. If you're above Cape Hatteras, the ocean is always going to be on the east. Below Cape Hatteras the ocean is to the southeast. Don't confuse the ocean with the sound (landlubbers do this from time to time). The ocean has breaking waves; the sound has only small ripples at shore.

Your biggest concern with getting around on these islands will be catching the ferry at the right time. See our Ferry Schedules section in this chapter, but be sure to supplement this information with a current schedule. Always try to be in line early (thirty minutes early is required for guaranteed placement on the reserved ferries). In the summer there is always a line for the Ocracoke-Hatteras Ferry, so don't expect to just drive up and hop right on a waiting ferry. Luckily the ferries leave every thirty minutes in the busy season. Don't stray far from your car when you're in a ferry line. On the Hatteras side is a shopping center that lures people away from their cars. On more than one occasion I've seen people lose their ferry position because they were shopping when the ferry boarded. The ferry staff, who are a relaxed and friendly lot, get really annoyed when this happens. The ferries board about ten minutes before the posted departure time.

There is no public transportation within Cape Hatteras National Seashore, so you'll need some kind of vehicle to get around. This is a predominantly drive-in park, so most people arrive by car and therefore have no worries about getting around. A four-wheel-drive vehicle is not necessary unless you want to drive on the beach (see our Off-Roading chapter). If you don't have a car, you can certainly get around by bicycle. The entire seashore is 72 miles long, and you can see it all or a portion of it on two wheels. (See our Cycling chapter). Ocracoke Island, where everything is accessible without a car, is the best place to be if you have only a bike.

If you have only your feet, say you boated or flew in, each of the individual villages is self-sufficient and you would have most everything you needed within walking distance.

Essential Park Information

Cape Hatteras National Seashore occupies three barrier islands—Bodie, Hatteras, and Ocracoke Islands. Although Bodie Island is not technically an island (it used to be, though now it's part of a barrier spit), you can think of it as beginning at the northern entrance of Cape Hatteras National Seashore.

Pea Island National Wildlife Refuge

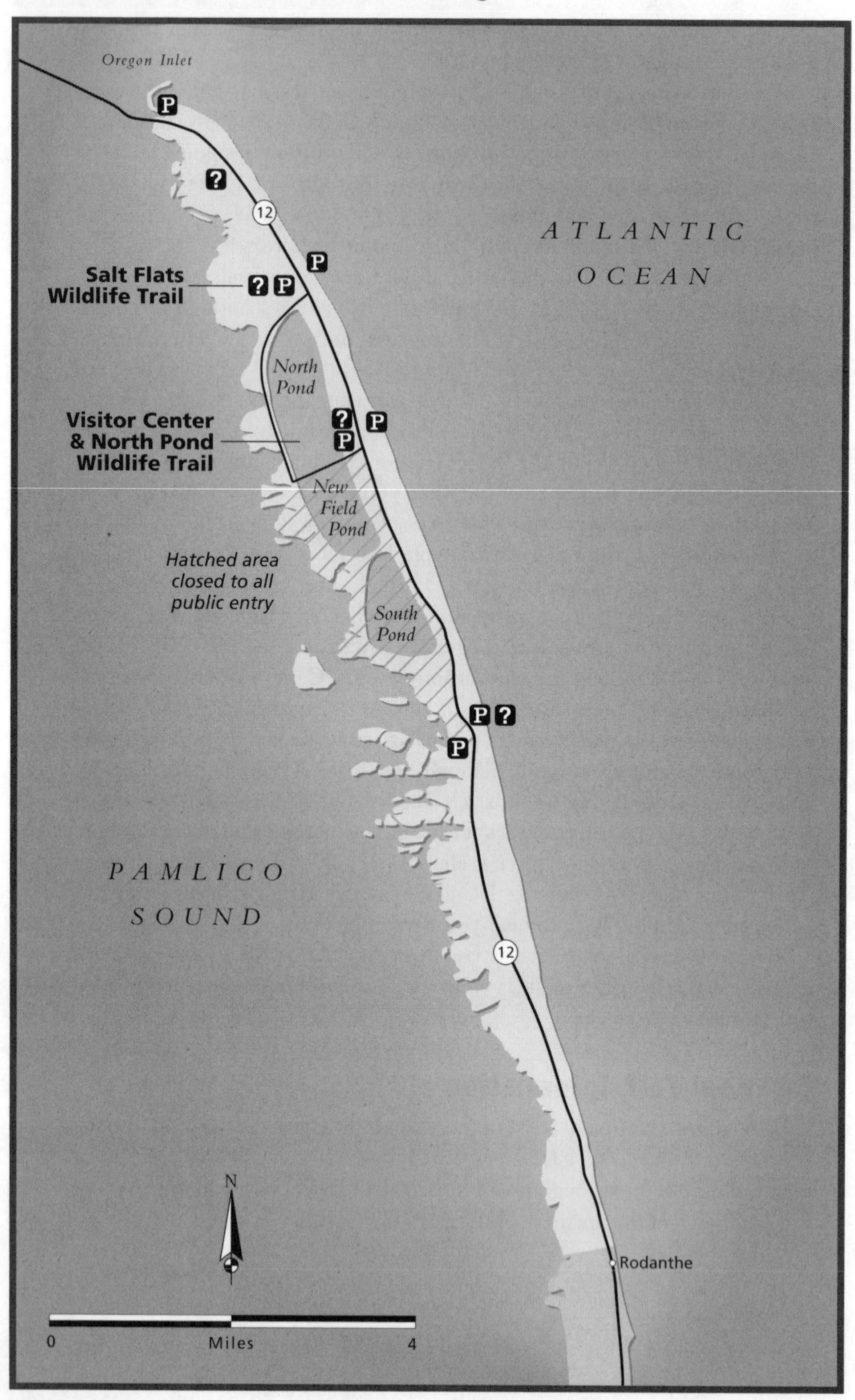

Cape Hatteras National Seashore shares its three islands with Pea Island National Wildlife Refuge and eight villages—from north to south these are Rodanthe, Salvo, Waves, Avon, Buxton, Frisco, and Hatteras Village in Dare County and Ocracoke Village in Hyde County. A portion of the town of Nags Head also abuts some Cape Hatteras National Seashore property on Bodie Island. The villages are not a part of the park and are subject to county and state laws. The beaches in front of the towns are part of the Cape Hatteras National Seashore. The U.S. Fish and Wildlife Service manages the land and beaches within Pea Island National Wildlife Refuge, so laws and regulations are slightly different than those of the park.

Contacting Park Personnel

Cape Hatteras National Seashore is operated by the National Park Service Outer Banks Group, which also oversees Fort Raleigh National Historic Site and the Wright Brothers National Memorial. The National Park Service Outer Banks Group headquarters are on Roanoke Island at 1401 National Park Drive, Manteo, NC 27954. You can call headquarters at (252) 473–2111 or visit the Web site at www.nps.gov/caha.

Bodie Island District Ranger — (252) 441–7425
Hatteras Island District Ranger, Buxton — (252) 995–5044
Ocracoke Island District Ranger — (252) 928–5111

Cape Hatteras National Seashore Visitor Centers

Bodie Island Visitor Center
Bodie Island Lighthouse Road at the Bodie Island Lighthouse Keepers' Quarters
(252) 441–5711

This visitor center at the base of Bodie Island Lighthouse stocks Cape Hatteras National Seashore information, has exhibits about Bodie Island and other lighthouses, and is also a bookstore. Programs are held here in the summer (programs are also held at the Environmental Education Center across the street). A nature trail (see our Hiking chapter) and observation platform (see our Birding chapter) are located here. It is open from 9:00 A.M. to 6:00 P.M. from Memorial Day to Labor Day and 9:00 A.M. to 5:00 P.M. the rest of the year.

Hatteras Island Visitor Center
Cape Hatteras Lighthouse, Buxton
(252) 995–4474

This visitor center is located in the keepers' quarters of the Cape Hatteras Lighthouse. The building itself is architecturally interesting, and the museum and video about moving the lighthouse are worth seeing. A great little bookstore with lots of books about the local area is also on-site. Programs are held here (or begin here) in the summer. It is open from 9:00 A.M. to 6:00 P.M. from Memorial Day to Labor Day and 9:00 A.M. to 5:00 P.M. the rest of the year.

Ocracoke Island Visitor Center
N.C. Highway 12 next to Cedar Island and Swan Quarter ferry docks
(252) 928–4531

The Ocracoke Island Visitor Center is on Silver Lake in a small building with rest rooms. The visitor center has park information, exhibits about natural and cultural history, and a small bookstore. The NPS docks and a boat ramp with parking are on-site. Programs are offered in the summer months. Behind the visitor center on the sound is an interesting war memorial. It is open from 9:00 A.M. to 6:00 P.M. from Memorial Day to Labor Day and 9:00 A.M. to 5:00 P.M. the rest of the year.

Other Visitor Centers

Whalebone Junction Information Center
N.C. Highway 12, northern entrance of Cape Hatteras National Seashore
(252) 441–6644

This information center is run by the Outer Banks Visitors Bureau. It stocks Cape Hatteras National Seashore maps and information, plus rack cards and brochures for businesses on Hatteras and Ocracoke Islands. You can also pick up touristy publications and free tabloid newspapers here. The center is staffed by knowledgeable people who can answer any questions you might have. It is open from 9:00 A.M. to 5:30 P.M. year-round.

Pea Island National Wildlife Refuge Visitor Center
MP 31, N.C. Highway 12 between Bodie Island and Rodanthe
(252) 987–2394

This visitor center introduces you to Pea Island National Wildlife Refuge. It has rest rooms, plus exhibits about local wildlife and books that relate to the entire area. A boardwalk and nature trail start here. It is open from 9:00 A.M. to 4:00 P.M. year-round.

Cape Hatteras Lighthouse is a beloved icon of the national seashore.

Park Fees

The only fees you will encounter within Cape Hatteras National Seashore are camping fees at Oregon Inlet, Cape Point, Frisco, and Ocracoke Campgrounds. At this writing, camping fees were $18 per night.

Park Hours

The visitor centers and buildings have specific hours (9:00 A.M. to 6:00 P.M. from Memorial Day to Labor Day and 9:00 A.M. to 5:00 P.M. the rest of the year). Otherwise you may be outdoors in the Cape Hatteras National Seashore at any hour as long as you are not camping in an undesignated area. Camping is allowed only in designated campgrounds, so sleeping on the beach or elsewhere in the park—in a tent, vehicle, or open air—is not allowed.

Park Rules

The National Park Service Act of 1916 directs the National Park Service to manage its parklands "to conserve the scenery and the natural and historic objects and the wildlife therein and to provide for the enjoyment of the same in such a manner and by such means as they will leave them unimpaired for the enjoyment of future generations."

So the park is here not only for human enjoyment, but also for the wildlife to have a safe place to live. The park is here for us today and it should be the same for the people of tomorrow. In order for that to happen, we can abide by a few simple rules, right?

Alcoholic Beverages: Open containers of beer and wine are allowed in Cape Hatteras National Seashore, but the laws of North Carolina do not allow distilled liquors such as whiskey and vodka or fortified wines to be consumed in public. Open containers of alcohol are not allowed in motor vehicles, including those on the beach. In North Carolina it is illegal to drive with a blood alcohol level of .08 or higher. The legal drinking age is twenty-one.

Camping: Camping is allowed only at designated campgrounds at Oregon Inlet, Cape Point, Frisco, and Ocracoke. See our Camping chapter. Camping on the beach is not permitted.

Climbing on the Dunes: Climbing on the sand dunes that line the oceanfront is strictly prohibited. The dunes are very fragile yet extremely important to the ground-nesting birds, and they prevent erosion. It is illegal to climb on the dunes or to pick any of the grasses, including sea oats, found on the dunes.

Driving on the Beach: Beach driving is allowed on many miles of Cape Hatteras National Seashore. All vehicles must be street legal and the driver

Marshmallows liven up the stark landscape.

must be licensed. The maximum speed limit is 25 miles per hour, seatbelts are required, and driving on dunes or in closed areas is strictly prohibited. Beach areas in front of the villages are closed to beach driving from May through September. See our Off-Roading chapter for a list of rules and an access map.

Fireworks: Fireworks are not allowed anywhere in Cape Hatteras National Seashore, including the beaches in front of the villages.

Fishing and Hunting: Fishing and hunting are allowed in Cape Hatteras National Seashore, but state laws apply to both. Fishing is regulated by size limits, bag limits, and seasons. Fishing licenses are required for commercial harvesting only. Contact the Division of Marine Fisheries at (800) 682–2632, www.ncdmf.net, or local tackle shops for information about fishing laws. For hunting, you must also observe seasons and bag limits set by the North Carolina Wildlife Resources Commission. Call (800) 675–0263 or visit www.ncwildlife.org.

Group Gatherings: Group gatherings that do not require the assistance of a ranger are welcome in the national seashore without a permit. Large organized events do require a permit and a fee (see Weddings, below).

Litter: Littering is illegal in the national seashore. Not only is litter harmful to wildlife, but also it is unsightly to park users and damaging to the ecosystem. Trashcans are provided at beach accesses and ramps. Always pack out whatever you bring in. Dump stations are provided at all four NPS campgrounds.

Metal Detectors: Metal detectors are not allowed anywhere in Cape Hatteras National Seashore, including the beaches and the campgrounds. The only items that can be collected from the land or the beach are driftwood and shells.

Open fires: Bonfires are permitted on the Cape Hatteras National Seashore beaches, and you don't need a permit. The fires must be at least 100 feet from any grasses or dunes and below the high-tide line. Use water to put the fire out. Otherwise, fires are allowed only in grills at designated campgrounds and picnic areas.

Personal Watercraft: The trailering, launching, or landing of personal watercraft of any kind (Sea-Doos, Jet Skis, Wave Runners) is prohibited within the boundaries of Cape Hatteras National Seashore. This includes ocean and soundside beaches and public boat ramps at Oregon Inlet and Ocracoke Island.

Pets: Pets are allowed in Cape Hatteras National Seashore as long as they are on a leash and under human control at all times. Pets are not allowed at designated swim beaches or in buildings. Horses are allowed to be ridden anywhere that vehicles can drive. Guide dogs are allowed to be with their owners at all times. Pets are not allowed on the trails at Pea Island National Wildlife Refuge, though they are allowed on the beach if leashed. Always clean up after your pet.

Surfing: Surfing is allowed everywhere except for within 300 feet of fishing piers and at designated lifeguarded swimming beaches in the summer.

Weddings: For weddings and other organized events at Bodie Island, Cape Hatteras, and Ocracoke Lighthouses or on the beach, you must get a permit from the National Park Service. The NPS charges $100 for group gatherings, possibly more if the event is very large and requires a ranger's assistance. You cannot bring in chairs, altars, flowers, music, birdseed, or any of the usual wedding accoutrements, so a wedding here must be very simple. The NPS does not allow receptions because there are no facilities. Call (252) 473–2111, ext. 121.

Important Phone Numbers

For all emergencies, dial 911

National Park Service–Cape Hatteras National Seashore (252) 473–2111

Outer Banks Hospital, Nags Head (252) 449–4500

HealthEast Family Care, Avon (252) 995–3073

HealthEast Family Care, Hatteras (252) 986–2765

Ocracoke Island Emergency Medical Services (252) 928–6580

Ocracoke Island Health Center (252) 928–1511

Albemarle Mental Health Center (252) 995–4010

Poison Control Center (800) 848–6946

Dare County Sheriff's Office (252) 986–2145

Hyde County Sheriff's Office (252) 928–7301

24-Hour Weather Forecast (252) 223–5737

U.S. Coast Guard Emergencies (252) 995–6411

U.S. Coast Guard Oregon Inlet (252) 441–1685

U.S. Coast Guard Hatteras Inlet (252) 986–2175

U.S. Coast Guard Ocracoke Inlet (252) 928–3711

Sea Tow Oregon Inlet (252) 473–3465

Dare County Hurricane Evacuation Information (252) 473–3355

Hyde County Hurricane Evacuation Information (252) 928–1071

Outer Banks Visitors Bureau (800) 446-6262, (252) 473–2138

Outer Banks Chamber of Commerce (252) 441–8144

Hyde County Chamber of Commerce (800) 493–3826, (252) 926–9171

Beach Wheelchairs

For disabled visitors, Cape Hatteras National Seashore has beach wheelchairs available on a first-come, first-served basis. The wheelchairs have large balloon-type tires that can maneuver easily in sand. You can check out the chairs from the lifeguards or ask about them at the visitor centers. You need to bring a driver's license or other proof of identification to check out the chair. At Coquina Beach, call (252) 441–5711; Cape Hatteras, (252) 995–4474; or Ocracoke (252) 928–4531.

Birding

The Cape Hatteras National Seashore harbors an incredible variety of birds, making it one of the East Coast's year-round birding hotspots. The park's open spaces provide habitat for birds who live here all the time and those that visit for only part of the year to breed, feed, rest, or nest. Salt marshes, tidal flats, salt ponds, impoundments, dunes, beaches, small pockets of maritime forests, and sound and ocean waters provide varied habitat for waders, shorebirds, waterfowl, landbirds, and songbirds. The area is especially interesting for watching migratory birds and waterfowl and pelagic birds.

The National Audubon Society named both Cape Hatteras National Seashore and Pea Island National Wildlife Refuge as Important Bird Areas, and it is easy to see why. More than 400 species of birds have been sighted in these areas and the surrounding waters. This impressive number is due to the varied habitats, the area's location along the Eastern Flyway, and the fact that strong winds and storms often bring in unusual "vagrant" birds. Pea Island and Cape Point are prime places for spotting accidental avian visitors.

If you are serious about birding, the definitive guide to the avocation in this area is *A Birder's Guide to Coastal North Carolina*, by John O. Fussell III (see the Bibliography). It is an excellent companion for birding in Cape Hatteras National Seashore and Pea Island National Wildlife Refuge. Fussell outlines specific tours, complete with exact mileages, for people who are interested in maximizing their birding experience. The book is a guide to finding birds, not a field guide, so you will need to bring your field guide with you as well.

Anyone who's remotely interested in birding and wildlife should make an effort to attend Wings Over Water, an annual celebration of wildlife and wildlands in eastern North Carolina. Held every October, Wings Over Water offers guided birding, paddling, and natural history trips, workshops, and speakers. There are dozens of programs and trips per day over a six-day period. The birding field trips are divided up according to level of experience, so beginners can stop and look at every bird along the way and experienced birders can move on to the unusual stuff. Some trips require strenuous

Marshes support a wide variety of wildlife.

walking or wading, and some require just a minimal amount of walking. Many of the events are held in Cape Hatteras National Seashore and Pea Island National Wildlife Refuge. For information visit www.wingsover water.org or call (252) 441–8144.

The three most popular places for birders in the seashore are Bodie Island, Pea Island National Wildlife Refuge, and Cape Point. Other areas, like Buxton Woods, the Hatteras Spit, and Ocracoke Island, offer excellent birding opportunities as well, but in this chapter we offer information only about the three areas that have the greatest numbers and variety of birds and the easiest opportunities for seeing them. Explore on your own, and you will see birdlife all over the islands. When you're on the water in the warmer months, you won't have to look hard to see brown pelicans and osprey hunting for fish.

Bodie Island

Serious birders like to combine trips to Pea Island with a trip to Bodie Island to explore a variety of habitats. The north end of the island is marshy and flat, where you might see a red-winged blackbird teetering on a tall blade of marsh grass or hear rails calling from the marsh. Raptors, including bald eagles and owls, are seen here as well. Avid birders may wade deep into these low marshlands to find the many species hiding within.

Coquina Beach is another popular location to find birds. Park at the access and walk over the ramps to the beach. Depending on the season, you may see scoters, loons, grebes, gannets, ducks, gulls, and shorebirds.

Around the Bodie Island Lighthouse, the habitat is more densely vegetated. In an effort to attract more waterfowl, members of an early nineteenth-century hunt club altered this habitat by planting pines and building impoundments and dams. The pine groves leading to the lighthouse host a variety of landbirds. In breeding season, from late April to late June, you'll see the biggest mix, including gray catbirds, common yellowthroats, pine warblers, and indigo buntings. In the fall and winter look for thrushes, woodpeckers, yellow-bellied sapsuckers, kinglets, and many others.

One of the best spots for birding on the island is the Bodie Island Lighthouse Pond. East of the lighthouse beyond the parking lot, two observation decks provide an overlook of the pond. Depending on the season and water levels, you may see ducks, waders, shorebirds, rails, terns, or raptors. The best time to see birds at the pond is late in the day or at sunset, when the sun will be behind you and not in your eyes. Bring a scope or binoculars because many birds will be far off.

The Bodie Island Dike Trail (see our Hiking chapter) is a footpath that winds through pine forest and back into the marsh, alongside tidal creeks and offering a view of the pond. Look for wading birds in the creeks and sound. The pine grove is a good place to spot songbirds in the autumn.

The beach and flats on the south end of Bodie Island, around Oregon Inlet, are a good place to look for shorebirds, including piping plovers, western sandpipers, terns, American oystercatchers, and gulls. Birding is best here in late spring and summer.

Pea Island National Wildlife Refuge

Pea Island National Wildlife Refuge is one of the top birding sites on the Atlantic Coast. The refuge habitats include impoundments, ponds, marshes, dunes, beaches, and the sound waters. The U.S. Fish and Wildlife Service manages the refuge's 5,834 acres to support shorebirds, waterfowl, and landbirds, with three impoundments that support migratory waterfowl. Pea

Island is a dream for both novice and experienced birders. A walk along the North Pond Trail or just a view from the observation platforms almost always provides sightings of something; casual observers will find many common species like ibises, egrets, or herons, while more knowledgeable birders have the opportunity for sightings of rare birds.

One of the most exciting times to visit is in late fall and early winter. One reason is the numerous waterfowl that descend on the refuge's ponds and salt flats. Tundra swan, snow geese, Canada geese, and dabbling and diving ducks fill the ponds and create an incredible feast for the eyes and ears. The North Pond Wildlife Trail and the Salt Flats Wildlife Trail (see our Hiking chapter for descriptions) provide the best views of North Pond, where these birds are active. The observation platforms provide a great overlook, but you'll want binoculars to see the birds more closely. A spotting scope can help you see birds up to a quarter mile away. The Fish and Wildlife Service provides binoculars and has a scope that can be used on guided bird walks.

Some birders come to Pea Island in the fall to look for unusual landbirds. Migrating hawks and peregrine falcons are also common autumn sightings.

Pea Island, the state's best site for shorebirds, has the largest regularly occurring flock of avocets and the greatest number of breeding black-necked stilts of any site in North Carolina. Many other species can be seen during autumn migration. For viewing ocean-going birds, the best times are late October through March. Some of the best viewing is in December, when you can see grebes, gannets, cormorants, gulls, and scoters.

Two areas of the refuge that are greatly populated with birds—New Field and South Pond—are closed to visitors. During Wings Over Water, the annual birding and wildlife festival in October, a tour of South Pond is offered.

Cape Point

At the tip of Cape Hatteras is Cape Point, one of the most exciting and important areas for birding. This point of land, referred to as The Point by locals, sticks far out into the ocean, with the Gulf Stream sweeping by within a few miles. They say that birding is best here in nasty weather, but this is not a problem because you can drive a four-wheel-drive vehicle out onto The Point.

As Pat Moore, director of the Cape Hatteras Bird Club, says, "The Point is like having a buffet of bird sightings laid out for you year-round." Sightings of pelagic species out on The Point are common, especially in late May. Hordes of gulls congregate here in winter, as do gannets, scoters, and cormorants. In the spring and summer, The Point is home to as many as seven species of terns, American oystercatchers, black skimmers, and piping plovers. In nesting season, you can get close enough to the terns to see their breeding plumage and watch their breeding behavior.

There are two ways to get to The Point, by vehicle or by foot. Just past Cape Point Campground, there is parking next to the fish-cleaning table. Park there and observe the nearby pond for ducks and wading birds. In order to reach the Salt Pond, an excellent place year-round for birding, you can walk or drive along the sandy four-wheel-drive road that leads over the dune at Ramp 44. From there you can view the Salt Pond and Cape Point. Continue your walk or drive to the eastern edge of the pond, where in the winter you might see snow geese, a variety of ducks, and possibly a peregrine falcon. In the autumn migration season, between July and October, you'll see a variety of shorebirds around the west end of the pond. On the east end look for gulls and terns. From the pond, turn to the beach. The nearby shoreline will produce foraging shorebirds at any time of year.

On your walk from the pond to The Point, you will pass the tern colony site. In nesting and fledging season, from April to August, the colony is posted to keep pedestrians and vehicles out. As you head out to The Point, you'll walk along the boundary of the colony, so you can get a good view of the terns and skimmers. In late fall the National Park Service opens the tern colony area, so you can walk through to see plovers and sandpipers.

The Point is most exciting from November through March. Gulls galore, gannets, loons, grebes, shearwaters, petrels, scoters, and jaegers are often seen on or passing over this area. Late May is the very best time to see pelagic species moving past. The Point offers the best chance for seeing something unusual at any time. Its position out in the Atlantic, its shape, and its constantly changing nature make it an excellent birding location.

Buxton Woods Nature Trail (see our Hiking chapter) offers a chance to see year-round landbirds, though you probably won't have any rare sightings. Warblers, marsh wrens, swamp sparrows, and common yellowthroats are often seen here. In Jennette's Sedge you might spot some wading birds.

Guided Bird-Finding Trips

Pea Island National Wildlife Refuge offers bird walks on North Pond Trail for beginner and experienced birders. From Easter to Thanksgiving, they are held in the morning hours (usually 8:00 to 9:30 A.M.) on Wednesdays, Thursdays, and Fridays. Meet at the Pea Island Visitor Center on N.C. Highway 12. Call (252) 987–2394.

Cape Hatteras Bird Club, a group of local birding enthusiasts, offers birding trips at The Point on Tuesdays year-round. From September through May, the bird club drives four-wheel-drive vehicles out to The Point. Participants meet at Cape Hatteras School at 8:00 A.M. or at Ramp 44 at 8:15 A.M. You can drive your own four-wheel drive or ride with one of the birders. You must make reservations so they can make sure that they have enough vehicles. From June through August, the bird club trips are walking tours sponsored by the National Park Service. Participants meet at Ramp 44 at 7:30 A.M. The walk goes from the ramp to the Salt Pond and over to the ocean, but not out to The Point. It's a hard walk through the sand, so bring comfortable shoes, sunscreen, a hat, and water. Both tours are led by a volunteer bird club member and are free. For the off-season tours, call ahead to make reservations with Pat Moore, Cape Hatteras Bird Club, (252) 995–4777. Reservations are not required for summer tours; for information call the National Park Service at (252) 995–4474.

Capt. Vic Berg offers tours of the backside of the island—the nearshore waters and salt marshes around the refuges. An experienced birder, he uses a shallow-draft boat that allows him to get to places that other people can't. For information call Outer Banks Waterfowl at (252) 261–7842; www.outerbankswaterfowl.com.

Pelagic Birding

Pelagic birds, those that live on the open ocean, are a fascinating aspect of coastal birding. They can be occasionally sighted from land, especially from Cape Point, but the best way to see them is to get out on the open ocean. Pelagic birding is best at the Gulf Stream or in deep waters of 100 fathoms or more. Going out into water that is 500 to 1,000 fathoms produces even more interesting sightings. Oregon and Hatteras Inlets provide easy access to the Gulf Stream and deep water.

The species seen most commonly on trips off the North Carolina coast are in the petrel and shearwater families. Depending on the season of your trip, you might see black-capped petrels; Wilson's, Leach's, and band-rumped storm petrels; greater, sooty, Cory's, manx, or Audubon shearwaters; Pomarine jaeger; and bridled and sooty terns. Less common sightings have included the herald petrel, white-tailed tropicbird, masked booby, South Polar skua, long-tailed jaeger, and white-faced storm petrel.

The pelagic birds look rather common and gull-like, but they are truly unusual. They live on the ocean, coming to land only to breed or when they are blown off course. They have tubular nostrils that allow them to drink salt water and expel the salt from their noses.

If you're serious about seeing pelagic birds, the best thing to do is to hook up with a professional birding guide on an organized trip. Guides advertise on the Internet, in birding magazines, and through the American Birding

Association. You can also charter a boat from one of the Outer Banks marinas. Some charter captains, who normally take out fishing parties, will take a party of birders out to sea. The cost is the same as for fishing—about $900 to $1,200 for a full-day charter. If you don't know the tricks of the trade, you'll want to have a guide with you.

A day of pelagic birding on the ocean is not like birding on land. Sightings will be occasional, possibly with long periods of time in between. But the sightings of other sea dwellers, like whales, dolphins, turtles, and sharks, will keep you entertained. Also, it is difficult to use binoculars (it is impossible to use scopes) in a rocking boat, so you might have to identify birds by their flight patterns and shapes. Bring low-powered binoculars (7 or 8x).

There are a few things to think about if you're chartering a boat. The first is seasickness, which, if you're prone to it, can make you absolutely miserable. There are several seasickness; remedies to try: over-the-counter medications, which may make you drowsy, prescription skin patches that go behind the ear; and wristbands that put pressure onto a point at the wrist. Always eat something light before going out and keep eating lightly throughout the day. Saltine crackers and ginger snaps are good stomach settlers. An empty stomach will often make you as nauseous as an overly full stomach. Another thing to think about is that you're going to be on the water all day: bring sunscreen, a hat, water, and food. Dress in layers of clothing, because it will probably be cool on your way to the Gulf Stream but warm once you get there. If you plan to photograph the birds, bring a telephoto lens.

Pelagic Birding Trips

Brian Patteson Inc. Pelagic Trips
P.O. Box 772, Hatteras, NC 27943
(252) 986–1363
www.patteson.com

Country Girl
Captain Allan Foreman
Docks at Pirate's Cove Marina in Manteo
Leaves out of Oregon Inlet
(252) 473–5577

Miss Hatteras
Captain Spurgeon Stowe
Docks at Oden's Docks in Hatteras Village
(252) 986–2365

Boating, Sailing, and Paddling

Boating is a way of life on the Outer Banks. There's much more water than there is land, so it's only natural to be afloat. Maybe it's the whipping wind in your face or the wake you leave behind, but being on the water can clear your head like nothing else. On a boat, you can easily forget about the problems of life on land.

Whether you're arriving by boat, trailering your own boat behind your car, or planning to rent one once you get here, you will find that Cape Hatteras National Seashore and the island villages are very accommodating to boaters. Free, public boat ramps with plenty of parking are available on Bodie Island and Ocracoke, though on Hatteras Island you'll have to pay to use a private boat ramp. In the villages you will find motorboat and sailboat rentals, plus marinas that offer docking space and sell gas and boating supplies.

Note that the trailering, launching, or landing of personal watercraft (Jet-Skis, Wave Runners, Sea-Doos) is prohibited within the boundaries of the national seashore.

When you're on the water, watch the weather with a close eye. Storms and winds come up quickly on the Outer Banks. Local weather is broadcast on VHF-FM at channel 2. For emergencies, call 911 on your cell phone or use VHF channel 16, the calling and distress channel.

Arriving at Cape Hatteras National Seashore by Boat

Ocracoke Island: Most pleasure boaters arriving in Cape Hatteras National Seashore by water look first to Ocracoke Island. The island's Silver Lake is a safe harbor that attracts multitudes of transient sailboats and pleasure boats. The National Park Service Dock has public docking facilities with several slips on Silver Lake. Slips are available on a first-come, first-served basis at a charge of 80 cents per foot from April through November and 40 cents per foot the rest of the year. There are water and electric hookups (no water in winter) for an extra charge. Stays at these docks are limited to two weeks in

Boating is a way of life on the Outer Banks.

summer. A couple of marinas also provide docking space on Silver Lake (see the list below). Boaters are allowed to drop anchor in the middle of the lake and rest awhile in the harbor without having to pay slip fees. If you have a dinghy to get to shore, this is a great option.

Hatteras Island: Transient boaters can find dockage space in Hatteras Village. Fishing boats make up the majority of the visiting boats here because this is one of the gateways to Gulf Stream fishing. Several marinas in the village accommodate transient boaters of all sorts and sizes. One marina in Frisco also accepts transients. (See the list below for marinas on Hatteras and Ocracoke Islands.)

Bodie Island: Oregon Inlet Fishing Center has mostly permanent dockage, but transient boaters can find a few slips in the off-season. Always call ahead (252–441–6301) to check availability if you're planning to come to these docks. Pleasure boats generally don't stop at this marina because the inlet is tricky and there are no nearby services, like restaurants or attractions, that you can reach without a car. Anglers on fishing boats are happiest here because Oregon Inlet is nearby and the whole place thrives around the fishing culture.

Marinas with Dock Space

The following marinas have dock space for transients or those who need a place to dock a small boat while they're here.

Frisco Cove Marina
N.C. Highway 12, Frisco
(252) 995–4242
www.boats@friscocove.com

Hatteras Harbor Marina
N.C. Highway 12, Hatteras Village
(252) 986–2166, (800) 676–4939
www.hatterasharbor.com

Hatteras Landing Marina
N.C. Highway 12, Hatteras Village
(252) 986–2205, (800) 551–8478
www.hatteraslanding.com

Oden's Dock
N.C. Highway 12, Hatteras Village
(252) 986–2555, (888) 544–8115
www.odensdock.com

Teach's Lair Marina
N.C. Highway 12, Hatteras Village
(252) 986–2460
www.teachslair.com

Anchorage Marina
Silver Lake Harbor
N.C. Highway 12, Ocracoke Village
(252) 928–6661

Community Square Docks
Silver Lake Harbor
N.C. Highway 12, Ocracoke Village
(252) 928–3321

National Park Service Dock
Silver Lake Harbor, Ocracoke Village
(252) 928–4531

Boating

Most people around here go boating because they are fishing, but others just like to ride around on the water enjoying the day. Waterskiing is not especially popular in the Pamlico Sound for a couple of reasons: The water is shallow, the wind is constant so waves are often a deterrent, and boat traffic is often heavy when the water is warm. This does not mean that people do not water-ski, but it's not a highly practiced sport here for good reason.

Large, deep-draft boats head through one of the inlets and go straight to the ocean. Most small boating is done in the Pamlico Sound, but when the ocean is calm some small boats leave through one of the inlets for the day. Be extremely cautious when operating a small boat in the ocean. Wherever you are boating, always make sure you have the required safety gear, flotation devices, and preferably a VHF radio or cell phone.

Getting through the inlets in any size boat can be tricky. Boaters should exercise extreme caution in all inlets, passing through slowly and staying well within the channel markers. Water depths can change drastically just outside the markers. Shoals in the inlets are the bane of all boaters, and they can occur without warning. If you're unsure of the inlet you plan to use, ask about its safety at local marinas or call the Coast Guard.

Oregon Inlet: This inlet is notoriously dangerous due to the narrowness of the channel and shoaling. The depth is controlled to 12 feet, which means the channel should never be less than 12 feet at low tide, unless there has been very recent shoaling and the dredge work has not yet been done to correct it. The Coast Guard does not recommend using the inlet at low tide if your boat draws more than 7 or 8 feet of water. Oregon Inlet is most dangerous in north or southeast winds.

Hatteras Inlet: This inlet is not always safe because of shoaling and shifting sands. Stay well within the markers and you should be fine, but the width of the channel is variable. The channel is a steady 9 to 13 feet deep, and the bar at the mouth of the inlet varies from 8 to 13 feet.

Ocracoke Inlet: This is a notoriously shoaly inlet, which is most dangerous when the winds are out of the southeast or southwest, especially at low water. The channel ranges from 10 to 12 feet deep. The depth is only about 1 to 2 feet just outside the channel on the green side, so be sure to stay within the markers.

The Pamlico Sound's shallow waters make it necessary for boaters—especially those who don't know the area well—to use a nautical chart book. Charts are available at tackle shops and marinas. And because the sound bottom changes so frequently, a depth-finder is an additional asset. Grounding your boat on a sandbar or shoal can make for a miserable day. If you get stuck at low tide, you can always wait for the tide to come in and possibly push off then. If that is not an option, contact the Coast Guard with a nondistress signal on VHF channel 16. The Coast Guard will not tow your boat off the bar, but they will help you contact someone who will.

Boat Ramps

Oregon Inlet Fishing Center
N.C. Highway 12
Bodie Island
Parking available for vehicles and trailers. Free.

New Inlet Primitive Boat Ramp
N.C. Highway 12
Pea Island National Wildlife Refuge
Best for kayaks, canoes, small sailboats, and very small skiffs or johnboats. Parking available. Free.

Scotch Bonnet/Frisco Cove Marina
N.C. Highway 12
Frisco
No parking for vehicles and trailers. Fee is charged.

Village Marina
N.C. Highway 12
Hatteras Village
Parking available for vehicles and trailers. Fee is charged.

Willis Boat Landing
N.C. Highway 12
Hatteras Village
Parking available for vehicles and trailers. Fee is charged.

NPS Boat Ramp
End of N.C. Highway 12
Ocracoke Island
Located at the end of the large parking lot next to the visitor center and ferry docks. Parking available for vehicles and trailers. Free.

Motorboat Rentals

A few local companies rent boats, mainly 19- to 21-foot Carolina Skiffs or other small, center-console boats with outboard motors. The people who rent the boats stock them with all the required safety equipment and flotation devices. They also can offer great advice about boating safety and good places to fish or swim.

Frisco Cove Marina
N.C. Highway 12
Frisco
(252) 995–4242
www.boats@friscocove.com

Island Rentals
Silver Lake Road
Ocracoke
(252) 928–5480

Restless Native Boat Rentals
Anchorage Marina
N.C. Highway 12
Ocracoke
(252) 921–0011; (252) 928–1421

Sailing

Small sailboats most often head to the Pamlico Sound, but you'll also see catamarans like Hobie Cats or Prindles being launched into the ocean on days that aren't terribly rough. Larger sailboats with deep drafts have to be extremely careful in the sound, which is quite shallow in many places. The farther offshore you are, the better off you'll be. Always use a nautical chart in the Pamlico Sound if your boat has any significant draft.

The shallowness of the Pamlico Sound is perfect for sailing in small catamarans and sailboats. If you tip over, you can usually stand in the sound to flip the boat. The sound is wide and spacious, so you can easily sail around all afternoon. Just remember that the wind is capricious here, often shifting directions and gaining or losing strength. For novice sailors this may affect your ability to return to your launch site. Always be sure to bring flotation devices with you and keep them where you can reach them easily.

Several outfitters on Hatteras Island rent small sailboats by the hour, day, or week. Some places also offer lessons. If you're bringing your own boat and want to launch here, see our Boat Ramps section. Depending on the size of your sailboat, you may also be able to launch at a public beach access ramp or via a soundside off-road vehicle (ORV) road. See our map in the Off-Roading chapter for locations.

Sailboat Rentals

Rodanthe Watersports and Campground
N.C. Highway 12, Rodanthe
(252) 987–1431
www.watersportsandcampground.com

Hatteras Island Sail Shop
N.C. Highway 12, Waves
(252) 987–2292
www.HISS-waves.com

Windsurfing Hatteras
N.C. Highway 12, Avon
(252) 995–5000
www.windsurfinghatteras.com

Paddling

Cape Hatteras National Seashore offers opportunities for some of the best paddling adventures anywhere. Whether it's gliding through mazes of marsh with the birds, steadily making time between islands in the open Pamlico Sound, fishing from the stern of a canoe, or surfing on the waves of the Atlantic Ocean, there is something for every paddler. There is so much water here that you could spend years exploring it all.

Paddling in the sound you might see waterfowl, wading birds, raptors, nutria, or otters. You also have a chance of seeing bottle-nosed dolphins, especially from July through October. You can stop at marsh or spoil islands and explore for signs of wildlife. You can bring your fishing gear and stop off at a structure or reef (see our Fishing chapter) to see what's biting.

Ocean paddlers might see dolphins, sea turtles, rays, or fish. You might want to kayak or canoe out to a near-shore ocean wreck and drop a fishing line. If you're an experienced paddler, you can get your adrenaline pumping by surf kayaking in the breaking waves. (If you're new to this, try it on a sit-on-top kayak first.)

The elements that most affect paddlers are wind and sun. Wind may switch direction or build in the course of a day, so it's important to stay abreast of weather reports and respect your limits as a paddler. Beginner paddlers should stay within sight of land, in case bad weather brews or winds build. You might want to consider bringing a weather radio on long trips. The sun can be brutal in any season. Remember that the sun reflects off the water, making your skin more susceptible to burning. Wear sunscreen, a hat, and lightweight long-sleeved clothing if possible.

Summer is great for paddling around Cape Hatteras National Seashore. The predominant wind is out of the southwest and usually picks up as the day goes on. Therefore, it's best to go on morning trips when the wind is likely to be lighter and the sun less intense. Fall is also a wonderful season for paddling here. The temperatures are mild, the water is warm, and the crowds are gone. Winter and early spring are generally cold and windy on the Outer Banks, but they still are good times to paddle the area. Dress accordingly and you'll have a fine time exploring on your own.

There are numerous paddling outfitters and tour guides near Cape Hatteras National Seashore. Some outfitters offer ecotours with narrative about the natural and cultural history of this area. The guides on these trips always offer some sort of paddling instruction to beginners and equip paddlers with all the gear they'll need. Other outfitters just rent the equipment and send you on your merry way. Some of these businesses are located right on the water, which makes it really convenient for launching the boat. Usually they provide you with the safety equipment you'll need as well.

If you're bringing your own kayak or canoe, you can put in just about anywhere that's not private land. Be sure to wear a flotation device (PFD), or at least have one on board. It's the law in North Carolina to have a PFD on board, even in kayaks and canoes. Never paddle alone and always notify someone of your intended route and estimated trip times. Safety equipment and things you should consider bringing on an extended trip include a compass, first-aid kit, cell phone or VHF radio, spare paddle, tow rope, whistle, drinking water, sunscreen, bug spray, flashlight, GPS, sponge or bilge pump, spray skirt, towel, and sunglasses.

Sea kayaking is a great way for experienced paddlers to island hop.
NORTH CAROLINA DIVISION OF TOURISM, FILM AND SPORTS DEVELOPMENT

Launching and Paddling Sites

Places to launch in the sound include:

- Oregon Inlet Fishing Center, public boat ramps or by the propeller
- South end of the Oregon Inlet bridge
- New Inlet Boat Launch, Pea Island National Wildlife Refuge
- Salvo Day-Use Area, immediately south of Salvo
- Canadian Hole, "Haulover," south of Avon
- Boardwalk behind Hatteras Landing shopping center
- Molasses Creek, Ocracoke Island
- Ocracoke Island Public Boat Ramp, next to visitor center
- National Park Service soundside ORV roads

If you're launching in the ocean, the best thing you can have is a four-wheel-drive vehicle so you can drive on the beach, unload your kayak, and hit the waves. If that's not an option, park at one of the beach accesses anywhere along Highway 12. The piers at Rodanthe, Avon, and Frisco are also good places to put in. Cape Point at Buxton near the lighthouse is a good place to surf kayak, but it can be crowded with kayakers, surfers, swimmers, and anglers.

If you're wondering where to paddle, the best information source by far is the *Guide to Sea Kayaking in North Carolina* by Pam Malec (Globe Pequot Press, 2001). This book outlines thirty-five trips along the North Carolina coast, twelve of them in Cape Hatteras National Seashore. The trips are very detailed, and the guide is easy to use. Another place to check is the Outer Banks Paddlers Club's Web site at www.outerbankspaddlersclub.org. It has a list of places that the club has paddled—some with detailed maps—and information about joining the club.

For casual day-paddlers, Pea Island National Wildlife Refuge has a paddling map that takes kayakers and canoeists through the marsh and sound at the refuge. Wings Over Water, the annual October celebration of wildlife and wildlands, offers guided kayak tours of Pea Island National Wildlife Refuge, Avon, and the southern portion of Hatteras Island.

A great trip for paddlers is the 8-mile trip from Ocracoke Island to Cape Lookout National Seashore's Portsmouth Island (North Core Banks). You have to cross Ocracoke Inlet to get there, so this trip is best for intermediate to advanced paddlers. You can do the trip out and back in a day, or camp on the island for a night or two.

Kayak Rentals and Tours

Pea Island National Wildlife Refuge Canoe Tours
Pea Island Visitor Center
N.C. Highway 12
Hatteras Island
(252) 987–2394
Guided canoe ecotours at the refuge

Kitty Hawk Kites Kayak Tours
N.C. Highway 12, Hatteras Island
(252) 441–4124 or (800) 359–8447 for reservations
Kayak tours at Pea Island National Wildlife Refuge and around Hatteras Village

Rodanthe Watersports and Campground
N.C. Highway 12
Rodanthe
(252) 987–1431
www.watersportsandcampground.com
Rentals only; sound access on-site

Hatteras Island Sail Shop
N.C. Highway 12
Waves
(252) 987–2292
www.HISS-waves.com
Rentals only; sound access on-site

Hatteras Watersports
N.C. Highway 12
Salvo
(252) 987–2306
Rentals only; sound access on-site

Kitty Hawk Kites/Carolina Outdoors
Island Shops, N.C. Highway 12
Avon
(252) 995–6060, (800) 359–8447
www.kittyhawk.com
Rentals only; sound access on-site

Windsurfing Hatteras
N.C. Highway 12
Avon
(252) 995–5000
www.windsurfinghatteras.com
Rentals only; sound access on-site

Carolina Outdoors
Hatteras Landing, N.C. Highway 12
Hatteras Village
(252) 986–1446
www.kittyhawk.com
Rentals only; sound access on-site

Ocracoke Adventures
N.C. Highway 12
Ocracoke Village
(252) 928–7873
Rentals and guided kayak ecotours

Ride the Wind Surf Shop
N.C. Highway 12
Ocracoke Village
(252) 928–6311
www.surfocracoke.com
Rentals and guided kayak ecotours

Camping

Camping is the logical extension of any outdoor experience, and it's the best way to get deeper into the nature of the Outer Banks. Sleeping on the soft barrier island sand, feeling the constant stickiness of the salt spray in your hair and on your skin, and falling asleep to the sounds of the ocean waves rolling in and wind rustling the roof of your tent—there's no better way to end an Outer Banks day.

Cape Hatteras National Seashore provides excellent accommodations for camping, with four designated National Park Service campgrounds at Oregon Inlet, Cape Point, Frisco, and Ocracoke Island. Camping is not allowed elsewhere in the national seashore, and that includes the beach. There are also commercial campgrounds in the villages that dot the islands between the Cape Hatteras National Seashore boundaries.

If you're looking to rough it primitive-style, you're out of luck here. While the Cape Hatteras National Seashore campgrounds aren't luxurious, they are stocked with many amenities like cold showers, rest rooms, potable water, grills, picnic tables, and pay phones. At least they don't have utilities. The commercial campgrounds have the full gamut of amenities.

A few things to keep in mind about barrier island camping:

Sand: If you're tent camping, you'll need extra-long stakes to secure your tent in the loose sand.

Sun: Since there are not many trees here (with exceptions), you will not have any shade. Consider bringing extra awnings or tarps or a screened tent for hanging out in during the day.

Wind: Strong winds can whip up out of nowhere. If you don't want to end up chasing your tarp, chairs, or what-have-you around the campground in the middle of the night, make sure all your belongings are secured at all times.

Bugs: If you're not prepared for them, mosquitoes can ruin a camping trip. Bring a tent with mosquito netting and plenty of insect repellent. Many families bring an extra, large screened tent to hang out in together during the day and then retire to separate tents at night. DEET-based repellents

Camping is one of the best ways to get close to nature. BRANT HARRISON

work the best, but there are other herbal methods, like Citronella, that work. Avoid using scented soaps and perfumes and wear light-colored clothing, as dark colors seem to be more attractive to mosquitoes. Permethrin is a water-based repellent that can be used directly on your tent. It will keep a few mosquitoes from flying in while you brush the sand off your feet and zip yourself in.

Cape Hatteras National Seashore Campgrounds

The national seashore campgrounds are all on the oceanside of the island, so it's just a hop over the dunes to the beach. Trees are absolutely scarce, so be prepared for your site to be in full sun. Sites are well spaced, but since there are no trees, each site is in full view of other sites. Parking is available at each site. The more secluded campsites are at Frisco and Cape Point. Those at Frisco are located among the dunes so they afford the most privacy, though they may not be level.

Tents, trailers, and motor homes are allowed at all these campgrounds. There's always a chance you'll end up next to a motor home with a generator, but it's not likely. Motor homes tend to be at campgrounds that have full hookups.

Pets are permitted at the Cape Hatteras National Seashore campgrounds as long as they are leashed. Because the possibility exists that your pet will escape your grasp, be sure your pet is wearing identification while you're here. Your local campground and site number or cell phone number will be much more useful than your home address and phone number. Some people write this information on the dog's collar with permanent ink or attach a film canister, with this information inside, to the dog's collar.

The national seashore campgrounds are seasonal, open only from late spring through early to mid-fall.

Oregon Inlet Campground

Location: N.C. Highway 12, Bodie Island, just north of Oregon Inlet

Information: (252) 473–2111; www.nps.gov/caha

Open: Late March through mid-October

Sites: 120

Each Site Has: Parking pad, grill, picnic table

Site Assignment: First-come, first-served

Group Camping Area: Yes

Reservations: Not taken for regular sites; taken for group camping area

Facilities: Rest rooms, unheated showers, potable water, recycling center, phone, dump station

Parking: At each site

Fee: $18 per night

Discounts: 50 percent off for Golden Age and Golden Access Passports

Maximum Stay: 14 consecutive days

Pets: Allowed on leash

Fires: Allowed in fire pits

Vehicles: Two per site

Stay at the Oregon Inlet Campground if you're fishing out of Oregon Inlet Fishing Center or planning to see the sights along the northern Outer Banks during your stay. It is directly across from the fishing center and close to Bodie Island Lighthouse, Coquina Beach, and Nags Head. An access for four-wheel-drive vehicles to drive on the beach by the inlet is next to this campground, and a boat ramp is across the street at the fishing center.

Sunrise is always stunning over the Atlantic Ocean. NORTH CAROLINA DIVISION OF TOURISM, FILM AND SPORTS DEVELOPMENT

Cape Point Campground

Location: Cape Point, near the Cape Hatteras Lighthouse
Information: (252) 473–2111; www.nps.gov/caha
Open: Late May through early September
Sites: 202
Each Site Has: Parking pad, grill, picnic table
Site Assignment: First-come, first-served
Group Camping Area: No
Reservations: Not taken
Facilities: Rest rooms, unheated showers, potable water, recycling center, phone, dump station
Parking: At each site
Fee: $18 per night
Discounts: 50 percent off for Golden Age and Golden Access Passports
Maximum Stay: 14 consecutive days

Pets: Allowed, on leash
Fires: Allowed in fire pits
Vehicles: Two per site

Cape Point Campground is popular with fishing and surfing enthusiasts who find the biggest fish and the best waves at Cape Point. The Point is on the widest spit of sand on Hatteras Island, stuck out to sea like an elbow. It is the largest of the four NPS campgrounds and is within walking distance of the Cape Hatteras Lighthouse, Buxton Woods Nature Trail, and Buxton village. To reach it, head toward the lighthouse off Highway 12 and look for signs directing you to the campground.

Frisco Campground

Location: Off N.C. Highway 12, Frisco
Information: (252) 473–2111; www.nps.gov/caha
Open: Late March through mid-October
Sites: 127
Each Site Has: Parking pad, grill, picnic table
Site Assignment: First-come, first-served
Group Camping Area: No
Reservations: Not taken
Facilities: Rest rooms, unheated showers, potable water, recycling center, phone, dump station
Parking: At each site
Fee: $18 per night
Discounts: 50 percent off for Golden Age and Golden Access Passports
Maximum Stay: 14 consecutive days
Pets: Allowed, on leash
Fires: Allowed in fire pits
Vehicles: Two per site

Frisco offers the most quiet, most secluded campsites of the four NPS campgrounds. Some sites are surrounded by little scrubby shrubs so that you can't even see the tent from the car. Frisco is a quiet little village, and the campground reflects the same ambience. The Frisco Fishing Pier is nearby, and the beach is secluded. This is the campground for getting away from the rest of the bustling beach.

Ocracoke Campground

Location: N.C. Highway 12, Ocracoke Island, about 3 miles from the village
Information: (800) 365–CAMP; www.reservations.nps.gov
Open: Late March through mid-October
Sites: 136
Each Site Has: Parking pad, grill, picnic table
Site Assignment: First-come, first-served
Group Camping Area: No
Reservations: Required
Facilities: Rest rooms, unheated showers, potable water, recycling center, phone, dump station
Parking: At each site
Fee: $18 per night
Discounts: 50 percent off for Golden Age and Golden Access Passports
Maximum Stay: 14 consecutive days
Pets: Allowed, on leash
Fires: Allowed in fire pits
Vehicles: Two per site

If you want to stay on the oceanfront on Ocracoke Island, this is your only choice. The entire oceanfront of the island is National Park Service property, so there are no private accommodations on the ocean here. The sites are just behind the dunes. The campground is only about 3 miles from the village, so bring your bike if you can and ride into the village to eat, sightsee, or shop.

Commercial Campgrounds

There are numerous commercial campgrounds on Hatteras and Ocracoke Islands, ranging from mega-parks where you need a map to find your site to low-key, quiet settings. The list below is not complete; rather it is a representation of the variety available.

Cape Hatteras KOA

Location: N.C. Highway 12, Rodanthe
Information: (252) 987–2307, (800) 562–5268; www.koa.com/where/nc/331.66.htm
Open: March 1 through November 30

Sites: About 300, including Kabin Kamps

Facilities: All hookups, tent sites, two swimming pools, hot tub, sundeck, soundside fishing pier, poolside cafe, bike rentals, minigolf, game room, playground, laundry facilities, rest rooms, dumpsters, convenience store, planned activities

Cape Hatteras KOA is a "camping" resort, far, far away from the backcountry. With about 300 sites, it is absolutely teeming with people. The Kabin Kamps make good rustic accommodations if you don't have a tent, camper, or RV.

Rodanthe Watersports and Campground

Location: N.C. Highway 12, Rodanthe

Information: (252) 987–1431

Open: Year-round

Sites: 25

Facilities: Water and electric hookups, tent sites, hot showers, picnic tables, grills, sound access

This small, simple campground supports recreational vehicles and tents. Because it is right on the sound, it's a popular site for water-sports enthusiasts, especially windsurfers and kiteboarders, kayakers, and boaters. Water-sports equipment can be rented here.

Camp Hatteras

Location: N.C. Highway 12, Waves

Information: (252) 987–2777; www.camphatteras.com

Open: Year-round

Sites: 370

Facilities: All hookups, tent sites, rest rooms, laundry facilities, ocean and sound frontage, three swimming pools, hot tub, clubhouse, planned activities, tennis court, minigolf, sailing center, playground, fishing ponds, volleyball court, dumpsters, ATM

Camp Hatteras is another camping resort with so many amenities you could live here for a week and never leave the place. About fifty sites for tent campers are on the soundside, and these are quite nice. They are much quieter and away from all the hustle and bustle across the street, and each one has a view of the sound.

Sands of Time Campground

Location: North End Road, Avon
Information: (252) 995–5596
Open: Year-round
Sites: 66
Facilities: All hookups, tent sites, hot showers, flush toilets, laundry facilities, dump site, picnic tables, pay telephone

Some of the sites at Sands of Time have full shade. Campers enjoy swimming, fishing, and sunbathing at the nearby beach.

Cape Woods Campground and Cabins

Location: Back Road, Buxton
Information: (252) 995–5850; www.capewoods.com
Open: Year-round
Sites: 130
Facilities: All hookups, tent sites, swimming pool, playground, volleyball-court, game room, bathhouse, hot showers, laundry facilities, ice, propane, fishing

Cape Woods Campground is on the Back Road in Buxton, not far from the Cape Hatteras Lighthouse. This is a clean and quiet campground, with trees scattered around the property. It's a little more low-key than some of the camping resorts on the island.

Frisco Woods Campground

Location: N.C. Highway 12, Frisco
Information: (252) 995–5208, (800) 948–3942; www.outer-banks.com/friscowoods
Open: March 1 through December 1
Sites: 150
Facilities: Swimming pool, picnic tables, hot showers, country store, propane, public phones, sound access

Frisco Woods is by far one of the best campgrounds on the island. On the soundside, it has a shady, wooded area with sound views. Windsurfers love this campground because they can launch near their sites.

Hatteras Sands Camping Resort

Location: Eagle Pass Road, Hatteras Village
Information: (252) 986–2422, (888) 987–2225; www.hatterassands.com
Open: March through November
Sites: Over 100
Facilities: Paved RV sites, all hookups, picnic tables, hot showers, heated and cooled bathhouses, laundry facilities, hot tub, Olympic-size swimming pool, fitness center, game room, minimart, planned recreational activities

Hatteras Sands is a luxury RV resort with all the amenities you'd ever need. It's set among a series of canals in Hatteras Village. The resort also offers several other accommodation options such as "Doll Houses," camping condos, and tepees.

Beachcomber Campground

Location: N.C. Highway 12, Ocracoke
Information: (252) 928–4031
Open: Late March through late November
Sites: 29
Facilities: Electricity and water hookups, tent sites, hot showers, rest rooms, picnic tables, grills

Beachcomber is at the north end of the village behind Ocracoke Station. Restaurants, tackle shops, stores, and the beach access are not far away.

Teeter's Campground

Location: British Cemetery Road, Ocracoke
Information: (252) 928–3135, (800) 705–5341
Open: March 1 through November
Sites: About 25
Facilities: Water and electricity sites, a few full-hookup sites, tent sites, hot showers, charcoal grills, picnic tables

Teeter's, a small, grassy campground tucked back in Ocracoke Village, provides a nice resting spot for campers.

Cycling

With its long, flat landscape stretching 72 miles down the coast of North Carolina, the Cape Hatteras National Seashore is a good destination for long, relatively easy rides. There is only one real hill in the whole seashore area, and that is the man-made humpback bridge spanning Oregon Inlet, so you don't have to have quads of steel to cycle here. Some people strap their gear onto their bikes and make their vacations a biking/camping event, cycling from campground to campground and enjoying the attractions and restaurants around them before moving on to the next one. Heading to or from Ocracoke Island, cyclists enjoy making a passage on the ferries, and pay only $3.00 on the toll ferries.

Although Cape Hatteras National Seashore is a good biking destination, it's unfortunately not a great one. What prevents it from being the quintessential flatlanders' dream are two elements: wind and traffic.

Wind makes up for the lack of hills on the Outer Banks. It can get you coming and going, and there's absolutely no way to predict which way it will be blowing when you start your bicycling trip. If the wind is in your face, depending on your cycling abilities and frame of mind, it will either be a welcome challenge or a dastardly foe. On the other hand, if the wind is at your back, you'll zip along with ease, thankful for the little push forward.

Ideally, you'll always have the wind at your back on a long bicycling trip. So if you're headed south, you'll want a northerly wind blowing and if you're headed north you'll want a southerly wind blowing. You can plan your trip according to the wind direction of the moment, but planning is often futile. Winds switch capriciously on the Outer Banks. This isn't meant to be discouraging; it's just the facts. As long as it's not blowing a gale, as they say here, you'll probably be fine. Be realistic about your riding abilities if you're starting out on a long trip into the wind. If the wind is blowing hard in your face, you'll be pedaling constantly. Strong riders who are used to hills and like a challenge won't be affected much by the wind.

Traffic, on the other hand, can be discouraging to all riders. N.C. Highway 12 is a marvelous scenic highway, stretching right down the spine of Bodie, Hatteras, and Ocracoke islands, alongside sound, marsh, and dunes. The oceanside dunes are high, so you don't see the ocean the whole time; but you do get peeks of it here and there, and you can taste, smell, and hear it during rides along any portion of this highway. Unfortunately, Highway 12 is a narrow, two-lane road, the majority of it without so much as a shoulder for bicyclists. This is a shame, because this would be one of the top bicycling destinations anywhere if there was only a safer place to ride.

Traffic speeds along at 55 miles per hour, often faster, between the villages, and drivers, even though they're supposed to be relaxed vacationers, always seem to be in a mad dash to get somewhere. Many drivers in this area do not realize that cyclists have a legal right to be on the road, or else they are just not used to sharing the road with bicyclists. Therefore, they tend to get annoyed when they have to slow down or wait to pass. Ignore them and cycle safely in the same direction as the traffic. Go ahead and use up your fair portion of the lane, but don't cop an attitude and prevent the cars from passing you safely.

All this about wind and traffic said, if you're a seasoned two-wheeler, come anyway and explore these beautiful islands. Just be sure to have your equipment in order, wear a helmet and bright clothing, and try not to waver when riding. Cycling on Highway 12 at night is not recommended because there are no streetlights along the remote stretches and it is very dark. It is not recommended that young children ride along the non-shouldered portions of Highway 12. One slight sway on the bike could cause an accident. Children are required to wear bicycle helmets in North Carolina.

Be especially careful on the Herbert C. Bonner Bridge over Oregon Inlet. There is a narrow shoulder lane on the bridge, but it is often littered with broken glass, sharp objects, and broken crab and clam shells dropped by seagulls. Any of these items could cause a flat tire in this most dangerous of places, so you need to look down to avoid them. Looking down is hard, though, because the view of the inlet from the top of the bridge is breathtaking.

Traffic is heaviest in the Cape Hatteras National Seashore in the summer, so it is not recommended that you attempt a cycling trip then. Fall is the next busiest season because of the fabulous fishing, but traffic levels are not prohibitive to a cycling trip. Spring is the ideal time for a cycling trip on the Outer Banks. Winter is mild here and not out of the question weatherwise for serious cyclists.

Jennette's Sedge supplies fresh water to Buxton Woods.

Where to Ride

One of the best ways to see the Cape Hatteras National Seashore is to bicycle the 72-mile length of Highway 12 from Bodie Island to Ocracoke, or vice versa. It's one of the most beautiful bike trips you can make anywhere and people do it safely all the time. Ocracoke Island is the best place to have an overnighter or two on a bike trip because you truly do not need a car in the village.

Below are several suggested cycling routes. Use your imagination, though, and come up with your own. There are numerous campgrounds, accommodations, and attractions that it would be fun to cycle between (see our Camping and Attractions chapters and the Services and Necessities section for a list of accommodations). Remember that all long Outer Banks bike trips require retracing your steps: Since there is only one main road (Highway 12), there is no possibility for a true loop, unless you leave the islands, take a ferry, and loop around on the mainland. If you've got someone who's willing to pick you up, you can cycle in one direction.

Bodie Island Lighthouse to Ocracoke Lighthouse or Ocracoke Lighthouse to Bodie Island Lighthouse

Distance: About 60 miles one way / 120 miles round-trip

This bicycle tour will take you past three lighthouses, plus numerous campgrounds and accommodations if you need to break up the trip.

If you're starting at the north end, park your car at the Bodie Island Lighthouse parking lot or right across the street at the Coquina Beach Access, where there are showers and rest rooms. You'll cycle over Oregon Inlet, past the Cape Hatteras Lighthouse, and through seven villages before approaching the end of the island at the ferry docks. Board the free ferry and enjoy the 40-minute break from pedaling. The ferry will drop you off on Ocracoke Island, where you'll pedal the final 16 miles of the trip before reaching the village. Plan to spend the night in the village, whether camping or renting a room. Have a good meal, go to bed early, and get up and retrace your path the next day.

If you're starting in the south at Ocracoke Island, park at the National Park Service Visitor Center near the ferry docks. You'll cycle only 16 miles before boarding the ferry. Heading north on Hatteras Island will be the longest part of your trip. If you're planning to spend the night before cycling back down, your overnight options are limited. You can stop at the NPS campground at Oregon Inlet, or cycle another 8 miles or so farther up to Nags Head.

Hatteras Village to Ocracoke Village

Distance: 13 miles one way / 26 miles return

For a much shorter cycle, you can drive down to Hatteras Village at the southern tip of Hatteras Island and park your car at the parking lot at the ferry docks. Leave your car behind and take your bicycle onto the ferry to Ocracoke. Once the ferry lands on the island, you'll have only a 16-mile ride to the village of Ocracoke. This is the most friendly village on the Outer Banks. You can explore the entire island casually by bicycle. A car is actually a burden here. You can certainly do this round-trip in a day, but why not spend the night on the island?

Pamlico Sound Loop

Distance: Outer Loop is 285 miles; Inner Loop is 140 miles

This bicycle route is mapped out by the Bicycle Program of the North Carolina Department of Transportation. The loops start and end at Whalebone Junction on Bodie Island (or anywhere you want to start and end, since they're loops). The Outer Loop goes all the way down N.C. Highway 12, across the Ocracoke–Cedar Island Ferry to the mainland, and loops back up through small towns along the Pamlico Sound. The Inner Loop takes the same route down Highway 12 to Ocracoke, then over the Ocracoke–Swan Quarter Ferry to the mainland. Both loops return on U.S. Highway 264, a road that is pleasantly deserted most of the time, and end up back at Whalebone Junction. To receive a copy of the bicycle map of this route, contact the Bicycle Program of the N.C. Department of Transportation, P. O. Box 25201, Raleigh, NC 27611; (919) 733–2804.

Cycling Outfitter

Island Cycles
N.C. Highway 12, Hatteras Island Plaza
(252) 995–4336
www.islandcycles.com

Bike Rentals

Island Cycles
N.C. Highway 12, Hatteras Island Plaza
(252) 995–4336
www.islandcycles.com

Ocean Atlantic Rentals
N.C. Highway 12, Avon
(252) 995–5868

Lee Robinson's General Store
N.C. Highway 12, Hatteras Village
(252) 986–2381

Slushy Stand
N.C. Highway 12, Ocracoke Village
(252) 928–1878

Island Rentals
N.C. Highway 12, Ocracoke Village
(252) 928–5480

Beach Outfitters
N.C. Highway 12, Ocracoke Village
(252) 928–6261

Fishing

Fishing is to Cape Hatteras National Seashore as surfing is to Hawaii, horseracing is to Kentucky, and eating is to New Orleans: You do it there because it's the absolute best place to do it. The Outer Banks is known the world over for its fishing opportunities, especially billfishing, thanks to the nearby sweep of the Gulf Stream. Surf fishing, pier fishing, and inshore fishing are equally renowned. Cape Hatteras is regarded as the transitional point between two fishing zones, the Mid-Atlantic Bight and the South Atlantic Bight, which means that the diversity of the fish caught and the length of the fishing season are greater here than anywhere else along the Atlantic coastline.

The fishing grounds around Cape Hatteras National Seashore seem endless—72 miles of ocean surf, including a knobby cape stuck far into the Atlantic; the vast reaches of the Pamlico Sound, over 80 miles long and up to 30 miles wide in some places; winding mazes of tidal creeks and marshy shorelines; and the endless expanse of Atlantic Ocean. It is still possible, though it gets more difficult every year, to fish in peaceful seclusion here, whether it's on a deserted stretch of beach or on the backside of a marsh island without sight of another angler.

Access to the fishing waters is easy; there are three inlets offering deep-water access to the Atlantic, numerous boat ramps, public beaches with access ramps, several marinas, and fishing centers, three ocean piers, two jetties, and one high-rise bridge structure with a catwalk for anglers.

What species lurk in these fishing grounds? Offshore in the Gulf Stream, you can angle for the thrill of fighting a blue or white marlin or sailfish, or you can reel in edible delights like dolphin (mahimahi), yellowfin tuna, king mackerel, wahoo, or mako shark. Inshore, in the near-ocean, inlet, and sound waters, you might catch bluefish, Spanish mackerel, king mackerel, cobia, bonito, speckled trout, flounder, croaker, or red drum. Standing in the surf's edge with a rod and reel might bring you pompano, spot, sea mullet, flounder, bluefish, red drum, striped bass, Spanish mackerel, or a gray or speckled

Cape Hatteras National Seashore has miles and miles of undeveloped beaches.

trout. Dangling a line from a pier or structure can yield croaker, spot, sea mullet, red drum, cobia, or possibly a sheepshead or amberjack.

And this is by no means a complete list of what might appear on your line—it all depends on where you are, when you're there, and what you're fishing with. The catch from the Pamlico Sound and Atlantic Ocean varies according to the season and the water temperatures, but something is almost always biting. Fishing is truly a year-round sport in the waters around Cape Hatteras National Seashore, though spring and fall are the absolute best.

Fishing around Cape Hatteras National Seashore can be overwhelming to novices, though anglers armed with a small amount of the right information and a bit of luck have a good chance of catching fish. Serious anglers, the sportfishermen/women who study fish and their habits and know exactly what to do, have a great chance of catching fish. Of course, not everyone has time to become an expert. This is where fishing guides and charters come in handy. Guides are anglers who know the fish, their habits, where they hang out, and what to use to catch them. One trip with a guide or on a charter can teach you a lot about coastal fishing. Many reputable guides and scores of charter boats operate out of the local villages. Of course, if you're pier or surf fishing, you'll have to go it on your own. The clerks and owners of the local tackle shops and piers are quite helpful with fishing advice, if they're not too busy. Remember, they want you to be successful so you'll buy more of their bait and tackle.

A license is not required for saltwater fishing in the Pamlico Sound or Atlantic Ocean, unless you are using commercial gear. However, the state of North Carolina regulates fishing with laws regarding size limits, bag limits (numbers of fish caught in a day), and seasons. It is up to the individual anglers to be informed about size and bag limits *before* they go fishing. Limit sheets are available at local tackle shops, on-line at www.ncdmf.net or by calling the North Carolina Division of Marine Fisheries at (800) 682–2632.

Marine patrol officers with the Division of Marine Fisheries make regular inspections for illegal catches. They are allowed to stop you on the water or to approach you on the beach to have a look in your cooler. Officers are sometimes waiting at boat ramps and docks to inspect your catches. Possession of undersize fish or too many of a species is grounds for a stiff fine. Besides, the regulations are there for the good of fishing, to help declining fish species build back up so that people will be fishing on the North Carolina coast for generations.

For more information about surf and pier fishing in Cape Hatteras National Seashore or along the Carolina coast, an excellent resource is the book *Coastal Fishing in the Carolinas from Surf, Pier, and Jetty* by Robert J. Goldstein (see our Bibliography). Make sure you get the third edition, which was updated in 2000. Another great book for surf anglers is Joe Malat's *Surf Fishing*. Malat also has a book called *Pier Fishing*. Both of these books deal with Outer Banks fishing. Visit www.joemalat.com to find out how to get these books, which are only available locally.

Surf Fishing

Cape Hatteras National Seashore is the most popular surf fishing spot on the North Carolina coast because it is easily accessible and off-road vehicles are allowed on the beach. Oh, the fishing is pretty good too.

In the fall, when the red drum, bluefish, and striped bass move into the area, thousands of starry-eyed surf anglers fill the Hatteras Island communities. Buxton especially teems with anglers fishing out on Cape Point and the nearby beaches. At this time of year, and again in the spring, the predominant catch is huge red drum and bluefish. Though it takes a hard-core angler to stand in the ocean's edge on a frigid winter day, those that do it are often rewarded with monster-size rockfish (striped bass), which frequent these waters from mid-November to March, and sometimes bluefish. As the waters warm up in late spring through summer, surf anglers catch fish like pompano, flounder, spot, sea mullet, snapper bluefish, Spanish mackerel, and speckled trout.

Of all the fish caught in the surf around Cape Hatteras National Seashore, anglers get most excited about red drum. The red drum, aka the channel bass or redfish, is actually the North Carolina state fish. These fish are caught in the surf between Oregon Inlet and Cape Lookout from mid-September through December and again from April through June. The all-tackle world-record red drum was caught on the beach around Avon in 1984—a 94-pound, 2-ounce monster that was almost as long as the man who caught him was tall. Red drum fishing is a specialty on Hatteras Island.

Big chopper bluefish (not the small snapper blues) are also much sought after by anglers because they are so exciting to catch. They are voracious, travel in packs, and, if they're in a feeding frenzy, will eat anything in sight. These feeding frenzies, often driving smaller fish right up onto the beach, are known as bluefish blitzes. These larger blues are caught here in the late spring and again in November and December and sometimes throughout the winter. The all-tackle world-record bluefish of 31 pounds, 12 ounces was caught off Cape Hatteras in 1972. Bluefish over 20 pounds are common, and 25-plus pounders are caught every December.

There are 72 miles of beach along which to surf fish in the Cape Hatteras National Seashore—all of it public and accessible to everyone. Most, but not all, of the beach is accessible to four-wheel-drive vehicles (see our Off-Roading chapter). In Cape Hatteras National Seashore, surf anglers have the convenience of being able to access portions of the beach in their trucks via seventeen maintained ramps; drive large portions of the beach looking for sloughs and sandbars; then park their vehicles precisely in front of the spot to which they are laying claim. Of course, some anglers come without a vehicle, but their numbers are dwindling. Serious surf anglers want a vehicle so they can cover more ground to find the best spots. You can spot the die-hard surf fishermen and women on Hatteras and Ocracoke Islands by their trucks and four-wheel-drive vehicles: Metal boxes for transporting coolers are attached to the front or rear bumper; rod racks are fitted to the front, back, or top of the vehicles, and rust is a given.

The shores along the inlets—Oregon, Hatteras, and Ocracoke—are excellent surf fishing spots because of all the baitfish moving through in the current. The beaches closest to the inlets tend to be very crowded with anglers on weekends year-round and practically every day during the frenzy of fall surf fishing. False Point, at the tip of Hatteras Island at the inlet, is a favorite fishing spot.

The north shore of Oregon Inlet is accessed via Ramp 4. You cannot

Rockfish, also known as striped bass or stripers, thrive in the waters off the Outer Banks.

drive to the south shore of Oregon Inlet, but you can reach it on foot from a paved parking area next to the old Coast Guard station. Many anglers wade into a protected bay on the south side of the inlet, while others fish from the rocks or the beach. The east side of Hatteras Inlet is accessible via Ramps 55 and 57 on Hatteras Island. It's a short drive out to the Hatteras Spit. You can also get to this inlet from a soundside ORV trail. The west side of Hatteras Inlet is accessible from Ramp 59 on Ocracoke Island. To fish in Ocracoke Inlet, use Ramp 70 or 72 and drive out to the end of the beach. The other side of Ocracoke Inlet can be reached from Portsmouth Island.

One of the favorite surf fishing spots in these parts is Cape Point, accessible via Ramp 44 or Ramp 45 (off-season only). Looking at Cape Point on a map, you can see why it's such a prime location for fish: It's the point on the Outer Banks that's stuck farthest out into the ocean. It's the best place to catch big red drum, but it's also the most crowded. In the fall, anglers line up neck and neck, and the web of fishing lines leading seaward is mind-boggling. The serious drum anglers fish Cape Point at night. If you're looking for drum, The Point is certainly not the only place to catch them. Ask around about other, less-crowded spots, but don't expect anyone to tell you about the very best ones.

Surf fishing is good along the entire length of the Cape Hatteras National

Seashore. If you don't know quite what to do, talk to people in the villages, especially at the tackle shops. See our list of tackle shops later in this chapter.

Pier Fishing

Pier fishing is popular for many reasons—it's inexpensive, anyone can do it, it lets you fish in deep water without getting in a boat, and the variety of fish it yields is impressive. There are three ocean piers operating as concessionaires within the boundaries of Cape Hatteras National Seashore—Hatteras Island Resort Fishing Pier in Rodanthe (880 feet), Avon Fishing Pier in Avon (710 feet), and Cape Hatteras Pier in Frisco (560 feet). See the listings at the end of this section for contact information.

Spending a day or night out on a wooden pier is delightful. All of your senses get wrapped up in the experience: the smell of salt air and cut bait, the sounds of sea gulls begging and waves slapping the pilings, the sight of water swirling deep beneath you, the anticipation of feeling that tug on the end of your line.

Although many of the anglers on a pier are quite serious about sportfishing, piers are also good, safe places to teach children how to fish. Many children are introduced to fishing on piers. The sight of other people catching fish around them usually keeps them interested. Generations can fish together on piers, and many families make it an annual tradition to return to the same pier year after year. Indeed, pier loyalty is an issue. Some anglers would never dream of betraying their favorite pier. Lasting friendships are often formed on the ends of fishing piers.

Depending on the time of year, the Hatteras Island piers yield croaker, flounder, spot, sea mullet, gray sea trout, puppy drum, red drum, bluefish, cobia, and occasionally tarpon, Spanish mackerel, king mackerel, sheepshead, or amberjack. The piers in Rodanthe and Avon are reputedly hotspots for fall red drum. The 94-pound, 2-ounce world-record red drum was caught about 200 yards from the Avon Pier in 1984. The previous record, a 90-pounder, was caught at the Rodanthe Pier eleven years earlier. The pier in Frisco is best known for king mackerel fishing in the summer and flounder fishing in the fall.

There's a sort of hierarchy that takes place on fishing piers. All the way at the end are the hard-core anglers trying for cobia, tarpon, amberjack, or sharks. Shark fishermen are the most intense, staying up all night for their sport. (Only Avon Pier allows shark fishing.)

About midway down the pier are the slightly less serious anglers hoping for a Spanish mackerel or bluefish. Closest to the shore are the happy-go-lucky fishermen and families catching flounder, spot, or pompano.

Fishing is very popular with kids. NORTH CAROLINA DIVISION OF TOURISM, FILM AND SPORTS DEVELOPMENT

A day of fishing on a pier costs only about $6.00. Weekly and family passes are usually available as well. All three of the piers sell everything you'd need for a day of fishing, such as tackle, bait, gear, food, drinks, and sunscreen. They also rent fishing gear if you didn't bring your own. In addition there are benches, rest rooms, fish-cleaning stations and sinks, lights, and scales. The piers are typically open from April through November, possibly into December, but they close for the winter months.

Piers

Hatteras Island Resort Fishing Pier
N.C. Highway 12, Rodanthe
(252) 987–2323
www.hatterasislandresort.com

Avon Golf and Fishing Pier
N.C. Highway 12, Avon
(252) 995–5480

Cape Hatteras Pier
N.C. Highway 12, Frisco
(252) 986–2533

Inshore Fishing

News flash: You don't have to go offshore to the Gulf Stream for a thrilling day of fishing around Cape Hatteras National Seashore. Offshore fishing gets all the hype and glory in these parts, and those who know how great inshore fishing is here like it that way. It keeps the crowds down. Inshore fishing yields a great variety of fish, challenges anglers' skills, is less expensive, and is generally a more relaxing day on the water.

In this guide "inshore" means the waters of the Pamlico Sound, the inlets, and the ocean up to about 12 miles offshore. Wading in the marsh, dangling a line from a structure, or fishing from small boats, even canoes or kayaks, is considered inshore fishing. Surf fishing and pier fishing are generally considered inshore fishing, but in this book, we have written about them separately. Inshore angling can be fly-fishing, light-tackle casting, bottom fishing, wreck fishing, structure fishing, and trolling. Head boats, large vessels that ply the inshore waters with numerous anglers on board, are an option. Numerous guides offer both half-day and full-day charters. But inshore fishing is most often done by the angler who has his own boat (or rents one) and does a little exploring on his or her own.

Inshore fishing, including saltwater fly-fishing, is getting quite popular around Cape Hatteras National Seashore. As more anglers hear about how good the inshore fishing is here, more guides begin offering their services. As more guides offer their services, competition increases, which is always good for the consumer. Inshore guides in this area are knowledgeable about the regional fisheries and are well equipped for charters.

When inshore fishing, anglers look for structural or geographical formations. Fish gather around bridges, pilings, markers, buoys, artificial reefs, wrecks, islands, marsh points, sandbars, and shoals. Open water is considered dead space. Man-made structures in the water provide a surface that attracts algae, sponges, barnacles, mussels, crabs, snails, and all kinds of sea creatures. These in turn attract hungry fish. Other fish hang out next to inlets or sloughs, where they can feed on baitfish that drift by in the current.

North Carolina has an artificial reef program that provides structures to support its fisheries. Concrete, steel, boats, and even old train cars are sunk on the sound or ocean floor to attract fish. Two artificial reefs are in the Pamlico Sound off the Cape Hatteras National Seashore, one at Frisco and one at Ocracoke, and there are several in the ocean. For information and locations, see www.ncdmf.net or use a nautical chart.

In the Pamlico Sound, depending on the season that you're fishing, you might catch striped bass (rockfish), red drum, speckled trout, or bluefish. If you're bottom fishing you might catch flounder, croaker, or spot. Wreck fishing might yield sheepshead, tilefish, black drum, triggerfish, or sea bass. In the nearshore ocean, on the ocean wrecks, or at Diamond Shoals you might catch amberjack, cobia, false albacore, barracuda, king mackerel, or Spanish mackerel.

Surf fishing for red drum is famous on Hatteras Island, but inshore red drum fishing in the Pamlico Sound is hot, too. Red drum leave the ocean in April and head through Hatteras and Ocracoke Inlets to the sound. Through the spring and again in the fall, red drum is an inshore catch in the sound around Hatteras and Ocracoke Islands.

Fishing in the inshore waters does not require a boat. Many anglers fish off the "catwalk" at Oregon Inlet bridge. You can park in the lot at the southeastern end of the bridge and walk out onto the catwalk anytime. Other anglers wade into the sound or along the marsh. If you have your own boat, see our list of boat ramp locations in our Boating chapter.

Tackle shops dot Hatteras Island from tip to tip. See our list of tackle shops later in this chapter.

If you don't have any idea where to start, consider hiring a guide to take you out the first few times or every time. There are numerous guides in the area offering light-tackle casting and fly-fishing opportunities. To find a guide, contact a local tackle shop or one of the marinas listed. Head boats are another option if you don't have your own boat or don't know where to go. Head boats take numerous passengers on half-day or full-day trips through inshore waters. Tackle and bait are provided; you bring food, drinks, and sunscreen.

Head Boats

Miss Oregon Inlet
Oregon Inlet Fishing Center
N.C. Highway 12, Bodie Island
(252) 441–6301
www.oregon-inlet.com

Miss Hatteras
Oden's Dock
N.C. Highway 12, Hatteras Village
(252) 986–2365
www.odensdock.com

Miss Ocracoke
Jolly Roger Marina
N.C. Highway 12, Ocracoke
(252) 928–6060
www.ocracokeisland.com/miss_ocracoke

Offshore Charter Fishing

This is the big-time fishing on the Outer Banks, rightfully famous for its sizable and numerous catches. Offshore fishing out of Oregon, Hatteras, and Ocracoke Inlets ranks among the best in the world. Billfishing off the coast of North Carolina has received worldwide attention, especially following the 1974 world-record catch of a 1,000-plus-pound Atlantic blue marlin from a boat out of Oregon Inlet. That record has since been broken and several 1,000-pounders and countless 700- to 900-pounders have been caught and released in the Gulf Stream waters off of North Carolina.

The local inlets offer easy access to the offshore fishing grounds. Hatteras Inlet is about 20 miles—about an hour to an hour and a half, depending on the speed of the boat—from the warm waters of the Gulf Stream. Oregon Inlet is 35 miles—about an hour and a half to two hours—from the Gulf

Annual Sportfishing School

Want to learn to fish like a pro? The Sportfishing School, which celebrated its fiftieth year in 2002, is held each year on Hatteras Island. The four-day school is offered by the North Carolina State University Office of Professional Development and is of interest to anyone who wants to learn more about offshore big-game fishing. It's open to anyone older than eighteen. The school includes two days of classroom instruction, two Gulf Stream fishing trips, and instruction by university professors, scientists, conservation experts, tackle representatives, and local charter captains and mates. For information see www.ncsu.edu/cpe/fishing.

Stream. A few boats operate out of Ocracoke Inlet, which is about 20 miles from the Gulf Stream.

Offshore fishing yields depend on the time of year. Yellowfin tuna are caught year-round, with the best seasons being April through June and September through December. Bluefin tuna run from December or January through March. The best time to catch bigeye tuna is May through December, and for dolphin (mahimahi) it's May through October. Wahoo are caught April through December, though the best fishing is in the fall. The season for blue marlin, white marlin, and sailfish is May through October. Blue marlin and sailfish catches peak in July and August and white marlin catches peak July through October.

On the Outer Banks offshore fishing is big business. There are scores of boats operating out of several marinas on Bodie, Hatteras, and Ocracoke Islands. Boats fishing out of Oregon Inlet leave from Oregon Inlet Fishing Center or one of the Roanoke Island marinas. Boats fishing out of Hatteras Inlet dock at several Hatteras Village marinas. There are a few offshore fishing boats that leave out of Ocracoke Inlet. Call a marina to inquire about offshore charters. (See the list of marinas in the chapter.)

Chartering a boat for an offshore fishing trip is an expensive endeavor. All charters are full-day and can take up to six people. Expect to pay from $900 to $1,200 for a full-day offshore charter, plus you need to tip the boat's mate at least 15 to 20 percent of the price of the chapter. It's worth the money, though, to go out on a deep-sea fishing trip, and if you split the cost of the charter with others it's not so bad. While on a deep-sea trip, you're likely to also see bottle-nosed dolphins, sea turtles, rays, flying fish, and pelagic birds. Trips typically leave about 6:00 A.M. and return in the late afternoon, about 4:00 P.M.

When you charter the boat, the captain and mate will supply all the tackle and bait you'll need for the day. The captain will take you to the best places to fish and the mate will set everything up and help you every step of the way. Because the mates are so helpful, anyone, even children or disabled people, can go on an offshore fishing trip. In other words, you don't have to be a world-class sportsman to catch the fish. Most of the time the boat will be trolling, but oftentimes you will cast as well. Fly anglers are welcome, but you should let the captain know beforehand if you plan to fly-fish. You will need to bring food, drinks, sunscreen, sunglasses, and extra clothes.

Offshore fishing is great fun unless you get seasick. There's nothing like nausea to ruin a good day on the water. The best thing to do is to take an over-the-counter motion sickness remedy the night before and in the morning. You can also try a topical patch. Greasy food, alcohol, and dehydration make seasickness worse. Eat lightly, drink water, and stay in the fresh air on deck if you feel sick. It's perfectly acceptable to throw up overboard instead of going into the head.

If you don't want to go offshore fishing, but you want to see the catches, show up at the boat docks in the afternoon between 3:30 and 5:30 P.M. You'll get to see all the fish being unloaded from the boats when they come in.

Tackle Shops

The Fishin' Hole
N.C. Highway 12, Salvo
(252) 995–2351

Frank and Fran's Fisherman's Friend
N.C. Highway 12, Avon
(252) 995–4171

Red Drum Tackle Shop
N.C. Highway 12, Buxton
(252) 995–5414

Frisco Rod and Gun
N.C. Highway 12, Frisco
(252) 995–5366

Tradewinds Tackle Shop
N.C. Highway 12, Ocracoke
(252) 928–5491

Inshore and Offshore Fishing Charters

Oregon Inlet Fishing Center
N.C. Highway 12, Bodie Island
(252) 441–6301, (800) 272–5199
www.oregon-inlet.com

Albatross Fleet
Foster's Quay, N.C. Highway 12, Hatteras Village
(252) 986–2515

Hatteras Harbor Marina
N.C. Highway 12, Hatteras Village
(252) 986–2166, (800) 676–4939
www.hatterasharbor.com

Hatteras Landing Marina
N.C. Highway 12, Hatteras Village
(252) 986–2205, (800) 551–8478
www.hatteraslanding.com

Oden's Dock Marina
N.C. Highway 12, Hatteras Village
(252) 986–2555, (888) 544–8115
www.odensdock.com

Teach's Lair Marina
N.C. Highway 12, Hatteras Village
(252) 986–2460
www.teachslair.com

Capt. Norman Miller
Ocracoke Harbor Inn, Ocracoke
(252) 928–6111

Ocracoke Fishing Center and Anchorage Marina
N.C. Highway 12, Ocracoke
(252) 928–6661
www.theanchorageinn.com/marina

Miss Kathleen Sportfishing and *Miss Tarheel* Community Store Docks
Ocracoke
(252) 928–4841, (800) 305–1472

Crabbing and Clamming

Blue crabs are one of the most delectable crustaceans found in Outer Banks waters. Their meat is delicate and sweet and worth every ounce of effort to get to underneath the crab's tough shell. Outer Bankers typically let someone else do the catching and the picking and buy their crabmeat at a local fish house or seafood store. But catching blue crabs and picking the meat yourself can be fun. And children like crabbing because it's easy for them and they can see the action. Blue crabs can be caught in a crab pot or by hand using a piece of string and some bait. Be sure to make yourself familiar with size and bag limit laws.

Crab pots are sold at tackle shops. If you buy a pot, you just put some bait in the middle and set the pot out in the sound and wait. Be sure to anchor the pot and tie a marked buoy to the top to identify that it's there and that it is yours. To catch blue crabs by hand, you need to find a creek or other place where the water is slower moving. To catch crabs, tie a chicken neck or fish head to a string and then dangle the bait in the water. After a while, a sideways-swimming blue crab will come along and nibble at the bait. When this happens, use a small net to scoop up the crab. If it is at least 5 inches long from tip to tip of its shell, put it in a bucket and continue catching. If it's not that long, throw it back. It's illegal to keep crabs smaller than 5 inches. You'll need a lot of crabs to make a meal, though there's a limit to the amount you can harvest (fifty per day at this writing).

Crabbing is done on the soundside, preferably in creeks or bays. A good place to try is the creek behind Bodie Island Lighthouse. Walk down the dirt road toward the sound and you'll come to a wide creek. Off to the right is a slower-moving creek with a little bulkhead that you can sit on and drop your bait. You can also try crabbing at the trailhead right on the little bridge.

Clamming is done by wading in the sound and raking the muddy bottom with a clam rake, which you can buy at local tackle shops. You might want to ask about a good location to clam as well, but you'll be lucky if someone really turns you on to a good place. Most locals keep the good places a secret. One is Sandy Bay just north of Hatteras Village and the shallow areas around Hatteras and Ocracoke inlets. There is a soundside access here with a paved parking lot and a sandy beach that you can use to access the water. Just walk around, dragging your rake in the mud until you hear the distinct clunk of clamshells on the bottom (you'll soon learn the difference between the sound of clamshells and other objects). You scoop the clams up in your rake, wash the mud off, and put them in a bucket. Be sure to make yourself aware of current size and bag limits.

Hiking

The beach at Cape Hatteras National Seashore is basically a 72-mile-long hiking trail. If you're looking for more structured day hikes, the Seashore has a few marked, cleared trails for hiking and getting deeper into the barrier island ecosystems, such as the salt marsh, hammocks, and maritime forests. The trails mentioned below are marked with interpretive signs that inform visitors about what they're seeing. Hiking (more like walking) in the Cape Hatteras National Seashore is easy due to the flat terrain. Pockets of deep sand are the greatest obstacles to walking that you'll encounter. These trails are rarely crowded, so you'll get the solitude you're craving. If you're looking for birds and wildlife, walk quietly and be ever vigilant.

If you're hiking from late spring through early fall, be sure to bring bug repellent for mosquitoes and biting flies. Ticks are also a concern. Always check for them after hiking in the marsh or woods. You might encounter a snake, but try not to panic. Stay calm and the snake will most likely get away from you as fast as it can.

Bodie Island Dike Trail

Location: Bodie Island Lighthouse grounds

Length: 3 to 4.5 miles, depending on your route

Type: Self-guided; brochure available

Pets: On leash

Hours: Daylight hours only

Information: (252) 441–5711

An extensive trail winds through the forest, hammocks, and marsh behind Bodie Island Lighthouse. For some reason this valuable resource is not clearly marked or otherwise advertised on-site, so you have to ask someone at the visitor center to point you in the right direction. The self-guided trail starts at the grey fence on the west end of the site, just before you reach the parking area. From the opening in the wooden fence, walk down the dirt road until you get to a little bridge over a creek and you'll see the first trail marker. The trail markers correspond to the numbers on the trail guide. The trail winds off to the left.

The trail guide tells the story of how people have affected the landscape of Bodie Island, causing it to change dramatically over the years. In the mid-1800s this part of Bodie Island consisted primarily of sand flats, grasslands, and marshes, with a few small sections of woodland. In the early 1900s the members of the Bodie Island Gun Club dammed the marshes, creating a large freshwater pond that attracted and supported great numbers of waterfowl. The gun club also planted trees to protect their duck pond from ocean overwash. The National Park Service later planted more trees here to prevent erosion. Thus, today there is a substantial stand of pine trees where there was once only open grassland. The trail takes you through this pine grove.

Farther along the trail you'll come to a dam that marks an ecological division between fresh water and salt water. The water on the north side of the dam is fresh and supports freshwater plants such as cattails. On the south side are saltwater plants like black needle rush.

This trail offers wide marsh vistas, views of the lighthouse, and glimpses of creeks and the sound bays as well as the Coast Guard Station and Bonner Bridge over Oregon Inlet. Along the way, look for egrets, herons, ducks, or ibis in the creeks and sounds. Look in the waters on the north and east sides for big turtles floating near the surface. Marsh rabbits are also common sights along the trail. Walk quietly if you want to see the most wildlife, because even the smallest noises will startle them into seeking cover. There are benches along the way at interesting viewpoints so you can stop for a rest.

The trail is an easy 1.5 miles to marker 12, at which point you have to decide whether to turn around and retrace your steps back to the dirt road you came from or continue on around to the left for another 2.5 miles to the lighthouse entrance on N.C. Highway 12. I recommend turning around for several reasons. The trail continues parallel to the highway and the noise of the traffic drowns out the cricket chirps and birdsongs. Plus, the trail along the highway is not as interesting. It is flat and grassy and follows the path of the electricity poles. There is a much better chance of seeing wildlife if you turn around and retrace your steps.

When you get back to the trailhead, don't go back to the lighthouse just yet. Take a left and head a little farther down the dirt road. This will take you down to a fast-moving slough that flows between Bodie Island and Off Island. This slough is a renowned Bodie Island fishing hole, and you'll likely see anglers on the shore or in boats. Across the way is the private Off Island Hunt Club building and an old dilapidated fishing shack. Crabbing is good here. It's just a short walk from the creek back to the visitor center parking lot.

Mosquitoes, ticks, and biting flies are a factor on this trail in the warmer months. Bring bug repellent and wear long pants if possible. The trail is only partially shaded, so bring sunscreen as well. Pets are allowed on the trail only if they are leashed. The grasses alongside the trail are full of little cacti, so be sure to keep your pets out of the tall grass.

North Pond Wildlife Trail and Salt Flats Wildlife Trail

Location: Pea Island National Wildlife Refuge

Length: 0.5 to 4 miles, depending on your route

Type: Self-guided, map available

Pets: Not allowed

Hours: Daylight hours only

Information: (252) 987–2394

A bird-watcher's paradise, Pea Island National Wildlife Refuge has two short trails that offer magnificent glimpses of waterfowl and wildlife. The North Pond Wildlife Trail begins at the Refuge Visitor Center, about 4 miles south of Oregon Inlet. It is a half-mile-long, disabled-accessible trail made of boardwalk and concrete. It has viewing platforms, overlooks, and mounted binoculars. The Salt Flats Trail is a little over a mile north of the Refuge Visitor Center. It is only a quarter mile long, but it does offer disabled accessibility on a boardwalk that runs down along North Pond. It has a nice viewing platform at the end.

If you're looking for a longer hike, start at either the Salt Flats trailhead or the North Pond trailhead and follow the sandy service road all the way around North Pond. You will end up at the other trailhead. You can turn around and retrace your steps or follow N.C. Highway 12 back to the trailhead where you started. For a more interesting trip, cross over the highway to the beach and walk back up to your trailhead along the ocean. If you want to add the beach walk into the mix, start at the North Pond trailhead at the visitor center. This way, you'll end your trail walk at Salt Flats and cross over to the beach there. The area of beach that corresponds with the visitor center beach access is marked by a shipwreck that is visible in the water. When you see a boiler looking like a smokestack sticking up in the water, it's time to climb back over the dunes to your car. The entire walk will be 4 miles or a little longer, depending upon which route you take.

The 5,915-acre Pea Island National Wildlife Refuge attracts nearly 400 species of birds. The trails are well worth exploring in any season, though winter is by far the best. The trails run along man-made ponds that support populations of migrating waterfowl. In the late fall and winter, swans, snow geese, Canada geese, and twenty-five species of ducks visit the ponds at Pea Island. The trails offer the perfect vantage point for watching these magnificent birds in their winter habitat. Literally thousands of birds—including more than 3,000 snow geese—occupy the ponds, and their constant activity is indescribable. Great white swans sleep with their heads tucked under their wings, while mallards and wood ducks tilt their tail feathers up into the air to get a bite of grass off the bottom of the pond. Cormorants hold their wings out like capes to dry in the wind, while Canada geese honk and squabble and snow geese forage along the water's edge. Bring binoculars and a field guide to birds and you could stay here for hours on a winter afternoon.

In other seasons you will hear songbirds whistling from the wax myrtles and live oaks and see herons and egrets stalking prey in the shallow pond or osprey and hawks flying overhead. You may also spot pheasants, nutria, muskrats, marsh rabbits, or turtles. You will certainly see some kind of wildlife on these trails whenever you come.

Dogs are not allowed on the trails at Pea Island National Wildlife Refuge. In the warmer months, bring insect repellent and check yourself for ticks after your walk. The Refuge Visitor Center has educational exhibits on the wildlife and also sells wildlife guides. It is open from 9:00 A.M. to 4:00 P.M. every day from late spring through early fall and on weekends only in winter. The visitor center has a wheelchair available for loan. The trails should be used only in daylight hours.

Buxton Woods Nature Trail

Location: Cape Point, Buxton, near the Cape Hatteras Lighthouse
Length: 0.75 mile
Type: Self-guided
Pets: On leash
Hours: Daylight hours only
Information: (252) 995–4474

Buxton Woods Nature Trail is a three-quarter-mile loop trail offering a glimpse into the most unique of the barrier island ecosystems—the maritime forest. To find the trailhead, head toward the Cape Hatteras Lighthouse from N.C. Highway 12. A sign will direct you to a right turn that leads to the trail

On the Buxton Woods Nature Trail, hikers will discover a rare maritime forest environment.

and the Cape Point Campground. There is a picnic area at the trailhead.

At 3,000 acres, Buxton Woods is the largest remaining piece of maritime forest in North Carolina and has been called the most distinctive region of the whole Outer Banks. This shady green forest of pines, oaks, ferns, and flowering dogwoods surrounded by the flat, sandy dunescape of Cape Point, is the farthest point of land in the Atlantic Ocean—30 miles out to sea from the mainland. The strangest thing about Buxton Woods is that while you're walking around in the quietness and coolness that is provided by the thick growth of trees, you can hear the faint roar of the ocean above the drone of the insects. It's a magical place.

A pine needle–covered path leads you back into the forest. Along the way, informational signs tell the story of how Buxton Woods developed, what sustains it, and why it is in danger. Along the trail is the incredibly beautiful Jennette's Sedge, an expanse of freshwater marsh and pond. You have to peek around the live oaks and pine trees to get a glimpse of this environment. A sedge is a naturally occurring freshwater pond that forms in small dips and valleys below the water table. The fresh water is essential to the birds and other animals that live in the forest.

Animals that live in Buxton Woods include the gray squirrel, white-tailed deer, nutria, mink, muskrat, Eastern moles, white-footed mouse, and a variety of birds and snakes. Trail users are warned to look out for Eastern cottonmouth snakes, which are poisonous. Around the back loop of the trail, look for the dwarf palmetto, a tropical-looking, fanlike palm. Buxton Woods is the northernmost habitat for this plant.

Buxton Woods appears to be a healthy forest, but unfortunately it is not. It is a severely stressed ecosystem due to nutrient-poor soil, sandy substrate, man's clearing of the forest, a low water table, wind, and salt. Compared to the normal beachy Outer Banks environment, however, it is lush and verdant and just about the only shady place on the island. A visit here offers a welcome respite from the sun and wind.

The Buxton Woods Nature Trail is relatively easy to walk, though it is not recommended for the disabled because of small hills, sand, and the necessity to climb over a fallen tree or two. Children can easily walk the trail. Pets are allowed on leashes only. The trail should be used in daylight hours only. Insect repellent is a must in the warmer months.

Hammock Hills Nature Trail

Location: Ocracoke Island, across from the NPS campground
Length: 0.75 mile
Type: Self-guided
Pets: On leash
Hours: Daylight hours only
Information: (252) 928–4531

Right across from the National Park Service Ocracoke Campground is a fun little nature trail that takes its trekkers through a cross-section of the island. The trail begins on the west side of the road on sand dunes, then heads back through a small maritime forest and ends up at the salt marsh. Along the way, hikers will have their legs tickled by errant grasses as they wind deeper into the island toward the marsh. Signs describe how the island plants adapt to Ocracoke's harsh barrier island weather and elements. The trail loops around to end up at the highway where you started. Bring insect repellent in the warmer months and always check yourself for ticks after you walk here. Walk quietly and you might get an up close view of an egret, heron, or other birds and animals.

Kiteboarding and Windsurfing

Wind is a dominant and driving force at the Cape Hatteras National Seashore. It shapes the islands and the trees and changes the disposition of the water, the air, and the humans every time it switches direction. Wind affects the quality of the day for everyone on the Outer Banks who does anything outdoors. This is why kiteboarding and windsurfing are so popular here. With just a kite or a sail, you can harness that ever-present wind and let it work for you.

Kiteboarding and windsurfing are part of the culture on Hatteras Island. If you look toward the sound on any windy day, you'll see kiteboarders and windsurfers in action. Colorful crescent-shaped kites hover in the air above the water, while bright triangular-shaped sails zip back and forth on the water's surface.

Kiteboarding is all the rage in the wind-sports world and its popularity has soared on the Outer Banks in the past couple of years. Just how happening is Hatteras Island kiteboarding? When *Good Morning America* did a segment on kiteboarding in July 2002, the riders of Buxton's REAL Kiteboarding were featured and interviewed.

Kiteboarding has eclipsed the sport of windsurfing, inspiring the bumper stickers "Windsurfing Has Been Cancelled." Of course, windsurfing is still practiced by a lot of people, but the up-and-comers in the sport are kite-only and many windsurfers are trading in their sails for kites. The benefits, kiteboarders say, are that the equipment is less cumbersome and can fit in your trunk, that jumps and airtime are way easier, and that kiting requires less wind. Therefore, a kiteboarder can go out on more days than a windsurfer.

The waters around Hatteras Island are widely regarded as the best kiteboarding destination in North America, and some say this place beats all others in the world. The island ranks high with windsurfers as well. What makes Hatteras Island so perfect for kiteboarding and windsurfing is the warm shallow water, wide-open with few obstructions, steady winds, plenty of access points to the water (thanks to the undeveloped areas of Cape Hatteras

Constant winds and shallow sounds make windsurfing a favorite sport on the Outer Banks. NORTH CAROLINA DIVISION OF TOURISM, FILM AND SPORTS DEVELOPMENT

National Seashore), and the presence of kiteboarding and windsurfing devotees. Wind fanatics are drawn to Hatteras Island like zealots to mecca, and many of them make their living teaching others how to do the sports.

If you've never done either of these sports, there are several outfitters who can get you going with lessons. You can rent windsurfing gear to practice on your own, but you cannot rent kiteboarding gear. Kiteboarding is considered an extreme sport and the liability is too great for renting gear. It requires lessons, so learn with an experienced instructor and then buy your own gear.

Kiteboarding used to be the domain of only young, fit extremists, but the sport is evolving to include everyday people. As teaching tactics improve and instructors become more adept at sharing their knowledge, kiteboarding is becoming accessible to everyone. In the summer of 2002, REAL Kiteboarding taught the sport to about thirty people a day, ranging in age from ten to seventy-five. With a good teacher, you can expect to be getting up on the board and pulled by the kite in one day. Within three days, you can expect to be self-sufficient with kiteboarding equipment on the water.

Pamlico Sound is the ultimate location for learning both of these sports. The sound is shallow, usually about waist deep, making it easy for beginners to practice without feeling panicky about drowning. The wind conditions are perfect. On average, a week's stay on the Outer Banks will bring at least five or six days with enough wind to get out and go.

Uncrowded sound and ocean access points abound in the park (see our Off-Roading map for access points), and there are many schools and rental outfits catering to the sports in the nearby villages. Most kiteboarding and windsurfing is done in the sound, but more and more people are doing it in the ocean, jumping ocean swells and doing downwinders (riding in one direction). There are enough soundside access points on the island that you never have to ride in a crowded spot (this is especially good for beginners who need a lot of practice space). When riding in the sounds, watch out for shoals (shallow areas), crab pots and fishing nets (marked by buoys), boat traffic, swimmers, and jellyfish. In the ocean look out for surfers, swimmers, piers, and fishing lines.

If you're bringing your own equipment, experts advise you bring everything you own because you're probably going to need it. The winds can change dramatically in the course of a week. Bring your wetsuits as well, more than one thickness if you have it, especially in the spring and fall.

The most important thing you'll need to know about is the wind and where to go based upon its direction du jour. Winds are referred to by the direction they are blowing *from*. One of the great things about Hatteras Island is that the island bends and twists enough so that there are places to ride in any wind direction. If you don't know where to go based on the day's wind direction, call an outfitter and inquire.

Where to Kite and Sail on Hatteras Island

Hatteras Island is the hub of wind sports. Around Cape Hatteras National Seashore, the outfitters are all on Hatteras Island, access to the water is easiest, and the people doing the sports conglomerate there. This doesn't mean you can't do the sports on Bodie or Ocracoke Islands. Ocracoke has several uncrowded soundside ORV roads (see the Off-Roading map). There are dozens of unexplored launching spots waiting for kiteboarders and windsurfers who have their own equipment, so explore on your own.

The traditional wind-riding spot has always been Canadian Hole, now referred to by its traditional name of Haulover. Just across the street is Ego Beach, where windsurfers and kiteboarders show off in the ocean. Haulover is good for being around like-minded people, but it's usually crowded.

The following list of places to kite and sail was compiled by Trip Forman of REAL Kiteboarding:

Salvo Day-Use Area, just south of Salvo on the sound. Good for kiting and windsurfing in south, southwest, northwest, and north winds.

Three Dirt Roads, the three sound access roads north of Avon. Good for kiting and windsurfing in southwest, northwest, north winds. South winds at two northern roads only.

Island Creek/Windsurfing Hatteras, on the sound behind Windsurfing Hatteras in Avon. Good for kiting and windsurfing in north, northwest, southwest winds. Good for beginners in southwest.

Askins Creek, south end of Avon, on the sound behind the BP gas station. Good for kiting and windsurfing in south, southwest, northwest, north winds.

Soundside Four-Wheel-Drive Access, soundside north of Haulover/Canadian Hole. Good for kiting and windsurfing in south, southwest, northwest, north winds.

Haulover/Canadian Hole/Kite Point, soundside north of Buxton. Good for kiting and windsurfing in south, southwest, northwest, north winds.

Soundside Restaurant, soundside in Buxton. Good for kiting and windsurfing in west, northwest, northeast, east winds.

Frisco Woods Campground, soundside in Frisco. Good for kiting and windsurfing in west, northwest, northeast, east-northeast winds. Must be a customer of the campground.

Sandy Bay Sound Access, soundside in Frisco. Good for kiting and windsurfing in west, northwest, northeast, east-northeast winds.

Hatteras Inlet, soundside. Good for kiting in southwest, west, northwest, northeast, east-northeast winds.

Hatteras Inlet eastward to Frisco Airport, ocean. Good for downwind kiting and windsurfing in southwest, west, east, east-southeast winds.

The Point northward to Salvo, ocean. Good for downwind kiting and windsurfing in south, southeast, northeast, north winds.

Rodanthe northward to Oregon Inlet, ocean. Good for downwind kiting and windsurfing in southeast, north, northwest winds.

The following outfitters offer windsurfing lessons, rentals, and sales and kiteboarding lessons and sales:

Hatteras Island Sail Shop
N.C. Highway 12
Waves
(252) 987–2292
www.HISS-waves.com
Windsurfing and kiteboarding

Windsurfing Hatteras
N.C. Highway 12
Avon
(252) 995–5000
www.windsurfinghatteras.com
Windsurfing and kiteboarding

Sailworld
N.C. Highway 12
Avon
(252) 995–5441
www.sailword.com
Windsurfing and kiteboarding

REAL Kiteboarding
Bilbo Plaza, N.C. Highway 12
Buxton
(252) 995–4740
www.realkiteboarding.com
Kiteboarding only

Off-Roading

Cape Hatteras National Seashore allows driving on the beach via seventeen vehicle access ramps. It might seem intrusive to purists, but driving on the beach is not necessarily harmful to the environment—if everyone follows the rules. The convenience factor is off-roading's biggest asset. You can pack the car full of fishing equipment, water-sports gear, food, drinks, chairs, umbrellas, toys, dogs, children, and whatever else you might want and not have to worry about lugging it all over the dunes. Anglers especially enjoy this because they can drive the beach and read the water to find the best fishing spot. Then if nothing happens in that spot, they just hop in the truck and find another place. Being able to drive on the beach is good for less ambulatory people too, like children, the elderly, and the disabled, because it makes their walk to the shore much shorter.

The seventeen vehicle access ramps span the length of Bodie, Hatteras, and Ocracoke Islands. See the Off-Roading map for access ramp locations; note that several of the ramps do not allow access from late May through mid-September. The ramps are numbered according to their approximate distance from the northern boundary of the national seashore, so the lower numbers are in the northern portion of the park and the higher numbers are in the southern portion. The last ramp, number 72, is on Ocracoke Island. There are also fifteen soundside off-road vehicle (ORV) roads—actually, cleared sand paths. You should follow only those paths that are marked ORV.

Some of the favorite (and most crowded) places to drive on the beach are at Oregon Inlet, Cape Point, Hatteras Inlet, and the south end of Ocracoke Island. These are all great fishing spots, so they tend to have the most usage.

While off-roading is fun for the people, it is not so for the wildlife. Turtles and birds nest on the beach, and off-road vehicles and humans can disturb their nests. This is why many portions of the beach are closed in nesting season. You must stay out of these areas and keep your pets out as well. The nesting areas are clearly marked with posts and signs. Beach driving also contributes to erosion, so it's important to stay off the dunes.

Cape Hatteras National Seashore Off-Road Vehicle Routes

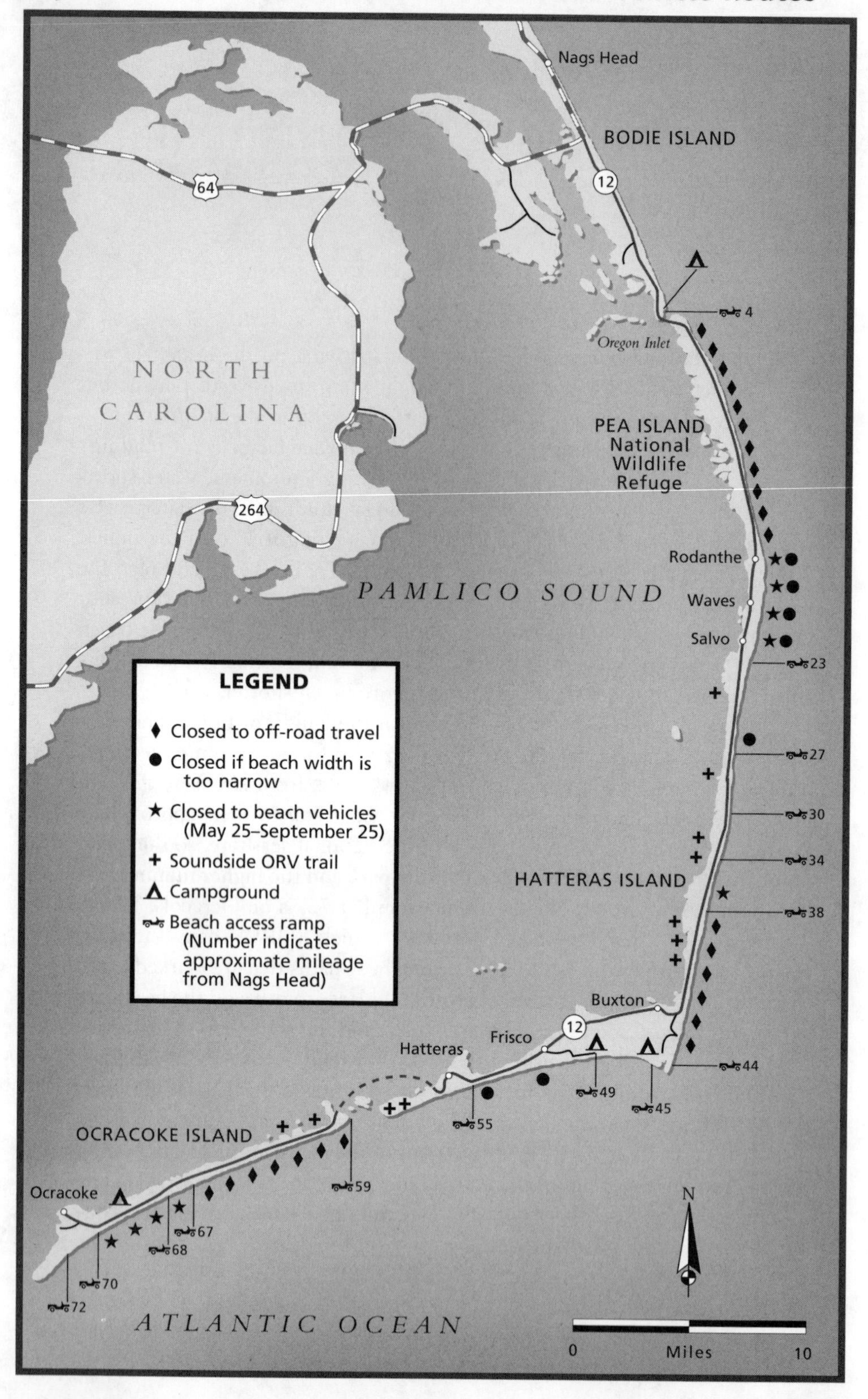

Consider It a Privilege

Not everyone is in favor of having vehicles on the beach. Several environmental groups are now seeking a ban on off-road vehicles in national parks. There are particular problems associated with beach driving on Cape Hatteras National Seashore, such as destruction of nesting areas for federally protected endangered species (piping plovers), dune destruction, and erosion on narrow beaches. Park rangers also have to deal with things like traffic violations, which include unsafe vehicle operation, operating without valid license or registration, speeding, driving under the influence of alcohol, underage drinking, open containers of alcohol, illegal camping, entering closed areas, etc. ORVs also cause beach-user conflicts. Swimmers, walkers, and beachgoers who come to the beach for peace and quiet are often annoyed and interrupted by the vehicles.

You can take it all when you drive onto the beach for a day of fishing.

National Park Service/Cape Hatteras National Seashore personnel are now working to develop an Off-Road Vehicle Management Plan. While they don't expect to ban ORVs from the beaches completely, they are looking at the possibility of requiring permits and fees for ORV users. This would help mitigate the damage to the beach and pay for the damage that is caused. This isn't likely to happen for a couple of years, if it happens at all. But while the management plan is being developed, NPS staff will be watching ORV users. To ensure that the privilege is continued, please follow the rules. See the list of beach driving rules and tips in The Basics chapter.

Scuba Diving

Nowhere could wreck diving be better than in waters known as the Graveyard of the Atlantic. Hundreds of wrecked vessels lie on the ocean floor between the barrier islands and the inner edge of the great oceanic "river" known as the Gulf Stream. Divers get a veritable history lesson exploring the shipwrecked vessels—everything from eighteenth-century schooners to tankers to luxury liners to World War II submarines and vessels that were torpedoed by German U-boats. Some wrecks are highly visible, while others are slowly being covered by sand. Some wrecks offer opportunities for artifact collecting, while others, like the USS *Monitor*, are federally protected shipwreck sites.

Marine life is an interesting part of wreck diving off Hatteras Island. The convergence of the Gulf Stream and Labrador currents at this particular area means that you can find both warm- and cold-water species on the wrecks, which actually act as reefs in an area where there are no natural coral reefs. The warm, 80-degree Gulf Stream waters bring valuable nutrients to the wrecks, which attracts fish and other marine life. The warm waters have a lot to do with the fact that you can find marine life here that is not normally found at this latitude. Sand sharks, tiger sharks, stingrays, amberjack, grouper, triggerfish, pompano, barracuda, sea turtles, spadefish, eels, and other fish are seen frequently on the wrecks. Tropical fish can be seen when the water temperature is right. Vivid coral growing on the shipwrecks is an interesting sight.

Capt. Art Kirchner of Atlantic Wreck Diving says diving on the Outer Banks is like a box of chocolates: You never know what you're going to get. Unpredictable currents and constant winds are challenges to divers in these waters. The ideal diving situation is no current and no wind, but the likelihood of that happening is very rare. Divers look for eddies, pools of still water that branch off of the Gulf Stream. Often divers have to contend with rough seas and low visibility.

Most of the wrecks off the Outer Banks lie in waters that are out of the depth range of most divers. However, there are plenty of wrecks that are in the recreational range, from 40 to 60 feet, and numerous deeper wrecks for more experienced divers.

Some of the most popular wreck-diving sites include the *Dixie Arrow*, a 468-foot tanker that was torpedoed by a U-boat in 1942 and lies on the bottom of the sea in 90 feet of water. The *Dixie Arrow* is in a good place geographically, so it's usually in clean water, and a lot of ship is visible, not yet covered by sand. Other torpedoed tankers and freighters on the ocean's floor are the *British Splendour*, *Empire Gem*, *F. W. Abrams*, and the *Cassandra*. The *Proteus*, 24 miles off the beach, is a 1917 luxury liner that had a collision at sea with a sailing vessel. Another popular site is the *Hesperides*, an ore carrier that went down on Diamond Shoals in 1886. Since it's only 40 feet down, it's a good site for recreational divers. The USS *Monitor*, a Civil War ironclad that sank 17 miles off Cape Hatteras in 1862, was the first site in the United States to be named a National Underwater Marine Sanctuary. Divers can visit the site only if they have a federal permit.

Most of the Outer Banks wrecks must be reached by boat. Some, however, you can swim to from the shore. In Rodanthe, about 100 yards from the fishing pier, lies the *LST 471*, in about 15 feet of water after sinking in 1949. The *Oriental*, a 210-foot federal transport vessel that sank in 1862, lies approximately 3 miles south of Oregon Inlet in about 20 feet of water. The wreck is only about 200 yards offshore, but it can be a difficult swim to reach it. If you're unfamiliar with the sites, it's best to take a guide with you the first time.

The landscape of the ocean floor is constantly changing due to hurricanes and storms. With each storm, wrecks can be covered or uncovered. This ever-changing aspect only makes the diving more interesting for returning divers. The folks at the two local dive shops can provide you with much information.

The following dive shops/outfitters offer scuba-diving certification and charter services. Cape Hatteras Diving and Nautical Training offers guides for beach dives.

Dive Shops

Cape Hatteras Diving and Nautical Training
Manteo
(252) 473–1356
Also offers guided beach dives.

Outer Banks Diving and Charters
N.C. Highway 12
Hatteras Village
(252) 986–1056

Atlantic Wreck Diving
Teach's Lair Marina
Hatteras Village
(252) 986–2835

Surfing

The Outer Banks is renowned as the best East Coast surfing location, and the best Outer Banks surfing, no doubt, is on Hatteras Island within Cape Hatteras National Seashore.

It wasn't until the 1960s that surfing really took off on the Outer Banks, though locals had been establishing the sport here before that. In the '60s, the word got out about Outer Banks waves, and surfers from all along the East Coast began making road trips to the area's deserted beaches. Many of those early surfers ended up staying for good. In the 1970s the hottest surfing action was focused around Cape Hatteras Lighthouse, which was known as the "Wave Magnet." In the '70s the Eastern Surfing Championships began here, which attracted more attention to the local surfing scene. When professional surfers visit, and they often do, cameras and media attention follow, and now there probably isn't a surfer alive who hasn't heard of North Carolina's Outer Banks.

Old-school surfers had a definite image: young, bleached-blonde kids driving surf wagons and VW buses, skipping school, and living for the next big break. Today, it's harder to stereotype surfers; one reason is that there are many more people doing it here than ever before. The teenagers who started the sport here are all grown up and working regular jobs, but they still like to surf and now their kids are surfing the Outer Banks breaks. Several generations of the same family can be found in the water at once. Many of the devout surfers on the Outer Banks are fun-loving high school and college kids, but others are lawyers, engineers, parents, artists, restaurateurs, contractors, business owners, and more professionals who consider surfing a necessary spiritual experience. Several of the locals have become professional surfers.

Why is Cape Hatteras National Seashore surfing so great? Swells and sandbars, mainly. These barrier islands are situated far out into the Atlantic, with nothing beyond to break up the swells coming from the deep sea. A narrow continental shelf allows the swells to hit the beaches unaltered. The beaches receive the full brunt of tropical storm swells, low-pressure systems,

Cape Hatteras waves are made for surfing. NORTH CAROLINA DIVISION OF TOURISM, FILM AND SPORTS DEVELOPMENT

and nor'easters. Tropical action sends southern swells rolling this way in late summer and early fall, which makes Buxton, Frisco, and Ocracoke surfing really take off. Swells from the south are best on the beaches below Cape Hatteras, while swells from the north or east are best on the beaches above the Cape.

Wind patterns greatly affect what happens with the swells when they roll in. If the wind is behind them, the surf builds but the water gets slurry and choppy. But if the wind is in the face of the waves, expect smooth, clean riding.

When the swells roll in, it's the offshore sandbars that cause the waves to break. Sandbars can amass anywhere, though they are predictable around piers, shipwrecks, or other structures like jetties or groins. Sandbars are constantly shifting, so wave breaks are constantly shifting. What was epic one season may be extinct the next.

Cape Hatteras National Seashore offers the ideal surfing situation for more reasons than just the waves. Unlike many East Coast beaches that restrict surfing to zones or certain hours of the day, Cape Hatteras National Seashore has no strict restrictions on surfing, other than common sense requirements that surfers have to be leashed to their boards and stay 300 feet away from piers. Surfers also like the seashore's remote and desolate stretches of beach, where it's still possible to have a break all to yourself. The best breaks are often crowded, but if you have a sense of adventure and a four-wheel-drive vehicle, you can often find a place of your own. Another good thing about Outer Banks surfing is that the surfers can't help being friendly most of the time. Of course some locals try to establish a pecking order on the breaks, but there aren't the turf wars you hear about in other places.

Surfing is a year-round sport on the Outer Banks. Unfortunately, when the water is warm in summer, the surfing is not always at its best, unless there are storms brewing in the tropics. Many people surf in the winter, wearing 4/3 wetsuits with a hood plus sealed booties and gloves. Fall tends to be the best time for surfing on the Outer Banks, and this is why the Eastern Surfing Championships are held at Buxton then. This brings together surfers from all along the East Coast, from Maine to Florida.

Where to Surf

The following list of surfing locations highlights some of the best-known and consistent breaks in Cape Hatteras National Seashore. There are many others, and some of these may be old news by the time you read this book. This is just to get you started. Ask around at local surf shops if you want more information—or just look around.

Pea Island National Wildlife Refuge: The beaches at Pea Island are well known for surf breaks. One good place to check is around the Boiler, part of a shipwreck that sticks up out of the water. Park at the Pea Island Visitor Center and use the access across the street to get to the beach. Pea Island offers lots of empty beach to explore to find your own spot. Surfing is best here when swells are from the southeast and winds are from the west.

S Turns: Called the S Turns or the S Curves, this area just north of Rodanthe is renowned. Look for the tall, funky houses and the sign welcoming you to Mirlo Beach and park just north of there. Everybody checks this place out, so it can get rather crowded, but the good news is that you can spread out. People just pull off along N.C. Highway 12 and run over the dunes. Be careful not to get stuck in the sand when you park. Swells from the south or southeast are best here, with winds from the west. While you're in Rodanthe, look at the waves at Rodanthe Pier, but it's not as good a spot as it used to be.

Waves and Salvo: If you have a four-wheel-drive vehicle, use Ramp 34 and drive on the beach to look for a spot. Parking is nil in Waves and Salvo, so it's best to have a vehicle to get onto the beach. Surfing is best when swells are out of the south or southeast and winds are out of the west.

Avon Pier: There are good breaks from just north and just south of the Avon Pier. There is a lot of parking at the pier. Surfing is best here on northeast and southeast swells and winds out of the west or northwest.

Buxton/Cape Hatteras Lighthouse: Surfing at the lighthouse ain't what it used to be. The sandbars have changed around the three groins, detracting from what used to be known as the Wave Magnet. The surfing location is actually at the groins where the lighthouse used to be before it was moved. Surfing is best here on west or northwest winds. If the swell is from the northeast, the first groin is best. If the swell is from the southeast, surfing is best off the third groin.

Frisco: When swells are from the south with a light northeast wind, surfing on the south-facing Frisco Beach is excellent. Park at the Frisco Pier parking lot and have at it.

Ocracoke: Ocracoke is another south-facing beach, so its best swells are from the south or southwest and winds are from the north or northwest. Some surfers say Ocracoke is not consistent but the waves are good. You can drive on the beach to find a spot or park at one of the beach accesses on the island.

To get a report on the day's surfing, call a local surf shop. Often the shops have recorded messages that give wind direction, water temperature, and all the information you'll need to figure out whether it's worth going that day. This is especially helpful if you're coming from any distance to surf here. Call Rodanthe Surf Shop at (252) 987–2435, or Natural Art Surf Shop at (252) 995–4646.

Surf Shops

If you want to learn to surf, there are outfitters in the villages around Cape Hatteras National Seashore who will teach you. You can take private lessons, participate in surf camps, or just rent a board and try it on your own. See the list of surf shops below:

Rodanthe Surf Shop
N.C. Highway 12
Rodanthe
(252) 987–2412
Rentals

Hatteras Island Surf Shop
N.C. Highway 12
Waves
(252) 987–2296
Rentals and lessons

Natural Art Surf Shop
N.C. Highway 12
Buxton
(252) 995–5682
www.surfintheeye.com
Rentals

Ride the Wind Surf Shop
N.C. Highway 12
Ocracoke
(252) 928–6311
www.surfocracoke.com
Rentals and lessons

Many sandy paths lead to the sea.

Swimming

With 72 miles of Atlantic Ocean beach, Cape Hatteras National Seashore is the ideal place for swimming. It also offers access to many miles of Pamlico Sound shoreline for wading and swimming. The national seashore beaches are clean and easily accessible and available to everyone. Ramps, walkover areas, and parking are plentiful, so getting to the beach is never a problem. In many parts of the Cape Hatteras National Seashore, you can drive a four-wheel-drive vehicle right to your favorite beach spot on the ocean or sound, bringing with you all the things you'll need for an entire day of water fun. (See our Off-Roading chapter.)

Water temperatures are the most comfortable from June through September, though May and October are not out of the question. Average water temperatures are: 68° F in May, 72° to 75° in June, 76° to 79° in July and August, 75° to 78° in September, and 68° to 72° in October.

Ocean swimming is for experienced swimmers only. For children and inexperienced swimmers, you may want to consider the Pamlico Sound, where waves are small or nonexistent and there is no threat of rip currents and undertows. Of course, Pamlico Sound swimming is really more like wading. The sound is knee- to waist-high in most areas. Be aware that the bottom can be littered with sharp objects like oyster shells, glass, or other debris, so wearing old shoes or water booties is a good idea. A popular soundside swimming area is Haulover, aka Canadian Hole, just north of Buxton. This is a well-known windsurf-launching area too. There's a nice little beach here, plus a bathhouse with showers, changing rooms, and rest rooms.

Cape Hatteras National Seashore's Coquina Beach is one of the best ocean-swimming areas on the entire Outer Banks. The beach is named for a tiny, delicately colored clam that's common on the North Carolina beaches. Just across from the entrance to Bodie Island Lighthouse, Coquina Beach has just about everything you could want: tons of parking (even for buses), a lifeguard, a bathhouse with showers, rest rooms and changing rooms, a picnic area, and easy access to the beach. Coquina Beach can be a little crowded

The Haulover access (aka Canadian Hole) just north of Buxton is a great place for soundside recreation.

in the summer, but you only have to walk a short way to find your own stretch of beach. Regardless of the crowds, the lifeguard will give you peace of mind about swimming. The beach is guarded daily from Memorial Day to Labor Day. Pets on leashes are allowed here.

Lifeguarded Beaches

The National Park Service operates three lifeguarded beaches in the Cape Hatteras National Seashore, one on each island. Lifeguards are on duty from Memorial Day weekend through Labor Day. They staff the beaches every day between 10:00 A.M. and 6:00 P.M. If red flags are flying at the lifeguarded beaches, it means that the ocean conditions are too dangerous for swimming.

Coquina Beach, on Bodie Island across from the entrance to Bodie Island Lighthouse.

Cape Hatteras Beach, Hatteras Island in Buxton at the lighthouse area, near the old lighthouse site.

Ocracoke Lifeguard Beach, Ocracoke Island, use the first beach access road past the Ocracoke airstrip.

See The Basics chapter for information on swimming safety.

Other Adventures

Flying

Unless you're piloting the plane yourself, you may not consider an airplane tour outdoor recreation. But seeing the barrier islands from the air is so thrilling and shocking that we had to mention it somewhere in the book. Your whole outlook will change when you see that the islands you've been depending upon for firm footing are nothing more than thin ribbons of sand awash in the sea. From the air it looks like the waves could swallow the islands whole at any moment. The vegetation patterns of the islands are very apparent, especially at Buxton Woods, where the line between the woods environment and the stark sand environment is abrupt. You also get to see another perspective of the water. Shoals and sloughs and inlets stand out in sharp contrast to deeper water. It all makes sense from up here. The following private flying services, one at Frisco and one on Ocracoke, offer air tours. Bring your camera.

Burrus Flying Service
Billy Mitchell Airstrip
N.C. Highway 12
Frisco
(252) 986–2679

Gale Force Advisory Aerial Tours
Billy Mitchell Airstrip
N.C. Highway 12
(252) 995–3797

Pelican Airways
Ocracoke Airstrip
N.C. Highway 12
Ocracoke
(252) 928–1661

Horseback Riding

There's something very romantic and appealing about riding horses along the beach, which is exactly what you can do here. Horses must enter the beach at the numbered vehicle access ramps; do not attempt to cross over the dunes. Horses are permitted anywhere that vehicles are allowed, which means that you might have to contend with recreational vehicles on the beach. Buxton Woods has a series of trails and is a good place for a shadier ride. You can also ride on the soundside of the island, where there are several sand roads leading to the water. If you aren't planning to bring your horse on vacation, there is a company in Buxton that offers guided horse tours through Buxton Woods and onto the beach.

Equine Adventures
N.C. Highway 12, Buxton
(252) 995–4897

Hunting

The Cape Hatteras National Seashore area is rich in historic hunting traditions. In the early 1900s, the sportsmen visiting the area weren't in search of fish but of waterfowl. Many wealthy outsiders established hunt clubs along Hatteras Island. Much of the land that now forms the national seashore was once private hunting grounds for wealthy shooting sportsmen. In the early twentieth century, Outer Banks waterfowl hunting was at its world-renowned peak. Sportsmen from all over the East Coast visited this area every fall and winter to get a piece of the action. The Bodie Island Club was a fixture on Bodie Island in the early twentieth century and beyond. In the early 1900s, the club basically changed the habitat around the lighthouse to attract more waterfowl. Its members planted trees, blocked the water flow within the marshes, and replaced a great portion of land with a large freshwater pond that supported great numbers of waterfowl. Back then, there were no limits or laws regulating hunting, and the sportsmen shot freely.

Today, of course, there are strict hunting regulations and not nearly as many waterfowl flying overhead. But hunters still have a good chance of shooting their limit of geese, swan, and ducks that frequent the food-rich marshes of Cape Hatteras National Seashore.

Waterfowl hunters must have a valid North Carolina hunting license with a waterfowl privilege and a Federal Duck Stamp, and they must comply with all state hunting regulations. Contact the North Carolina Wildlife Resources Commission at (800) 675–0263 or www.ncwildlife.org.

Bodie Island: There are twenty permanent blinds available for hunting at Bodie Island. Hunting is by registration request only, and hunters are chosen by lottery. Those who are chosen in the lottery are assigned a blind and must use that blind only.

To register for the lottery, write to HUNT, Cape Hatteras National Seashore, 1401 Park Road, Manteo, NC 27954, or visit the Web site at www.nps.gov/caha. The lottery is handled by mail only and must be postmarked *after* September 25 and received before October 6. If you aren't registered in the lottery, there's still a possibility you can hunt at Bodie Island. Show up at the Whalebone Visitor Center at 5:00 A.M. during hunting season. If there are any no-show hunters, the remaining blinds are divvied up on a first-come, first-served basis.

Pea Island National Wildlife Refuge: Hunting is not allowed here, on land or in the adjacent sound waters.

Hatteras Island: Hunting is permitted within 250 feet of the Pamlico Sound shoreline, between the villages of Salvo and Avon, Avon and Buxton, Frisco and Hatteras, and Hatteras Village and Hatteras Inlet. Temporary blinds are permitted.

Ocracoke Island: Hunting is permitted on the Pamlico Sound side of N.C. Highway 12, within 250 feet of the shoreline, excluding Ocracoke Village, Hammock Hills Nature Trail, and the posted area near the Ocracoke Pony Pens. Temporary blinds are permitted.

For information about hunting, call the NPS main office at (252) 473–1101 or visit the Web site at www.nps.gov/caha.

For hunting gear, supplies, or information, the local resource is Frisco Rod & Gun on N.C. Highway 12 in Frisco, (252) 995–5366.

The following private hunting guides are available to take you waterfowl hunting in the waters around Cape Hatteras National Seashore.

Outer Banks Waterfowl
4740 Elm Court
Kitty Hawk, NC 27954
(252) 261–7842, (252) 441–3732
www.outerbankswaterfowl.com

Ken Dempsey
P.O. Box 156
Hatteras Village, NC 27943
(252) 986–2102

Ocracoke Waterfowl Hunting
P.O. Box 193
Ocracoke Island, NC 27960
(252) 928–5751

Hatteras Island's old live oaks are inviting places to climb.

Cape Hatteras National Seashore Summer Programs

Every summer rangers at Cape Hatteras National Seashore lead a variety of family-oriented nature and cultural programs that help visitors better understand their surroundings while they're here. Programs are held at each of the three visitor centers: Bodie Island Visitor Center at the Bodie Island Lighthouse, (252) 441–5711, Cape Hatteras Visitor Center at the Cape Hatteras Lighthouse, (252) 995–4474; and the Ocracoke Visitor Center in the village at Ocracoke Island, (252) 928–4531.

The programs at each of the visitor centers vary, but they always include a lighthouse program, a walking tour of some sort, a history program, an activity, a creature feature, an evening program, and a kids' program. You can always expect something to interest each member of the family. Some programs are wheelchair-accessible.

Programs last from thirty minutes to two hours throughout the day and are free. They are held from early June through Labor Day. Some of the programs, especially the activities, are limited to a certain number of participants, so if you're really interested in something you may want to sign up ahead of time. Stop by or call the visitor center nearest you to see which programs are being held while you're here or pick up a copy of the *In the Park* newspaper at an NPS visitor center.

A special seashore program for kids is the Junior Ranger Program. Anyone between the ages of five and thirteen can earn a Junior Ranger patch at Cape Hatteras National Seashore by going to programs and completing a booklet. Rangers at any of the visitor centers can give you information about this program.

Wildlife-Watching

A variety of wildlife share these islands with locals, tourists, and migrating birds. While you're out hiking, birding, paddling, or doing any other outdoor activities, you might come into contact with reptiles, amphibians, or small mammals. Cape Hatteras National Seashore and Pea Island National Wildlife Refuge were established to provide habitat for a variety of wildlife and birds. Rangers manage diverse habitats—which include beach, dunes, salt marsh, fresh and brackish ponds, and maritime forest—for these animals to live in.

When you're observing animals and wildlife here, think about the dynamic nature of barrier islands and how difficult it must be to survive in winds, storms, and the salty environment while staying out of the path of three million human visitors and avoiding a variety of nonnative predators.

Bring binoculars and report any unusual sightings to a park ranger.

Amphibians: Look for frogs at freshwater ponds and damp forest floors, like those at Buxton Woods. You might see a green treefrog, bullfrog, soutern leopard frog, or Fowler's toad.

Reptiles: Look for reptiles lying in the sun on colder days. Otherwise, they tend to hide out in cool shady places or in shallow water where they can regulate their body temperatures. You might find turtles, including common snapping turtles, eastern mud turtles, or a diamondback terrapin. Skinks you might see include a five-lined skink, a ground skink, a six-lined racerunner, or eastern glass lizard. Snakes in this area include a black racer, corn snake, rat snake, eastern hognose snake, eastern kingsnake, Carolina salt marsh snake, rough green snake, brown snake, eastern garter snake, and eastern cottonmouths (poisonous).

Mammals: Mammals are often wary of humans so you usually won't see them just out in the open, though you'll probably see marsh rabbits munching grasses on the roadsides. Try looking for animal tracks, trails, or scats. Field guides that identify these signs are available in bookstores. Mammals you might see include opossums, southeastern shrew, bats, eastern cottontails, marsh rabbits, voles, mice, nutria, river otters, gray fox, mink, raccoon, and white-tailed deer.

Marine Mammals: On the water you might encounter sea turtles or marine mammals, like bottle-nosed dolphin, porpoises, whales, or seals. The sea turtles here include loggerhead sea turtle, Atlantic green sea turtle, Kemp's ridley sea turtle, leatherback sea turtle, or the hawksbill sea turtle. Whale and seal sightings are pretty rare, though they're sometimes found stranded on the beaches. If you're out on a deep-sea fishing boat, your chance of seeing these marine mammals increases exponentially. Bottlenosed dolphins are very commonly seen in the ocean near the shore and in the sound. When you're boating or paddling, keep a lookout for their telltale curved fins rolling through the water. Sometimes you can find a boat that takes passengers out on dolphin-watching trips. One such boat is the *Miss Hatteras* at Oden's Dock in Hatteras Village; call (252) 986–2365.

Local Attractions

Bodie Island Lighthouse
N.C. Highway 12, Bodie Island
(252) 441–5711
www.nps.gov/caha/bodielh

On the soundside of the island amid tall pine trees, a lush green lawn, and freshwater marsh and ponds, the Bodie Island Lighthouse occupies an unusual setting for an Atlantic lighthouse. The portion of Cape Hatteras National Seashore on which it sits—Bodie Island—is largely undeveloped, so you can get a pretty good idea of the isolation the lightkeeper must have experienced when the lighthouse was first lit on October 1, 1872. Even today, the lone beam projects far over the dark landscape, the only sign of civilization for miles around. When the lighthouse was built, the landscape around it was typical of the rest of the Outer Banks with sand dunes, hammocks, and low vegetation. In the early 1900s the members of a nearby hunt club altered the ecosystem around the lighthouse, planting pines and damming the marsh to attract waterfowl.

This is the third lighthouse to bear the name of Bodie Island Lighthouse, though the first two were actually south of Oregon Inlet on Pea Island. The first, ca. 1846, was built by an engineer with no lighthouse experience. That 54-foot tower began to lean within two years and was abandoned in 1859. The second lighthouse, an 80-foot tower, was built nearby in 1859. During the Civil War, in 1861, quick-thinking Confederate forces blew it up so that advancing Union forces would not be able to use it as an observation post.

For ten years after, the coast between the Cape Hatteras Lighthouse and Virginia remained dark. Construction on the final Bodie Island tower was begun in 1871 and completed in 1872 with the installation of a first-order Fresnel lens. The light on the 156-foot tower beamed 19 miles out to sea, providing a welcome beacon north of Cape Hatteras. The double keepers' quarters was completed soon thereafter. The light was electrified in 1932, and an on-site keeper was no longer needed.

The Bodie Island Lighthouse stands sentinel north of Oregon Inlet.

Today the site is incredibly scenic. A long drive toward the west takes you back to the lighthouse compound with its perfectly whitewashed outbuildings and horizontally striped black-and-white tower, all set against an expanse of lowlands. The lighthouse is not open for climbing because it needs interior restoration work. The National Park Service is hoping to restore the tower, and Cape Hatteras National Seashore has received a grant and state funds to begin the work. Even though you can't climb, it's still a great place to visit. The double keepers' quarters is open as a visitor center, museum, and bookstore, and the grounds have a nature trail (see our Hiking chapter), an observation platform (see our Birding chapter), and a lucrative fishing hole (on the back of the property near the sound). There are rest rooms on-site. Nature and history programs are held here in the summer months. The visitor center is open from 9:00 A.M. to 6:00 P.M. from Memorial Day to Labor Day and from 9:00 A.M. to 5:00 P.M. the rest of the year.

Oregon Inlet Fishing Center
N.C. Highway 12, Bodie Island
(252) 441–6301, (800) 272–5199
www.oregon-inlet.com

Oregon Inlet Fishing Center is an Outer Banks sportfishing institution with a prime location next to Oregon Inlet. Even if you're not into sportfishing, this is an interesting place to visit to get a feel for the magnitude of recreational fishing on the local economy and culture. One of the intriguing things to see is the center's fishing fleet. Almost all of the vessels are locally built Carolina boats, their flared bows reflecting a bright rainbow of colors in the harbor water. If you want to see all the boats at the docks, be sure to come in the late afternoon or on a very windy day when the boats can't go out fishing. Another cool thing to see is the daily unloading of the catches. If you come to the docks between 3:30 and 5:00 P.M., you'll see the mates throwing tuna, dolphin, wahoo, or other fish onto the docks to be picked up for cleaning. You might be lucky enough to see a giant blue marlin come in to be weighed, but these fish are usually released. You can see a preserved blue marlin—a 1,030-pound one caught in 1973—in a display case next to the store. Also on display is a huge propeller, salvage from the USS *Dionysus* shipwreck. The on-site fishing center store has snacks, drinks, bait, tackle, and souvenirs.

Oregon Inlet is the prime place to begin a fishing trip, offshore or otherwise. If you want to charter an offshore or inshore boat, talk to the reservations people at the fishing center. Or you can reserve a spot on the *Miss Oregon Inlet* head boat. A well-maintained public boat ramp is here with plenty of parking for trucks and trailers. You can also wade into the sound from here; start near the propeller and work your way around the shoreline. If you're driving on the beach alongside Oregon Inlet, come to the fishing center afterward to reinflate your tires. The fishing center is a concessionaire in the Cape Hatteras National Seashore.

Pea Island National Wildlife Refuge
N.C. Highway 12, between Oregon Inlet and Rodanthe
(252) 987–2394 (visitor center), (252) 473–1131 (administrative office)
http://peaisland.fws.gov

With 5,834 acres of barrier island land and 25,700 acres of Pamlico Sound waters, Pea Island National Wildlife Refuge is a safe haven for wildlife and a wonderland for wildlife-watchers. This 13-mile stretch of Hatteras Island is separate from Cape Hatteras National Seashore and is managed by the U.S. Fish and Wildlife Service instead of the National Park Service. Pea Island, which really was an island long ago when other inlets were open, was formerly hunting, farming, and livestock grounds. The island was named for its wealth of delicately flowered dune peas, which are the favorite food of visiting snow geese. The U.S. government acquired the land and established a refuge here in 1937. The Fish and Wildlife Service built the artificial ponds and impoundments, making the area an oasis for waterfowl. Today the refuge consists of ocean beach, dunes, fresh- and brackish-water ponds, salt flats, salt marsh, and sound waters.

If you like watching birds and wildlife, don't miss Pea Island. Wintering waterfowl, migrating shorebirds, raptors, waders, migratory songbirds, occasional bald eagles, the threatened piping plover, and hundreds of other birds are seen here. The bird list boasts more than 265 species (see our Birding chapter). The wildlife list includes twenty-five species of mammals, twenty-four species of reptiles, and five species of amphibians. Loggerhead turtles nest on the beaches here in the summer. In a refuge like this, so devoted to nature, it's a good feeling to know that the creatures feel safe, that they have a place to come where they don't feel threatened. At Pea Island you definitely feel like the land belongs to the wildlife, and the animals are letting you visit for a while, instead of the other way around.

Other things to do on Pea Island include kayaking, beachcombing, surf fishing, surfing, nature photography, and hiking. This is the perfect place for quiet outdoor activities and communion with nature. The refuge has miles of ocean beach, a visitor center with wildlife exhibits, a gift shop, a bookstore with nature-related books, rest rooms, hiking trails (see our Hiking chapter), plenty of parking, informational kiosks, observation platforms and photography blinds, a small boat-launch ramp, and weekly ecotour programs in the summer like bird walks, turtle talks, and canoe tours. The visitor center is open from 9:00 A.M. to 4:00 P.M. every day from March through November. The rest of the year it's open from 9:00 A.M. to 4:00 P.M. Thursday through Sunday. The National Wildlife Refuge System is celebrating its hundredth year in 2003, so special events will be held here throughout the year. Ask at the visitor center about the celebratory events.

Chicamacomico Life Saving Station
N.C. Highway 12, Rodanthe
(252) 987–1552
www.chicamacomico.org

The hard-to-pronounce Chicamacomico Life Saving Station is a thriving example of Outer Banks maritime history. The weathered stations and their attendant outbuildings are important vestiges of lifesaving history. The 1874 Chicamacomico station was one of the original seven lifesaving stations built on the Outer Banks (others followed later) to look out for and aid the shipwrecks that occurred with regularity along the Outer Banks. The precursor to today's Coast Guard, the U.S. Life Saving Service had an important presence on the Outer Banks. The Chicamacomico station operated for seventy

This ornate building, the original Chicamacomico Life Saving Station, now serves as the surf boat house.

years, until 1954. It has since been restored and is now an intriguing museum and historic site.

The compound includes the ornately trimmed 1874 Chicamacomico Life Saving Station (now a boathouse for the surf boat), the larger 1911 Chicamacomico Life Saving Station, and five support buildings—two cookhouses, a shop, a stable, and a building that now houses a collection of shipwreck artifacts. In addition, there are several types of cisterns. Inside the 1911 station house you'll see exhibits about lifesaving and shipwreck history, plus a museum shop. The fascinating thing to see at the site is a reenactment of the old lifesaving drills on Thursdays at 2:00 P.M. from June through August. In the drills you get to see a crew use the historic beach apparatus. On other summer days you might catch another program, like a storytelling session or a knot-tying class. One evening a week, a beach bonfire is held at 8:00 P.M., with someone telling shipwreck and lifesaving stories around a campfire. All programs are held in the summer months. Chicamacomico is run by a nonprofit organization and volunteers. The station is open from Easter weekend through Thanksgiving weekend, Tuesday through Saturday, from 9:00 A.M. to 5:00 P.M. Admission is free, but donations are much needed. There are picnic facilities on-site.

Cape Hatteras Lighthouse
Lighthouse Road, off N.C. Highway 12, Buxton
(252) 995–4474
www.nps.gov/caha

The nation's tallest brick lighthouse, the 208-foot Cape Hatteras Lighthouse is the symbol of the Outer Banks and Cape Hatteras National Seashore. It is one of the most loved and well-known lighthouses on the East Coast, especially since it survived a highly publicized move in 1999. The tower's daymark or painted pattern, is two black and two white spiral stripes, a rare pattern for lighthouses.

The original Cape Hatteras Lighthouse was built in 1803, but mariners complained that it was barely bright enough to be of any use. The current-standing 1870 tower was built 600 feet north of the original location to keep it safe from erosion. A fixed testament to the rate of beach erosion, in 1870 the tower was originally 1,500 feet from the sea, but by 1935 the ocean was lapping at its base. Erosion-control efforts failed and the lighthouse was closed. A temporary structure was established on-site, but soon the erosion subsided and the Cape Hatteras Lighthouse was reopened in 1950.

By the 1980s the Cape Hatteras Lighthouse was again facing serious erosion concerns. Storms and strong currents had continued to erode the sand that buffered the lighthouse from the sea, and it was in danger of falling into the ocean. Government officials spent millions of dollars researching ways to save the structure, piling up sandbags at its base and reinforcing the surrounding jetties. In 1987 the National Park Service decided that the only way to save the lighthouse was to move it. Many people vehemently opposed moving the lighthouse, claiming it would never survive such an ordeal. In the end the government prevailed, and Congress appropriated $9.8 million to perform the task.

The highly complex move required months of engineering, planning, and design by experts in numerous fields. To state a complex situation quite simply, the lighthouse was jacked up, lifted onto steel beams, and nudged by hydraulic jacks toward its new home. The 2,900-foot move took place from June 17 to July 9, 1999—only 23 days and about three weeks ahead of schedule. About 20,000 visitors a day, as well as the national media, watched the historic event. The Cape Hatteras Lighthouse arrived at its new location safely and intact. The beacon was relit in November 1999.

The Cape Hatteras Lighthouse is the most popular attraction at Cape Hatteras National Seashore. The picturesque tower hovering over the village of Buxton lures lighthouse lovers from all over the world. Its light, visible 24 nautical miles out to sea, sweeps across the village with comforting regularity.

The Cape Hatteras Lighthouse is the only one of the three Cape Hatteras National Seashore lighthouses that is open for climbing. The view from the top is absolutely unforgettable. The lighthouse is typically open for climbing from the Friday before Easter through Columbus Day. Call ahead for current climbing hours and fees. Children under 38 inches tall cannot climb the lighthouse.

Also on-site is a visitor center, called Museum of the Sea, housed in the historic keepers' quarters. Even if you don't climb the tower, the museum is worth a visit to learn about lighthouse history. A bookstore is housed in another keeper's building. Rest rooms and plenty of parking are on-site and you can access the beach from here.

Frisco Native American Museum & Natural History Center
N.C . Highway 12, Frisco
(252) 995–4440
www.nativeamericanmuseum.org

Hatteras Island is rich in Native American history, as the Croatoan Indians, later known as the Hatteras Indians, lived on the island (west of Cape Hatteras) prior to English settlement. This enchanting museum celebrates the Native American culture of Hatteras Island and the nation with authentic collections

The new Graveyard of the Atlantic Museum in Hatteras Village was designed to resemble a ship.

of artifacts and artwork from ancient to modern times. The museum's collection includes an ancient dugout canoe that was found on the property. You can beat a Hopi Kiva drum and see numerous displays of Indian artifacts like pipes, stones, tools, and musical instruments. The variety and amount of artifacts here is amazing. In the gift shop are handcrafted beadwork, pottery, basketry, weaving, toys, educational materials, and jewelry. In the Natural History Center, there are educational exhibits, a small theater, and displays. Self-guided nature trails are outdoors. Admission is charged. The museum is open year-round, Tuesday through Saturday, from 11:00 A.M. to 5:00 P.M.

Graveyard of the Atlantic Museum
End of N.C. Highway 12, Hatteras Village
(252) 986–2995
www.graveyardoftheatlantic.com

Next to the Hatteras ferry docks is an unusual modern building with nautical curves, porthole windows, and shipwreck-style beams and timbers. This is the new Graveyard of the Atlantic Museum, a nonprofit labor of love for the maritime history of North Carolina. Years of fund-raising, research, planning, and design have gone into the establishment of this museum, which interprets maritime history through the artifacts and stories of shipwrecks, particularly from the time period of 1524 to 1945. The coast of North Carolina, known as the Graveyard of the Atlantic, has one of the highest densities of shipwrecks in the world. The state-of-the-art museum is expected to be fully finished in 2004, but in the meantime a portion is open to the public with some exhibits. A special exhibit in 2003 on Brigadier General Billy Mitchell commemorates flight on the Outer Banks. In 1923 Mitchell and U.S. Army airmen under his command took off from an improvised airstrip near Hatteras Village and sank the obsolete Navy battleships USS *Virginia* and USS *New Jersey*, anchored near Diamond Shoals. Thus, Mitchell was instrumental in convincing the U.S. Navy that aerial bombing was necessary in modern warfare. No fees will be charged to enter the museum until it is fully operational, though contributions are greatly needed.

Ocracoke Pony Pens
N.C. Highway 12, Ocracoke Island
(252) 928–5111
www.nps.gov/caha/oc_ponies

The National Park Service maintains a herd of about thirty ponies in a 180-acre penned pasture about 5 miles north of Ocracoke Village. Visitors can walk up to a platform at the edge of the pen to get a look at them. The ponies' ancestors used to run free on Ocracoke Island. Legend has it that the wild ponies came to the island by way of sixteenth-century shipwrecks. At one time there may have been as many as 300 free-roaming horses on the island. The island residents used the ponies for work and play, and the U.S. Life Saving Service used them to haul heavy equipment to the surf and to patrol the beaches. In the 1950s the local Boy Scouts cared for the ponies and rode them for fun. In 1959 all of the free-roaming animals were penned, because they were being hit by cars on the newly paved N.C. Highway 12

Wild horses are part of the mystique of the Outer Banks.

and they were eating up all the dune vegetation, contributing to erosion. The National Park Service cares for them now. The ponies have distinctive physical characteristics: five lumbar vertebrae instead of the six usually found in horses; seventeen ribs instead of eighteen; and unique size, shape, posture, and color. It's free to visit the ponies, but you can only look. Don't try to feed or pet them; they may not be running wild, but they are not tame.

Ocracoke Preservation Society Museum
N.C. Highway 12, Ocracoke
(252) 928–4531

The Ocracoke Preservation Society Museum, which is dedicated to the history and culture of the island, occupies an old village home that was moved to this site to save it from demolition. Many of the original architectural elements of the turn-of-the-century home are intact, and the house is decorated with furnishings donated by the locals. A 1930–40s kitchen, bedroom, and living room are set up in the house. The museum also has photographs, exhibits, maritime relics, decoys by local carvers, Civil War artifacts, shells, a video presentation, and a small gift shop. Upstairs is a small research library that can be used with permission. It's free to visit the museum, which is open from Easter through November, but donations are encouraged.

British Cemetery
British Cemetery Road, Ocracoke

A poignant attraction on Ocracoke is a small cemetery honoring four British seamen whose bodies washed ashore on the island in 1942. The seamen were four of the thirty-three sailors and four officers aboard the HMS *Bedfordshire*, a British vessel patrolling the coast between Norfolk and Cape Lookout. The *Bedfordshire* was sent to the American coast when German U-boats began to hinder shipping in the early stages of World War II. The vessel escorted convoys and aided torpedoed ships. On May 11, 1942, a German U-boat torpedoed the *Bedfordshire* from 600 meters. Three days later two Coast Guardsmen patrolling the Ocracoke beaches found and retrieved the bodies of two soldiers, a Lieutenant Cunningham and Stanley Craig. The Williams family of Ocracoke donated a plot of its family cemetery, and the islanders gave the seamen a respectful burial. Two more unidentified British soldiers were found a week later and buried alongside their fellow seamen on the island.

Ocracoke Island Lighthouse
Lighthouse Road, Ocracoke
www.nps.gov/caha/ocracokelh.htm

The oldest and the shortest of the Outer Banks lighthouses, Ocracoke Island Lighthouse is a pristine little tower dressed all in white. In all its 75-foot glory, the 1823 lighthouse still functions in the heart of Ocracoke Village. It is the second-oldest operating lighthouse in the nation. When it was built, the tower's whitewash daymark was created by blending lime, salt, Spanish

The Ocracoke Island Lighthouse is the second-oldest operating lighthouse in the nation. NORTH CAROLINA DIVISION OF TOURISM, FILM AND SPORTS DEVELOPMENT

whiting, rice, glue, and boiling water and applying the mixture while it was hot. The keepers' quarters on-site is the original building, though a second story was added in 1897 to house an additional keeper and another section was added in 1929. Also on-site is a generator house, which was once the oil supply shed. The lighthouse is not open for climbing, but it is a picturesque, charming site just begging to have its snapshot taken. It's a great stop on a bicycle tour of the island. Occasionally in the summer there may be a volunteer on-site to talk about the lighthouse or answer questions. Ask at the NPS Ocracoke Island Visitor Center about the possibility.

Services and Necessities

Where to Eat

Owens' Restaurant
N.C. Highway 12, MP 16.5,
Nags Head
(252) 441–7309

Sam & Omie's Restaurant
N.C. Highway 12, MP 16.5,
Nags Head
(252) 441–7366

BoardWok South
N.C. Highway 12, Rodanthe
(252) 987–1080

Tiki Grill
N.C. Highway 12, Salvo
(252) 987–1088

Hodad's
N.C. Highway 12, Avon
(252) 995–7866

The Pickled Steamer
N.C. Highway 12, Avon
(252) 995–3602

Orange Blossom Bakery and Cafe
N.C. Highway 12, Buxton
(252) 995–4109

The Tides Restaurant
N.C. Highway 12, Buxton
(252) 995–5988

Gingerbread House Bakery
N.C. Highway 12, Frisco
(252) 995–5204

South Shore Grill
N.C. Highway 12, Frisco
(252) 995–5535

Austin Creek Grill and Austin Creek Baking Company
Hatteras Landing, N.C. Highway 12, Hatteras Village
(252) 986–1511 (grill), (252) 986–1578 (bakery)

The Breakwater Restaurant
N.C. Highway 12 at Oden's Dock,
Hatteras Village
(252) 986–2733

The Back Porch Restaurant
1324 Country Road, Ocracoke
(252) 928–6401

Café Atlantic
N.C. Highway 12, Ocracoke
(252) 928–4861

Howards Pub
N.C. Highway 12, Ocracoke
(252) 928–4441

Jason's Restaurant
N.C. Highway 12, Ocracoke
(252) 928–3434

Ocracoke Coffee Co.
Back Road, Ocracoke
(252) 928–7473

Where to Stay

If you're visiting the northern end of the Cape Hatteras National Seashore (Bodie Island or Pea Island National Wildlife Refuge), you might want to consider staying in Nags Head or one of the northern Hatteras Island villages (Rodanthe, Waves, or Salvo). Avon and Buxton are in the middle of Hatteras Island; Frisco and Hatteras Village are at the southern end.

Comfort Inn South
N.C. Highway 12, MP 17,
Nags Head
(252) 441–6315, (800) 334–3302

Quality Inn Sea Oatel
N.C. Highway 12, MP 16.5,
Nags Head
(252) 441–7191, (800) 440–4386

Hatteras Island Resort
Atlantic Drive of N.C. Highway 12,
Rodanthe
(252) 987–2345
www.hatterasislandresort.com

Avon Motel
N.C. Highway 12, Avon
(252) 995–5774, (800) 243–5774
www.avonmotel.com

Cape Hatteras Motel
N.C. Highway 12, Buxton
(252) 995–5611, (800) 995–0711
www.capehatterasmotel.com

Lighthouse View Motel
N.C. Highway 12, Buxton
(252) 995–5680, (800) 225–7651
www.lighthouseview.com

Outer Banks Motel
N.C. Highway 12, Buxton
(252) 995–5601, (800) 995–1233
www.outerbanksmotel.com

Durant Station Motel
N.C. Highway 12, Hatteras Village
(252) 986–2244, (888) 550–2244
www.durantstation.com

Holiday Inn Express Hatteras
N.C. Highway 12, Hatteras Village
(252) 986–1110, (800) 361–1590
www.outerbanksholidayinn.com

Seaside Inn of Hatteras Bed and Breakfast
N.C. Highway 12, Hatteras Village
(252) 986–2700
www.seasidebb.com

Berkley Manor B&B
N.C. Highway 12, Ocracoke
(252) 928–5911, (800) 832–1223
www.berkleymanor.com

Boyette House
N.C. Highway 12, Ocracoke
(252) 928–4261, (800) 928–4261
www.boyettehouse.com

The Lightkeeper's Guesthouse
Creek Road, Ocracoke
(252) 928–1821

Weekly House Rentals

Midgett Realty
N.C. Highway 12, Rodanthe, Avon and Hatteras Village
(252) 986–2841, (800) 527–2903
www.midgettrealty.com

Sun Realty
N.C. Highway 12, in all Hatteras Island villages
(800) 334–4745
www.sunrealtync.com

Surf or Sound Realty
N.C. Highway 12, Rodanthe and Avon
(252) 995–5801, (800) 237–1138
www.surforsound.com

Ocracoke Island Realty
N.C. Highway 12, Ocracoke
(252) 928–6261
www.ocracokeislandrealty.com

Sandy Shores Realty
N.C. Highway 12, Ocracoke
(252) 928–5711
www.ocracoke-island.com

Grocery Stores

Food Lion
Hatteras Island Plaza, N.C. Highway 12, Avon
(252) 995–4488

Conner's Supermarket
N.C. Highway 12, Buxton
(252) 995–5711

Burrus Red and White Supermarket
N.C. Highway 12, Hatteras Village
(252) 986–2333

Ocracoke Variety Store
N.C. Highway 12, Ocracoke
(252) 928–4911

Medical Services

HealthEast Family Care
N.C. Highway 12, Avon
(252) 995–3073
N.C. Highway 12, Hatteras Village
(252) 986–2765

Ocracoke Health Center
Back Road, Ocracoke
(252) 928–1511

Veterinarians

Hatteras Island Animal Clinic
N.C. Highway 12, Avon
(252) 995–5062

Ocracoke Animal Clinic
British Cemetery Road, Ocracoke
(252) 928–3443

Kennel

Sandy Paws Bed & Biscuit
136 West End Road, Ocracoke
(252) 928–3093

Nearby Attractions

Cape Hatteras National Seashore is close to numerous attractions that shouldn't be missed when you're visiting the area.

Wright Brothers National Memorial, Milepost 8, U.S. Highway 158, Kill Devil Hills; (252) 441–7430; www.nps.gov/wrbr. Site of the world's first powered airplane flight by Wilbur and Orville Wright on December 17, 1903. Memorial, museum, bookstore, and special programs. First Flight Centennial Celebration held here December 12–17, 2003, with centennial events throughout the year.

Jockey's Ridge State Park, Milepost 12, U.S. Highway 158, Nags Head; (252) 441–7132; www.jockeysridgestatepark.com. Largest sand dune on the East Coast.

Fort Raleigh National Historic Site, Roanoke Island; (252) 473–5772; www.nps.gov/fora. Historic site honoring the beginning of English settlement in North America.

Elizabethan Gardens, Roanoke Island at Fort Raleigh; (252) 473–3234; www.elizabethangardens.org. Ten and a half acres of Elizabethan-style botanical gardens to commemorate the first English settlement in America.

The Lost Colony, Waterside Theatre, Roanoke Island at Fort Raleigh; (252) 473–3414 or (800) 488–5012; www.thelostcolony.org. The nation's longest-running outdoor drama depicting the historical account of the legendary colony of English settlers that disappeared in 1587.

North Carolina Aquarium on Roanoke Island, 374 Airport Road, Roanoke Island; (252) 473–3494; www.ncaquariums.com. A 68,000-square-foot facility with aquariums representing the waters of the Outer Banks and surrounding areas.

2003: A Year to Celebrate on the Outer Banks

Several milestone events are being commemorated on the Outer Banks in the year 2003. For starters, Cape Hatteras National Seashore is celebrating its fiftieth anniversary. Cape Hatteras National Seashore was established January 12, 1953, as the first national seashore in the United States. The National Park Service plans to celebrate the event with special activities throughout the year. For more information call (252) 473–2111 or visit www.nps.gov/caha.

In 2003 the National Park Service Outer Banks Group has its hands full with another huge milestone event: the First Flight Centennial Celebration at the Wright Brothers National Memorial in Kill Devil Hills. This yearlong, statewide celebration, which climaxes the week around December 17, 2003, at the Kill Devil Hills Memorial site, honors the historic first flights of Wilbur and Orville Wright on December 17, 1903. On location at the Wright Brothers National Memorial will be temporary pavilions housing exhibits about flight. During the week of December 12–17, several flyovers will occur and aviation dignitaries will speak at the site. December 17 will feature a huge, media-filled celebration and re-creation of the first flight. In honor of the first flight celebration, several events are planned on Hatteras Island. Call (252) 995–4440 for information. For more information visit www.outerbanks.org or call the Outer Banks Visitors Bureau at (252) 473–2138 or (800) 446–6262.

Another event worth celebrating in 2003 is the hundredth anniversary of the National Wildlife Refuge System. Pea Island National Wildlife Refuge on Hatteras Island will celebrate the event in special ways. Contact it at (252) 473–1131 or http://peaisland.fws.gov.

Roanoke Island Festival Park, Manteo; (252) 475–1506; www.roanoke island.com. *Elizabeth II* representative 1585 sailing ship, hands-on museum, film, art gallery, live performances.

Annual Events

Wings Over Water, throughout the Outer Banks, Cape Hatteras National Seashore and Pea Island; (252) 441–8144; www.wingsoverwater.org. Annual festival celebrating wildlife and wildlands in eastern North Carolina. Birding, hiking, paddling, and natural history field trips, plus workshops, programs and speakers related to the natural world. Held in October.

East Coast Kite Surfing Championships, Frisco Woods Campground, Frisco; (252) 995–5208 or (252) 441–4124; www.outerbanks.com/frisco woods.com or www.kittyhawk.com. Annual kiteboarding competition. Held in April.

Inner Tribal Powwow "Journey Home," Cape Hatteras School, Buxton; (252) 995–4440; www.nativeamericanmuseum.org. Annual inner-tribal celebration on ancestral ground in Hatteras. Crafts, drumming circles, storytelling, dancing, food, bonfire. Held in April.

Eastern Surfing Championships, Cape Hatteras Lighthouse, Buxton; (866) SURF-ESA; www.surfesa.org. Annual surfing competition for all ages.

Cape Lookout National Seashore

Cape Lookout National Seashore

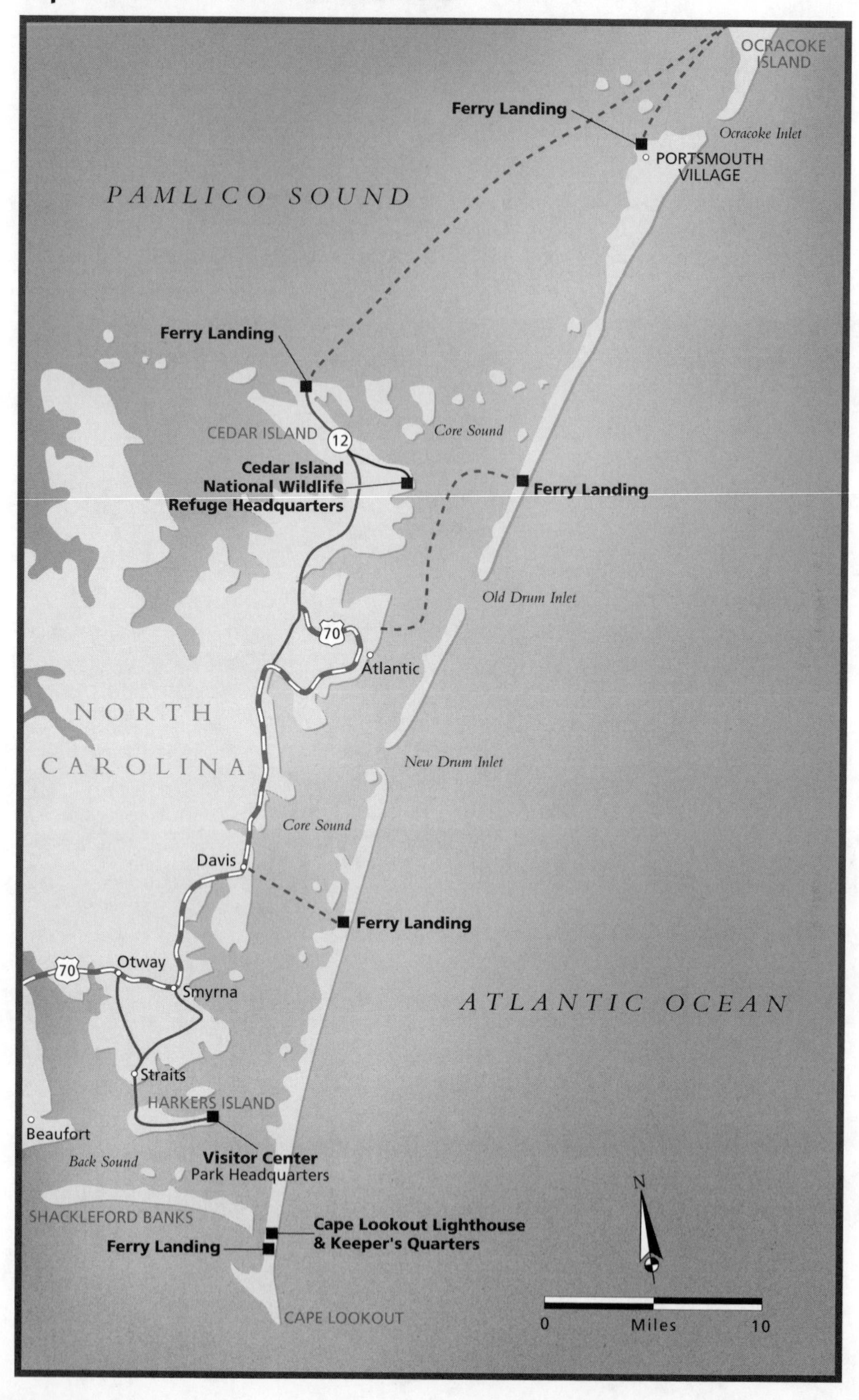

OCRACOKE ISLAND
Ferry Landing
Ocracoke Inlet
PORTSMOUTH VILLAGE
PAMLICO SOUND
Ferry Landing
CEDAR ISLAND
12
Core Sound
Cedar Island National Wildlife Refuge Headquarters
Ferry Landing
Old Drum Inlet
70
Atlantic
NORTH CAROLINA
New Drum Inlet
Core Sound
Davis
Ferry Landing
70
Otway
Smyrna
ATLANTIC OCEAN
Straits
HARKERS ISLAND
Beaufort
Back Sound
Visitor Center
Park Headquarters
N
SHACKLEFORD BANKS
Cape Lookout Lighthouse & Keeper's Quarters
Ferry Landing
CAPE LOOKOUT
0
Miles
10

Overview

Far, far away from the modern world, floating in the sea with no tangible link to the continent, is Cape Lookout National Seashore. Its detachment from the mainland is its essential quality, not only geographically but also vitally. The essence of these islands is rugged and unadulterated. Here, nature takes its course with freedom.

The seashore islands are honest, offering nothing but what they are in their natural state—raw, beautiful, desertlike islands. They are aloof—no catering to the masses here; tourists or no tourists, the islands remain essentially the same, for the most part unaltered by man's intentions.

Cape Lookout National Seashore embraces four slender barrier islands along the central coast of North Carolina. These islands, generally considered the southern Outer Banks, are for the most part undeveloped, with no paved roads, no permanent residents, and no commercialism. Cape Lookout National Seashore is a remote barrier island environment, which includes 56 miles of deserted beaches, impermeable marsh, a rare maritime forest, a forsaken village, an unmanned working lighthouse, and free-roaming wild horses. The Atlantic Ocean crashes against one side of the islands, while sound waters lap at the other. At some points on the islands it is only a shell's throw between sound and ocean; the greatest width of the islands is only a mile and a half.

For the outdoors enthusiast, this environment is an unbelievable dream. Anglers, surfers, shell-collectors, hikers, campers, sunbathers, birders, paddlers, and wanderers are most attracted to Cape Lookout National Seashore, as are geologists and biologists. Visitors need to be of the self-sufficient variety. There are few amenities or facilities and the recreation opportunities are very unstructured. The environment is harsh and hostile, with little shade or protection from the wind, no fresh water, and plenty of bugs. These elements, combined with the remoteness of the islands, make visitation at this seashore much lower than at its northern neighbor, Cape Hatteras National Seashore. Cape Lookout National Seashore sees 450,000 visitors a year,

Cape Lookout National Seashore is remote and rugged.

while Cape Hatteras sees more than three million. Of course, lower visitation is alluring to the rugged outdoorsy types who prefer Cape Lookout to Cape Hatteras.

The Lay of the Land

At the northern end of Cape Lookout National Seashore is **North Core Banks,** oriented from northeast to southwest. This 18-mile-long island borders Ocracoke Inlet and is visible from Ocracoke Island. The island is often referred to as Portsmouth Island after the abandoned village on its northern end called Portsmouth Village. When Whalebone and Swash Inlets were open, the north end of the island became totally separate from the south end, resulting in Portsmouth Island in the north and North Core Banks in the south. These inlets are now closed. It's quite confusing because inlets are constantly opening and closing on the north end of this island. Regardless, the national seashore staff calls the stretch from Miles 0 to 18 North Core Banks, while most everyone else calls it Portsmouth Island.

Portsmouth Village, at mile 0, is an abandoned historic village. At one time it was the most prosperous village on the whole Outer Banks, but its residents left a few at a time until there was no one left in the early 1970s (see the Brief History section in this chapter or the Attractions chapter). The National Park Service has restored several of the buildings, including the post office, the school, the church, a home, and Life Saving Station. Visitors are welcome to tour these buildings on their own. Some of the old homes are leased to private caretakers who upkeep the buildings; do not tour those buildings.

North Core Banks is a tenuous island, constantly being broken into pieces and soldered back together by opening and closing inlets. In September 2002 Tropical Storm Gustav opened two new inlets at Miles 2 and 7, chunking up the northern end of the island into small bits. At this writing, the inlets were still open at high tide and the areas were only traversable at extreme low tide. The usual southern migration and closure of the inlets was expected, but no one ever knows what will happen with inlets.

At Miles 16 and 17 on North Core Banks is the Long Point cabin area, where twenty cabins are operated by a mainland concessionaire. The cabins are available for rent and offer an alternative to camping. The cabins were here before this island became a part of Cape Lookout National Seashore, but they are now owned by the National Park Service and leased to the concessionaire.

On the south end of North Core Banks at mile 18 is **Old Drum Inlet,** a historic inlet that was open from 1933 to 1971 and then reopened in 1999 thanks to Hurricane Dennis. The opening of this inlet formed a small island that the NPS calls **Middle Core Bank.** It's a 4-mile chunk of land (Mile 18 to 22) located between Old and New Drum Inlets. Old Drum Inlet is closing slowly and is wadable at low tide, so the island is not entirely inaccessible. The inlet will probably close completely within a few years, giving North Core Banks its detached, 4-mile tail back, but you can never talk with any certainty about inlets.

South of the Middle Core Bank at Mile 22 is **New Drum Inlet,** an artificial inlet opened in the 1970s to provide mainland fishermen with a passageway to the sea. The Army Corps of Engineers blew the inlet open with dynamite, but it has never been a stable inlet, proving that you can't mess with Mother Nature. The inlet widened to almost 4,000 feet and was much too shallow to use. They say the inlet has a mind of its own, that the Corps of Engineers couldn't get a straight channel through it no matter how much they dredged. The Corps eventually gave up on the expensive task of maintaining it, and mainland fishermen go north to Ocracoke Inlet or south to Barden Inlet to access the sea.

Below New Drum Inlet is **South Core Banks,** a 24-mile-long island stretching from Miles 23 to 47 and oriented northeast to southwest. Before it was part of the national seashore, this island was called Core Banks, without the directional moniker. Like the other islands of the national seashore, South Core Banks is largely empty. Its areas of development are the Great Island cabin area at Miles 29 to 30, run by a mainland concessionaire; the Cape Lookout Lighthouse compound; and Cape Village, a historic area of fishing cottages and the old Life Saving and Coast Guard Stations. South Core Banks is the most visited of the seashore islands, mainly because of the easy ferry access to the Cape Lookout Lighthouse area and Cape Point.

The Cape Lookout Lighthouse, at Mile 41, is a working aid to maritime navigation, but it is not open to public climbing. Its keeper's quarters are open with a small visitor center and exhibits. Ferries dock in the sound in front of the lighthouse, and this is also a popular area for visiting boaters. On summer afternoons and fall weekends, the sound in front of the lighthouse is downright packed with boaters. A boardwalk leads from the sound to the lighthouse and on to the ocean beach.

A few miles down the island, around Miles 43 to 44, is **Cape Lookout**, one of North Carolina's three famous capes. Cape Point at Mile 44 is a sharp spike of land that juts out into Lookout Shoals, a dangerous, shallow area that contributes to the coast's moniker of Graveyard of the Atlantic. The Cape Lookout Lighthouse was built to guard ships off these formidable shoals.

From Cape Point, the land hooks around and faces southwest. A spit of land with the ineloquent name of Power Squadron Spit shoots off from the point and forms a snug bight called Lookout Bight. This protected area of water is deep, wide, and safe from all weather. Sailors love to tie up here, and both fish and fishermen frequent it. A groin wall was built here in 1915 to try to widen Lookout Bight, and it worked. The bight and Cape Point are wider than they used to be. Fishing cottages sit on the shore along Lookout Bight. These cottages, along with the 1888 Life Saving Station building and the 1916 Coast Guard station building, constitute a National Historic District.

Shackleford Banks, the southernmost island of Cape Lookout National Seashore, runs perpendicular to the Core Banks. With its beaches facing directly south, the 9-mile-long island is the most remote of them all. It is separated from Core Banks by shallow Barden Inlet, aka The Drain; before the inlet opened in 1933, Shackleford was attached to Core Banks. Shackle-

Wild horses roam the dunes of Shackleford Banks.

ford is a wilderness of sand and shrub, home to a herd of more than one hundred free-roaming wild horses. The island is also home to one of North Carolina's most distinctive maritime forests. Shackleford Banks is bordered on the west by Beaufort Inlet.

Creation of Cape Lookout National Seashore

The islands of Cape Lookout National Seashore were originally intended to be part of Cape Hatteras National Seashore. In the 1930s, during early talks about the first national seashore, planners envisioned a park stretching from the Virginia line to Beaufort Inlet. But by the time Cape Hatteras National Seashore came into being two decades later, it was a third of the size originally proposed—Core and Shackleford Banks were not included. It soon became apparent that at Cape Hatteras National Seashore, recreation and visitation came first, due to the easy access to the park and the proximity of the island villages. In his book, *An Outer Banks Reader*, David Stick writes that Cape Lookout National Seashore was created to satisfy an environmental preservation void that Cape Hatteras National Seashore could not fulfill because of its high visitation.

In the 1960s, while other coastal areas were seeing rapid development, Core and Shackleford Banks miraculously remained undeveloped. The National Park Service recognized the opportunity to preserve these coastal islands in their natural state, and an act of Congress established Cape Lookout National Seashore in 1966. The state of North Carolina took over the responsibility of acquiring all the lands from private owners—a task that took ten years. In 1976 the National Park Service took ownership of 28,500 acres on the islands.

By 1976 there were hundreds of fishing/hunting camps and shacks on the islands, built by mainland residents, many of whom had squatted on the state-owned property. Camp owners who could prove land ownership were paid for their property and granted leases to continue using it. The National Park Service conducted a survey of the condition of the structures, and most of the shacks were condemned. But some of the fish camps in North Core and South Core Banks were deemed habitable; these were contracted to concessionaires Morris Marina Kabin Kamps and the Alger Willis Fish Camps to rent to visitors, as is still done today.

Also on the islands were nearly 2,500 junked, rusty vehicles. Prior to 1976, it was common for visitors to ferry over a used four-wheel-drive vehicle, run it on the beach until it died and then leave it behind on the island. The National Park Service at first undertook the task of removing the vehicles, but this proved to be too expensive and they stopped. In the end it was a recreational fishing club that took over the task of removing the vehicles.

On Shackleford Banks, the National Park Service had to deal with feral livestock—pigs, goats, sheep, and horses—that were destroying the vegetation of the island. They removed all the domestic animals but the horses, which proved to have historic, culturally significant lineage. Today they manage the number of horses on the island to keep the herd healthy.

With the removal of junked cars and rundown shacks, the National Park Service began the task of converting the islands into a park. In 1978 the National Park Service registered Portsmouth Village on the National Historic Register and began to preserve and restore the abandoned community's buildings. Many of the buildings are leased to owners who promise annual upkeep on the buildings. Over the years the park established visitor centers and exhibits at Portsmouth Village, the lighthouse keepers' quarters and on the east end of Harkers Island. They established a few facilities for visitors, like compost toilets, picnic areas, and ferry docks. They hired biologists and ecologists to help protect sea turtles, piping plovers, wild horses, and the barrier island environment, and rangers to educate the public and interpret the islands' history.

Geology and Geography

(See the Cape Hatteras Overview chapter for an explanation of how the North Carolina barrier islands were formed.)

Once a barrier island forms, it migrates, changes shape, and evolves in its own unique way. Barrier islands are ephemeral and dynamic. No two are the same, and one is never the same as it was in the past. The barrier islands of Cape Lookout National Seashore are no exception.

The Core Banks, running northeast to southwest, are low and narrow with almost no dunes, and they are overwashed by the ocean in almost every major storm. Shackleford Banks, running east to west, is higher, with extensive vegetated dunes. Elevation ranges from sea level to 10 feet on Core Banks and up to 35 feet on Shackleford Banks, where the extreme highs create lows between the dunes, called swales.

The predominant north-south winds in the area affect the islands differently. On the Core Banks, wind blows the sand up and down the islands, flattening out any dune formation. The Core Banks are retreating, or eroding, on the ocean side because of the rise in sea level, while at the same time accreting, or growing, on the sound side. Therefore, the islands are moving to the west, toward the mainland. On Shackleford, wind blows sand back and forth across the island, building up the dunes and adding width to the island. The blowing sand has actually submerged trees, and when it blew away again, the dead trees reappeared, resulting in the "ghost forest" on Shackleford's west end. You'll see the ancient-looking dead trunks protruding from the sand.

Because of the undeveloped status of the islands, it is easy to see the geological processes at work. The changing nature of the islands is apparent at Cape Lookout, says NPS Ranger Karen Duggan. "The Cape switches back and forth like a dog wagging its tail," she says. Cape Lookout has migrated to the east and widened since the 1800s, though this was partially affected by a man-made jetty.

The low, narrow islands of Core Banks are frequently overwashed by storm waves, meaning the ocean water comes clear over the islands to the sound. This is a healthy barrier island process. The barrier islands on the northern Outer Banks, from Ocracoke Island to the Virginia line do not receive overwash because of high man-made dunes on the ocean beach. These dunes were built to protect the island from erosion, but now it is clear they contribute to it. The Core Banks, however, do not have the artificial dunes that prevent overwash; subsequently, they are not eroding as fast as their northern counterparts. The lack of man-made dunes on these islands keeps them in their unaltered state, and geologists frequently use the islands as a laboratory to learn more about barrier islands.

Islands oriented northeast-southwest like Core Banks are low-lying and narrow and subject to the creation of inlets. At least six different inlets have cut the Core Banks at the Old Drum Inlet location. Numerous inlets have opened and closed between Portsmouth Village and Old Drum Inlet. The inlets usually migrate south and close, unless humans work to keep them open.

Shackleford Banks, because of its east-west orientation, is less susceptible to inlets. The east and west ends of Shackleford are very different places. The west end is high dunes and shrubs and there is even a maritime forest here. The east end is low and marshy. The natural process of change at Shackleford is erosion on the ocean side of the island, overwash on the low eastern end of the island, and accretion on the western end of the island. Shackleford Banks has some freshwater marsh and springs, a freshwater pond, and a maritime forest.

Habitats of Cape Lookout National Seashore

Ocean Beach: The Atlantic Ocean meets the shores of Cape Lookout National Seashore, and its sealife is often visible from the beach. Sea turtles lay eggs on Core and Shackleford Banks in summer. Shackleford attracts loggerhead turtles exclusively, while Core Banks sees loggerhead, green, leatherback, and Kemp's ridley turtles. Bottle-nosed dolphin are often seen in the ocean in winter, and occasionally a whale or shark may wash up on the shore. Crabs, fish, starfish, jellyfish, seaweed, shells, and egg sacks are often seen in the water or washed up on shore, offering a peek at the incredibly rich life in the sea. Although the sandy beach appears desolate, it's actually quite alive. A variety of microscopic plants and animals live beneath the surface of the wet sand, mole crabs (a k a sand fleas) and coquina crabs burrow in the sand, ghost crabs scurry all along the beach. Shorebirds flit and hop around the tide line, dining on worms and other creatures that live in the sand, while great gulls fly overhead or rest on the beach. Ground-nesting and colonial waterbirds make their nests directly on the sandy beach. The amount and variety of seashells on the beaches of Cape Lookout is astounding. Unbroken sand dollars, Scotch bonnets, whelks, olives, and many more interesting shells are waiting to be found.

Dunes: The dunes at Cape Lookout National Seashore vary in height. On Core Banks they are low, while on Shackleford they are higher. A variety of salt-tolerant beach grasses grows on these dunes, including plants like salt-

Soundside marshes are nutrient-rich breeding grounds for sea life.

meadow hay and American beachgrass. The most prominent residents of the dunes (and other areas) are the Shackleford Banks horses, which graze on these grasses and drink from a freshwater pond and springs.

Shrub Zone: Herbs and shrubs like wax myrtle, yaupon, live oak, red cedar, marsh elder, and bayberry thrive in this zone. There is little diversity of species on the islands of Cape Lookout National Seashore, so there are few residents of this environment. Raccoons, shrews, mice, marsh rabbits, cottontail rabbits, lizards, a few nonpoisonous snakes, and a few frogs inhabit this area.

Salt Marsh and Tidal Flats: The tidal flats, great expanses of sand that flood at high tide, are breeding grounds for a variety of waterbirds, while the salt marsh, on the back side of the islands at the sound, is the most productive ecosystem in the barrier island environment. Together, these are prolific breeding grounds for fish. The marsh, which produces essential vegetation and adds nutrients to the marine food chain, is alive with worms, crustaceans, lichens, and algae plus leaves and stems breaking down to produce carbon.

Smooth cordgrass, wax myrtle, marsh elder, bayberry, and saltmeadow hay sway at the shores. Fiddler crabs burrow in the sulfurous mud; baitfish and minnows flit in the water; oysters, mussels, and clams conglomerate on the bottom; herons, ibis, and egrets wade at the shore.

Sound: The vast Pamlico Sound and sheltered Core Sound back up to the Core Banks, while the tiny Back Sound snuggles behind Shackleford Banks. These sound waters are fed fresh water by inland rivers and salt water by ocean inlets, creating a brackish mix of water that supports many fish species. Crabs, oysters, mussels, clams, and shrimp also thrive in these waters. Bottle-nosed dolphin breed in the sound waters in the summer. A variety of birds, including pelicans and ospreys, fish in the sound waters.

Maritime Forest: The west end of Shackleford Banks is home to a rare ninety-acre maritime forest, within sight of both the ocean and the sound. What keeps this forest alive in such a harsh environment is the canopy of salt-tolerant trees, like loblolly pine and live oak. Under this canopy, less tolerant species are able to grow and in turn stabilize the soil. In the nineteenth century, a maritime forest covered almost the entire island, but an 1899 hurricane destroyed much of it. Other storms drove so much sand over the island that most of the forest was submerged under dunes. It reappeared in shifting winds and now there is a "ghost forest" of standing dead trees on the west end of the island. Shackleford Banks's maritime forest is dense and difficult to explore, but you can enter it via the horses' paths.

Brief History

The history of the islands that make up the Cape Lookout National Seashore exemplifies the difficulty of living on a barrier island. Every attempt at permanent settlement failed. The Native Americans had the right idea early on: Use the islands as fishing and hunting grounds but live in a more protected area.

The Coree Indians resided on Harkers Island and spent a great deal of time fishing in Core Sound and hunting in the Cape Lookout section of Core Banks. The Corees' seafood-gathering abilities were revealed when a great shell midden, a mound of oyster shells, was discovered on the east end of Harkers Island where the Cape Lookout National Seashore Visitor Center stands today. Shell Point, as it's known, was cleared out in the 1920s and the oyster shells were used in construction projects all over Carteret County. The Corees, however, were a "a bloody and barbarous people," as described by Englishman John Lawson. They and other local tribes decimated each other's numbers with much warring and infighting. In 1713 the Corees participated in an Indian attack on the white settlements at Roanoke Island, but the settlers eventually succeeded in killing almost all of them.

The first ownership of the islands of the present-day Core and Shackleford Banks was recorded in 1713, when John Porter acquired the islands. Settlement was a long time coming, however, as Porter kept his residence on the mainland. The subsequent owners, Enoch Ward and John Shackleford, were also nonresident property owners. It wasn't until 1734 that Shackleford's heirs and Ward began to sell off small parcels of land.

One of the first known people to spend a season on these barrier islands was a Josiah Doty, who arrived in 1727 to set up a whaling camp at Cape Lookout. Doty killed several whales, which provided him with 300 barrels of oil and a thousand pounds of whalebone. His success captured the attention of other whalers, and Cape Lookout became known as a whalers' camp for vessels from the mainland as well as New England.

In the mid-1700s Ocracoke Inlet became an important place of entry for the port towns of the northeastern North Carolina mainland. The hundreds of vessels using the inlet were supported by Ocracoke Village, but more support and fort protection were needed at the inlet. In 1753 the North Carolina Assembly decided to establish a new town on Core Banks near Ocracoke Inlet. The act directed five North Carolina residents to act as commissioners and to lay out fifty acres of land on Core Banks for a town called Portsmouth. The commissioners were to divide the town into half-acre lots and streets and oversee the construction of a fort called Fort Granville. The fort was to protect the town from "the Depradations of an Enemy in Time of War, and Insults from Pirates and other rude People in Time of Peace."

In 1757 the fort became active and troops were stationed there until 1764, though there is no record of a gun ever being fired. In the meantime, the pre-planned town of Portsmouth grew. A tavern opened, lots were sold and homes built, and a minister came to town to baptize the children. By the 1770s the two largest villages on the Outer Banks were the ones that served Ocracoke Inlet—Portsmouth and Ocracoke villages. These villages prospered while the rest of the Core Banks were sparsely populated by livestock raisers, whose sheep, cattle, horses, and hogs openly grazed on the islands.

During the American Revolution, Ocracoke Inlet was important for getting supplies to the mainland. The British were determined to block the Carolina inlets, but the Carolinians held a valiant defense. The Revolutionary War was active in and around Ocracoke Inlet. Fort Hancock, constructed at Cape Lookout during the war, was active. However, there was never any contact with the enemy at the fort, and it was disbanded before the war was over.

In 1800 Portsmouth Village had 246 residents, whose main occupation was piloting vessels through Ocracoke Inlet and catering to the visiting seamen. Ship captains who were unfamiliar with the inlet hired local captains to navigate their ships through the narrow channel. The few people scattered about on South Core Banks and Shackleford raised livestock or fished for whales and porpoise.

In 1806 a surveyor was sent to study the North Carolina coast. In that year he reported that four poor families lived at Cape Lookout and made a living at fishing for porpoise and other fish. He also reported a fishing operation up on the central Core Banks. Meanwhile the live oak and cedar forests of Shackleford Banks were being decimated for use in the shipbuilding industry in Beaufort. In 1812 the first lighthouse at Cape Lookout was constructed.

In 1840 Portsmouth got a post office, and by 1850 the town had 505 residents. However, times were getting hard for the Portsmouth villagers. Shipping traffic was being routed away from Ocracoke Inlet to Hatteras Inlet, which opened in 1846. During the Civil War many residents of Portsmouth Island fled to the mainland and, when the war was over, they did not return because there was no work to return to. In 1894 Portsmouth got a lifesaving station, which brought a few government jobs to the area. A menhaden plant was established, but it did not last. With no traffic in the inlet and no industry, the population of the town decreased quickly. By 1950 only fourteen people remained. By 1971 there were only three residents left. When one of them died, the last two reluctantly left the town.

Meanwhile, the middle Core Banks between Portsmouth Village and Cape Lookout was as vast and lonely as it is today. In 1896 the Core Banks Life Saving Station was established about midway down the islands, near present-day Drum Inlet. What a isolated outpost this must have been! The building is no longer there; it burned down in 1968.

On the south end of the Core Banks, whaling and government jobs kept a small population alive. In 1857 a new lighthouse was commissioned for Cape Lookout and was put into service in 1859. In 1887 the Cape Lookout Life-Saving Station was established, though it wasn't fully operational until 1888.

As the prospect of good whaling off Cape Lookout in February, March, and April became widely known, small whaling settlements began to grow around Cape Lookout and Shackleford Banks, which were at that time attached. By the late 1800s there were two communities on Shackleford Banks—Diamond City on the east end and Wade's Hammock on the west end. As soon as Diamond City, named after the pattern on the lighthouse, was fully established and named, however, it fell prey to storms that drove its residents away. In 1899 the final blow—a hurricane—drove all of the residents off the island. They moved across the sound to Harkers Island, Marshallberg, or Morehead City, taking their houses with them. Much of the land that was Diamond City is now submerged in Barden Inlet, which opened in 1933.

The last permanent residents of Core Banks were Coast Guardsmen, who weren't really permanent, and Les and Sally Moore. The Moores lived on the island for nearly twenty years, operating a store and renting out fishing cottages and beach buggies. They had to leave when the national seashore was established in 1976. Today there are people who live on the islands for extended periods of time—cabin caretakers, park volunteers, biologists—but no one lives there year-round.

Human Effects on Cape Lookout National Seashore

Humans have affected the landscape of Core and Shackleford Banks over the years, though not nearly as much as at other coastal islands. Historically, mainlanders allowed their livestock to freely roam the islands, and the animals ate up the natural vegetation and altered the habitat. Though most of the livestock was removed from the islands, wild horses still graze on Shackleford's natural vegetation. The herd is managed to a size of about one hundred so it will not damage the island environment with overgrazing. Shackleford has also endured the destruction of its maritime forest—early island and Beaufort residents cut down much of it for use in the local boatbuilding and housing industries.

Man has tried to tried to control the flow of water and the shapes of the islands by opening artificial inlets, dredging natural ones, and building jetties to widen Cape Lookout. The artificial inlet, New Drum, has never been a stable inlet.

The greatest threat to the natural environment today is the visitation and recreation of humans. Cape Lookout National Seashore sees more than 450,000 visitors a year, though because it is remote it has less of a problem than other national parks. Misuse of off-road vehicles is the biggest threat, disturbing bird and turtle nests and altering the habitat. Unleashed pets and nonnative predators cause problems for wildlife as well. The NPS tries to manage recreation to keep the park environment as close to its natural state as possible.

Some Things to Know

How to Get Here

Traveling to Cape Lookout National Seashore is not simple, and therein lies the park's appeal for many people. There are no bridges spanning the stretch of Core and Back Sounds between the mainland and the barrier islands, so the only way to get there is by boat. Nearly a dozen toll-ferry services transport visitors over to the islands; two of them even take four-wheel-drive vehicles and ATVs over to Core Banks. Taking a vehicle over allows you to explore much more of the islands than you can see on foot, though it is much more costly.

You can also reach the islands by private motorboat or kayak. Traveling in your own boat allows you the freedom to depart and land wherever and whenever you would like, but it is very important to know something about sound navigation before you boat over. Due to varying water depths and shoals, chart books are a must for safe navigation in the sound waters. The backsides of the Core Banks are marshy and shallow, so access is limited to certain areas. Paddlers must be strong and aware of the potential dangers of traversing open water. Please read our chapter on Boating and Paddling before attempting to cross Core or Back Sounds to the islands on your own.

Getting to the Gateway Communities

Before you can get to Cape Lookout National Seashore, you have to get to one of the gateway communities—Ocracoke, Atlantic, Davis, Harkers Island, Beaufort, or Morehead City—and that is an experience in itself. The coastal plain of North Carolina is interlaced with rivers, marshes, and swamps, so the roads never lead in a straight shot to anywhere you want to go. Driving through the Down East area to Atlantic, Davis, or Harkers Island is a treat, a chance to experience the fast-fading coastal heritage of North Carolina. In the slow-paced small towns, you'll see the accoutrements of life on the water: fishing trawlers docked along ditches, crab pots stacked in yards, boatbuilding sheds, fish houses, decoy carvers selling their wares, and commercial fishermen wearing boots and waders. You'll even hear a bit of an old brogue in the accents of some locals, particularly on Harkers Island. Morehead City and Beaufort are tourist-driven coastal towns, each with a vibrant waterfront area.

For directions to Ocracoke Island, see our Cape Hatteras National Seashore section.

The Down East communities of Atlantic, Davis, and Harkers Island have ferry service to Cape Lookout National Seashore. To get to these towns from the north, you can take the Cedar Island–Ocracoke Ferry from Ocracoke Island and then follow N.C. Highway 12 to U.S. Highway 70, which leads to Atlantic and Davis. To get to Harkers Island, stay on US 70 until you get to Otway, where you can turn off on Island Road to head toward Harkers Island, which is connected to the mainland by a bridge. To get to these communities from the west, take US 70 East off Interstate 95. Stay on US 70 through Morehead City and into the Down East communities.

To get to Morehead City and Beaufort from I–95, take the U.S. Highway 70 East exit at the town of Selma. US 70 East heads through Goldsboro, Kinston, New Bern, and Havelock before reaching Morehead City and then Beaufort. Both of these communities offer ferry service to the islands of Cape Lookout National Seashore.

Getting to Cape Lookout National Seashore

North Core Banks or "Portsmouth Island"

North Core Banks, colloquially known as Portsmouth Island, is most easily accessed via ferry service from Ocracoke Island and the town of Atlantic on the mainland. The Ocracoke ferries drop passengers and/or ATVs off at the northern tip of the island at Portsmouth Village. Morris Marina Kabin Kamps and Ferry Service in Atlantic takes passengers and vehicles to the Long Point ferry landing and cabins on the lonely southern end of the island (Miles 16–17). From there it's about a mile and a half south to Old Drum Inlet or 17 miles north to Portsmouth Village, assuming you can get there. Inlets open and close frequently on North Core Banks, and at this writing there were inlets open at high tide at Miles 2 and 7, limiting access to Portsmouth from the south to times of extreme low tide. These inlets were expected to close soon; ask a ranger or cabin caretaker about the possibility of driving to Portsmouth Village from the south. If you're boating to North Core Banks on your own, the safest places to land are at the ferry landing at the Long Point area or at one of the two docks on the northernmost tip of the island.

South Core Banks

South Core Banks is most easily reached by ferry service from Harkers Island and the mainland town of Davis. Alger G. Willis Fishing Camps and Ferry Service takes passengers and vehicles from Davis to the Great Island ferry landing and cabins in the northern portion of the island (Miles 29–30). From the ferry landing it is about 6 miles to New Drum Inlet and about 15 miles to Cape Lookout at the south end of the island. Four passenger ferries take visitors from Harkers Island to Cape Lookout, where the lighthouse and shelling on Cape Point draw the most attention from visitors. A couple of ferries also run from Beaufort to South Core Banks, but the trip is longer than from Harkers. If you're boating to South Core Banks on your own, the safest place to land is at the ferry docks in front of the lighthouse or at the ferry landing or NPS dock at the Great Island area.

Shackleford Banks

Numerous ferries offer service to Shackleford Banks from Harkers Island, Beaufort, and Morehead City. The trip takes just fifteen minutes from Harkers Island and Beaufort. If you're boating to Shackleford Banks on your own, there is a ferry landing on the western end.

Ferry Services

Several toll-ferry services take passengers to Cape Lookout National Seashore. Passenger ferries cost between $10 and $15 round-trip. Vehicle ferries cost $75 and more, depending on the length of the vehicle. Making ferry reservations is a good idea. Most ferries have set pick-up and drop-off times in the busy seasons, but ferry operators are more flexible in the winter when there is less business. All of the ferries drop off passengers on the islands and then establish a time for pick-up, either later the same day or another day. Be sure to arrange that time with your ferry service before you disembark, or bring a cell phone so you can call to arrange a time.

Remember that ferry services run in good weather only and reserve the right not to run in inclement weather or high winds that would make the crossing dangerous. Be sure to call ahead if weather is an issue. Also, call ahead in the off-season (winter and early spring) to make sure the ferries are running. A few ferries operate by request at those times.

When visiting Cape Lookout National Seashore, you need to take everything you'll need with you—water, drinks, food, rain gear, extra clothing, sunscreen, etc. Nothing is available on the islands. You'll also need to bring everything out. This is a trash-free park; there are no trashcans on the island.

Portsmouth Island ATV Tours
Jolly Roger Marina, N.C. Highway 12, Ocracoke Island
(252) 928–4484
www.portsmouthislandatvs.com
Guided ATV tours and birding trips of Portsmouth Village and beaches

Rudy Austin's Ferry Service
Silver Lake Harbor, Ocracoke Island
(252) 928–4361
Passenger ferry to Portsmouth Village on North Core Banks

Morris Marina Kabin Kamps and Ferry Service
1000 Morris Marina Road (off U.S. Highway 70), Atlantic
(252) 225–4261
www.portsmouthisland.com
Passenger and vehicle ferry to North Core Banks

Alger G. Willis Fishing Camps and Ferry Service
Willis Road (off U.S. Highway 70), Davis
(252) 729–2791
www.drumwagon.com/awfc
Passenger and vehicle ferry to South Core Banks

Calico Jack's Cape Lookout Ferry
Island Road, Harkers Island
(252) 728–3575
Passenger ferry to lighthouse area of South Core Banks, Shackleford Banks

Harkers Island Fishing Center
Island Road, Harkers Island
(252) 728–3907
Passenger ferry to lighthouse area of South Core Banks, Shackleford Banks

Local Yokel Ferry
Island Road, Harkers Island
(252) 728–2759
Passenger ferry to lighthouse area of South Core Banks, Shackleford Banks

Sand Dollar Ferry
Barbour's Harbor Marina, Island Road, Harkers Island
(252) 728–6181, (800) 281–3978
Passenger ferry to lighthouse area of South Core Banks, Shackleford Banks

Island Ferry Adventures
618 Front Street, Beaufort waterfront
(252) 728–7555
Passenger ferry to Shackleford Banks; will go to Cape Lookout Lighthouse by request

Lookout Express
Front Street, Beaufort waterfront
(252) 728–6997
Passenger ferry to lighthouse area of South Core Banks, Shackleford Banks

Outer Banks Ferry Service
Front Street, Beaufort waterfront
(252) 728–4129
Passenger ferry to Shackleford Banks

Waterfront Ferry Service
Portside Marina, 209 Arendell Street, Morehead City
(252) 726–7678
www.portsidemarina.com
Passenger ferry to Shackleford Banks

Getting Around Once You're There

The only ways to get around on land at Cape Lookout National Seashore are on foot and in four-wheel-drive vehicles—and there are no paved roads to assist with either of those methods of transportation. Be prepared with everything you could possibly need while you're there. Driving is allowed on North and South Core Banks but not on Shackleford Banks. For more details on hiking and driving, see our Hiking and Off-Roading chapters.

On-Island Taxis and Tours: In the summer, other ways to get around include taking a guided tour in a four-wheel-drive vehicle or hitching a ride with one of the transportation services. On South Core Banks, a couple of four-wheel-drive "taxis" offer visitors a ride from the lighthouse area to Cape Point. Most of the taxis are big pickup trucks with bench seats and canopies in the back. Take the taxi if time is an issue or you can't make the 2-mile trek in the sand, but walk if you can, as you'll get to see a lot more of the island. Some of the taxi companies also offer guided driving tours of the Cape Village area and then drop off passengers at the beach for an hour or so. The problem with these summer taxis and tours is that they gather up everyone and dump them off at the same place on Cape Point. If you're looking for solitude, this isn't the way to go. As an option, you can take the taxi to Cape Point and walk the 3 miles around the hook of the Point to Power Squadron Spit, where there are fewer people. There are guided ATV tours of Portsmouth Village on North Core Banks.

Portsmouth Island ATV Tours
Jolly Roger Marina, N.C. Highway 12, Ocracoke Island
(252) 928–4484
www.portsmouthislandatvs.com
Transportation to island and guided ATV tours and birding trips of Portsmouth Village and beaches

Cape Lookout Beach Tours/Sand Dollar Ferry
Island Road, Harkers Island
(252) 728–6181
Passenger ferry to South Core Banks; taxi to Cape Point or guided tours

Mule Train Beach Tours
South Core Banks: Cape Lookout Lighthouse area and Cape Point
(252) 504–4121
Two-hour driving tour of lighthouse area, Cape Village, and Cape Point. Must use a ferry service to get to the island

Essential Park Information

Park Visitor Center and Personnel Headquarters
Cape Lookout National Seashore Visitor Center
131 Charles Street (off Island Road), Harkers Island, NC 28531
(252) 728–2250
www.nps.gov/calo

On the far east end of Harkers Island at an area known as Shell Point is the Cape Lookout National Seashore Headquarters and Visitor Center. The visitor center has several exhibits on the natural and cultural history of the islands, including Portsmouth Village, Cape Lookout Lighthouse, the U.S.

The Cape Lookout National Seashore visitor center on Harkers Island welcomes visitors with information about the seashore.

Life Saving Service, sea turtles, wildlife, birds, and seashells. You can see the Cape Lookout Lighthouse from the visitor center. You can also talk to a staff person or park ranger about the details of your trip to the barrier islands. Numerous brochures, field guides, and books are available. The visitor center has rest rooms, plenty of parking, and a picnic area. The land is right on the sound and offers a scenic place to watch gulls and ducks or have a picnic lunch. The sound beach is a good place launch a kayak, canoe, or small sailboat. The visitor center is open from 8:00 A.M. to 5:30 P.M., May 25 through Labor Day, and from 8:00 A.M. to 4:30 P.M. the rest of the year.

Park Facilities

North Core Banks or "Portsmouth Island": Portsmouth Village, at Mile 1, has a seasonal ranger station, rest rooms, and two boat landings. Around Mile 9 about halfway between the village and the Long Point ferry landing and cabin area, is a picnic shelter. The Long Point area, at Miles 16–17, has a boat landing, seasonal ranger station, showers, rest rooms, gas, cabins,

Solitude awaits you at Cape Lookout National Seashore.

parking, a dump station, and seasonal water. Cabins, ferry service, gas, and water are handled through Morris Marina Kabin Kamps and Ferry Service (see Ferry Services, above).

South Core Banks: The Great Island area, at Miles 29–30, has a ferry landing, boat dock, a seasonal ranger station, parking, rest rooms, showers, picnic shelter, gas, cabins, dump station, and seasonal water. Cabins, ferry service, gas, and water are handled through Alger G. Willis Fishing Camps and Ferry Service (see Ferry Services, above). The Cape Lookout Lighthouse area, about Mile 41, has a ferry landing/boat dock, seasonal ranger station, rest rooms, picnic shelters, boardwalks from sound to ocean, and parking. In the lighthouse keepers' quarters is a visitor center with a ranger on staff to answer questions as well as several exhibits on natural and cultural history. Programs are held here in summer. At Cape Point, at Mile 44, there are composting toilets.

Shackleford Banks: Shackleford is the most remote of all the Cape Lookout National Seashore islands. Its only amenities are a boat-landing dock and primitive composting toilets on the western end.

Park Fees

Visiting Cape Lookout National Seashore is free, but unless you have your own boat you will have to pay someone to take you over. Ferry fees typically run about $10 to $15 round-trip for passengers, much more for vehicles. There is no charge for camping on the islands, unless you plan to rent one of the cabins on North or South Core Banks from a private concessionaire (see the Camping/Cabins chapter). Ranger-led park programs are also free. The park charges $10 per week (or portion of a week) for any vehicles left unattended for more than 24 hours.

Park Hours

Cape Lookout National Seashore is open 24 hours for campers and anglers. Visitor center hours are from 8:00 A.M. to 5:30 P.M., May 25 through Labor Day, and from 8:00 A.M. to 4:30 P.M. the rest of the year. The visitor centers at Portsmouth Village and Cape Lookout Lighthouse are open from April through November only. Picnic shelters, rest rooms, and other facilities are for use during daylight hours only.

Park Rules

Alcohol: Open containers of beer and wine are allowed in Cape Lookout National Seashore, but the laws of North Carolina do not allow such distilled liquors as whiskey, vodka, etc., or fortified wines to be consumed in public. Open containers of alcohol are not allowed in motor vehicles, including those on the beach. In North Carolina it is illegal to drive with a blood alcohol level of .08 or higher. The legal drinking age is twenty-one.

Camping: All camping is primitive style as there are no designated camp-

Trash-Free Park

Cape Lookout National Seashore is a trash-free park, meaning that there are no trashcans or trash pick-up service anywhere in the park. This means that visitors are responsible for taking out any trash they accrue while visiting, including food scraps, bait scraps, cans, bottles, wrappers, paper, napkins, tissue, and used fishing gear and fishing line. Small trash bags are available in dispensers at various places in the park, but you must take the bags and trash off-island when you leave.

sites. Camping is free, but you must obtain a permit from the NPS at the Harkers Island Visitor Center, Portsmouth Village, Cape Lookout Lighthouse, Rudy Austin's Ferry Service, Morris Marina Ferry Service, Alger Willis Ferry Service, or Crystal Coast Visitor Center in Morehead City. See the Camping/Cabins chapter. The Cape Lookout location is a self-registration site where you drop your permit in a box.

Driving on the Beach: Four-wheel-drive vehicles and ATVs are allowed on North and South Core Banks but not on Shackleford Banks. See the Getting Around section earlier in this chapter for details. Note that motorcycles and dirt bikes are not allowed anywhere in the national seashore.

Fireworks: Fireworks are illegal in all national parks. They may not be used anywhere in Cape Lookout National Seashore, including Shell Point on Harkers Island.

Fishing and Hunting: Fishing and hunting are allowed in Cape Lookout National Seashore, but state laws apply to both. Fishing is regulated by size limits, bag limits, and seasons. Fishing licenses are required for commercial harvesting only. Contact the Division of Marine Fisheries at (800) 682–2632 or www.ncdmf.net for information about fishing laws (see the Fishing chapter). For hunting, you must observe seasons and bag limits set by the North Carolina Wildlife Resources Commission. Contact it at (800) 675–0263 or www.ncwildlife.org. For more information see the Hunting section of the Other Adventures chapter.

Metal Detectors: Metal detectors are illegal in all national parks. The only items that can be collected in the seashore are shells and driftwood.

Open Fires: Campfires are permitted only below the high-tide line, not on the dunes. Bring your own firewood because there is very little on the islands. You can collect driftwood or dead wood that is on the ground if you can find it. Shipwreck wood may not be used, nor can the standing dead wood at Shackleford Banks, which is part of a historic "ghost forest." Always use water instead of sand to put out a fire. A fire will still burn under sand.

Personal Watercraft: Personal watercraft—Jet Skis, WaveRunners, Sea-Doos, and the like—cannot launch from or land on Cape Lookout National Seashore property, including Shell Point on Harkers Island.

Pets: Pets are allowed on Cape Lookout National Seashore as long as they are on a 6-foot leash at all times. Make sure your ferry service will transport pets; not all of them do. Remember to bring water for your pets as well as for yourself.

Swimming: Swimming is at your own risk at Cape Lookout National

Seashore. There are no lifeguards anywhere on the islands. You should know that swimming in the Atlantic Ocean is potentially dangerous. Waves and currents are always at work. If you plan to swim in the ocean, make sure you are a strong, confident swimmer. Never swim alone, at night, or near inlets. Swimming is safer on the sound sides of the islands. Do not jump or dive from any of the boat docks on the islands, as the sound water is shallow. See the Basics section for swimming safety information.

Water: Bring drinking water with you! Fresh water is not available on the islands, except at the cabin areas on North and South Core Banks, and that is available only when the caretaker is on-site. Visitors without water will have a miserable day in these desertlike conditions.

Wildlife: Do not feed, disturb, or harass wildlife, including the Shackleford horses. It is illegal to touch, feed, take anything, or cause a change in a wild animal's behavior. Feeding wildlife upsets the natural balance of the ecosystem and exposes you to potentially dangerous animals. Disturbing and harassing wildlife includes letting your dog chase birds or dig up turtle nests, which is one reason the leash law is enforced. Remember, Cape Lookout National Seashore was provided as much for the rest and relaxation of wildlife as for humans.

Emergencies

If possible, bring a cell phone with you to Cape Lookout National Seashore. In such a remote area, it can be very difficult to find assistance in an emergency—a cell phone could save your life. Cell phones will work in most locations. If you call 911, tell the dispatcher that you are calling from a cell phone, give your cell phone number in case you get cut off, give as exact a location as possible, and tell the nature of your emergency.

In season, you can find emergency assistance at the ranger stations at the Cape Lookout Lighthouse keepers' quarters and Portsmouth Village Visitor Center. You can also get assistance from the caretakers at Morris Marina Kabin Kamps on North Core Banks or Alger Willis Fishing Camp on South Core Banks.

Important Phone Numbers

In all emergencies, dial 911

National Park Service–Cape Lookout National Seashore (252) 728–2550

Morris Marina Kabin Kamps and Ferry Service, Atlantic (252) 225–0366

Alger G. Willis Fishing Camps and Ferry Service, Davis (252) 729–2791

Ocracoke Island Emergency Medical Services (252) 928–6580

Eastern Carteret Medical Center, Sea Level (252) 225–1134

Carteret General Hospital ER, Morehead City (252) 247–1540

Poison Control Center (800) 848–6946

Carteret County Sheriff's Office (252) 504–4800

24-Hour Weather Forecast (252) 223–5737

U.S. Coast Guard Emergencies (252) 247–4545

U.S. Coast Guard Ocracoke Inlet (252) 928–3711

U.S. Coast Guard Fort Macon (Drum, Barden, and Beaufort Inlets) (252) 247–4511

Sea Tow (252) 728–6551

Carteret County Hurricane Evacuation Information (252) 728–8470

Carteret County Tourism Development (800) SUNNY NC

Carteret County Visitor Center (252) 726–8148

Carteret County Chamber of Commerce (800) 786–6962

Birding

The open wildlands of Cape Lookout National Seashore are excellent places to see a variety of birds, especially during spring and fall migrations. The diversity and numbers of birds at this national seashore don't quite compare to those of the Cape Hatteras National Seashore to the north. Cape Hatteras, with a bird-sighting list of over 400, gets more pelagic species because of its location farther out to sea and more waterfowl because of the impoundments and fresh water at Bodie Island and Pea Island National Wildlife Refuge. Cape Hatteras National Seashore is also a more popular birding location because it is so much easier to get to.

Nevertheless, Cape Lookout has a bird-sighting list of 275 species and, as the last uninhabited stretch of barrier island in North Carolina, is an important resting spot for birds during their spring and fall migrations. It is one of the most important areas in the state for the threatened piping plover. Most of the birds in Cape Lookout National Seashore are seen on North and South Core Banks; Shackleford Banks has a low diversity of birds. Migrating waterbirds are the predominant species on Core Banks.

Though there is a great variety of birdlife at Cape Lookout National Seashore, the park is not a popular place for birders primarily because of its remoteness. If birders are going to go to great lengths to get to Cape Lookout with a vehicle or if they are going to walk a great deal of the island in search of birds, they usually want to be rewarded with more than what Cape Lookout National Seashore offers. Birders can see all the same birds at Cape Hatteras National Seashore, and many more, without the hassle and expense of ferrying over. What makes it worth coming to Cape Lookout National Seashore for birding is the knowledge that you might be the only one doing it and, of course, the chance to see one of the few last remaining stretches of undeveloped oceanfront. Work the other elements of the island into your trip—remote camping, shelling, fishing, hiking, or off-road driving, as well as visiting historic Portsmouth Village or the Cape Lookout Lighthouse complex.

If you bring a vehicle over to North or South Core Banks, you'll obviously be able to cover more area, from inlet to inlet. If you're going to be on foot, Portsmouth Village or the Cape Lookout area are the most easily accessible areas and offer a good diversity of birds without too much walking. If you're fit, consider hiking an entire island in search of birds.

Two-thirds to three-quarters of the state's nesting pairs of piping plovers nest within Cape Lookout National Seashore. The birds prefer to nest on the ground in the sand flats around the inlets or at old inlet sites, especially New Drum Inlet. They like areas with little vegetation and low dunes, which is exactly the landscape of the Core Banks. The sand-colored birds are tiny and blend into their environment so most visitors won't notice them unless specifically looking for them. The birds are most often seen here in nesting season (spring and summer) on the ocean beaches. If you're looking for them, look around the inlets on North and South Core Banks, including the spit at Cape Lookout. Because these birds are nationally threatened, much of the park's conservation efforts are aimed at piping plovers (along with sea turtles).

Other ground-nesting birds that use the park in spring and fall are American oystercatchers and Wilson's plovers. These species, along with the piping plovers, do not build nests. Instead, they lay their eggs directly on the sand, out in the open, and away from other birds. The eggs as well as the chicks are sand-colored and well camouflaged from predators like raccoons and gulls.

Also near the inlets from April through August are colonial waterbirds like least terns, common terns, gull-billed terns, Forester's terns, and black skimmers. These species nest in large colonies, so they are easier to spot. If you get too close to a tern's nest you'll know, as terns aggressively defend their nests.

All of these species of beach-nesting birds are especially vulnerable to disturbance by humans. They blend in with the sand-colored beach environment and their nests are especially hard to see. Cape Lookout National Seashore manages its land to protect its ground-nesting birds. For this reason, portions of the beach are often closed. These closures keep out people, pets, and vehicles, but you can walk up to the edge to have a look at the birds. When the chicks are old enough to fly and escape danger, the areas are opened up again. To protect beach-nesting birds, it is important that visitors keep their pets leashed, do not leave garbage or food scraps on the beach (which attracts predators), and stay out of closed areas.

During the spring and fall migrations, a variety of shorebirds frequent the vast tidal flats on North Core Banks and both sides of New Drum Inlet.

The Cape Lookout National Seashore beaches are home to a variety of shorebirds.

These shorebirds include red knots, willets, ruddy turnstones, dowitchers, sanderlings, and sandpipers. The Portsmouth Flats, a 3-by-1.5-mile expanse of sand and mud flats on the northern end of the island, are especially good for seeing shorebirds. You need to visit the flats when they are flooded, however; when they're dry they're not especially good for birding. Try to visit after a rainy period or after a good northeast blow.

Fall brings peregrine falcons, merlins, and kestrels, most of them in October. These birds are best seen around inlets and at Cape Point. You might also spot a few of the resident ring-necked pheasants in the low scrub areas on North Core Banks or around Cape Village.

Waders like egrets, herons, and ibises are seen in the park year-round. Their nesting is primarily on spoil islands in Core Sound. One, called Morgan Island, is in the sound along the main channel from Harkers Island to Cape Lookout; ask your ferry operator to point it out to you. Ninety-nine percent of the national seashore's wading birds nest on this island, says a park ranger. Brown pelicans are also a common sight on the sound's spoil islands and shoals. When boating in the sound, also keep an eye out for osprey hunting and diving in the waters. Look to the tops of channel markers to get sight of the ospreys' sprawling nests.

At Cape Lookout, out on Cape Point, you can see gannets and scoters from fall through spring, and possibly jaegers, petrels, and shearwaters if the conditions are right. Rare gulls and terns have made appearances on Cape Point, and plovers often nest out on Power Squadron Spit. The best time to see a variety of shorebirds is during the fall migrations. In the pine trees around the lighthouse might be some landbirds like warblers, woodpeckers, and kinglets. Also look for ring-necked pheasants in the shrub thickets around Cape Village. In the marshes look for rails, migrating hawks, and wading birds. All the way out on the spit, you'll see cormorants, pelicans, gulls, and shorebirds, plus many loons in winter. In breeding season this is a good place to spot plovers, American oystercatchers, terns, and black skimmers.

Shackleford Banks can be a good birding spot for sighting shorebirds and wading birds in the warm seasons. East Shackleford Banks has great mudflats that attract rails and shorebirds. West Shackleford Banks is not as good for birding, but if you're there, look for plovers and other nesters on the beach in the breeding season. In the maritime forest on the west end, you might spot warblers, wrens, and kinglets, but don't enter the woods in the warm months if you're not prepared for ticks.

If you can't make it out to the islands, birding is not bad at the NPS Visitor Center at Shell Point on Harkers Island. From April through August at sunrise and sunset, you're likely to see a variety of wading birds, which nest on the sound islands. From April through July you'll probably see royal and sandwich terns. In spring you might see ducks, shorebirds, gulls, loons or terns. Anytime you visit here you'll likely see an enormous variety of gulls, many of them begging for food in the picnic area.

Those interested in learning more about birding on Cape Lookout National Seashore should read John O. Fussell's *A Birder's Guide to Coastal North Carolina* (University of North Carolina Press, 1994).

The Cape Lookout Environmental Education Center, which holds a variety of educational programs for kids and adults at Cape Lookout, has a birders' weekend led by John Fussell every October. Call (336) 292–0774 or visit www.cleec.org for more information.

Core Sound Kayaks conducts birding/kayaking trips by request. Capt. Dennis Chadwick, co-owner of the company, is an avid birder who enjoys sharing his knowledge with others. Chadwick also spearheads an informal club of birders that takes birding trips once a month. If you're interested, give him a call at (252) 728–2330 or visit www.clis.com/chadstscn.

Boating, Sailing, and Paddling

The only way to get to Cape Lookout National Seashore is by boat. You can take a ferry, but if you have a boat or kayak, why not take yourself over? Personal watercraft like Sea-Doos, Jet Skis, and WaveRunners, however, are not allowed to launch or land at Cape Lookout National Seashore. When you're on the water, watch the weather with a close eye. Storms and winds come up quickly on the Outer Banks. For emergencies, call 911 on your cell phone or use VHF channel 16, the calling and distress channel.

Boating

Getting to the banks by private boat allows you the freedom to come and go as you like, assuming the weather and water levels permit. Boaters need to understand basic sound navigation before heading out to the islands from the mainland or from Harkers and Ocracoke Islands.

Looking at a map, it appears that you can just zip over to the islands, anchor, and access the island as you please. However, much of the sound is very shallow and you can't cross it anywhere you wish. Stay within marked channels or use an up-to-date chart book and depth-finder—otherwise you risk getting stuck on a shoal. Much of the soundside of the islands is impenetrable marshland. Unless you know what you're doing, come ashore near one of the designated boat dock areas, where the land has been cleared to allow access. The best landing areas in the national seashore are on the sound sides around Cape Lookout and the west end of Shackleford Banks. These areas have flat sound beaches with just enough water to anchor in. Of course, because they are so perfect, they're often crowded. A summer day or fall weekend in front of the lighthouse or at Shackleford can be packed with partying boaters and families. If you're looking for solitude, you won't find it here.

If you plan to anchor in the sound for an extended period of time, you might consider bringing two anchors for extra security. And keep in mind that wind direction switches often, bad weather brews up quickly, and tides can bring a 2- to 4-foot change in water depth. At times the wind can blow so much water out of the sound that anchored boats are left high and dry. If this happens, all you can do is wait for the wind to switch and the water to come back in. It could be days. Bring extra provisions, especially water, in case this happens to you.

If you want to head from sound to ocean, Ocracoke, Barden, and Beaufort Inlets are the only safe passageways. New Drum Inlet between North and South Core Banks is not a safe inlet to cross because it does not have a straight channel. Locals use Ocracoke or Barden Inlets instead.

Ocracoke Inlet: Located between Ocracoke Island and North Core Banks (a k a Portsmouth Island), this is a notoriously shoaly inlet. It is most dangerous when the winds are out of the southeast or southwest, especially at low water. The channel ranges from 10 to 12 feet deep. Just outside the channel on the green side, the depth is only about 1 to 2 feet, so be sure to stay within the markers.

Barden Inlet: Locally known as The Drain, Barden Inlet is a marked channel that is safe and painless to cross in daylight hours. The lighted navigation aids are few and far between, so locals recommend that boaters not familiar with the inlet use it only during the daytime. The shoals in this inlet are moving and changing with each storm. Follow the channel buoys to avoid running onto the shoals. This inlet is used as a safe entry for Back Sound during some weather conditions that make Beaufort Inlet difficult to navigate. Barden is not a deep inlet; its consistent depth is only about 5 feet. Keeled sailboats or large vessels that draw more than 4½ feet of water should not use this inlet.

Beaufort Inlet: This is a very deep, wide, and safe inlet, which serves as the main shipping channel for the Morehead City State Port. It is highly trafficked, mainly with small boats, but every so often huge freighters come through here heading to the port. The narrow channel can get rough and dangerous in some wind conditions, especially nor'easters. Boaters should be aware of conditions and act accordingly.

Launching and Landing Sites

Places to launch when boating to Cape Lookout National Seashore include:

- Ocracoke Island Public Boat Ramp, next to NPS Visitor Center. Parking available.
- Wildlife Resources Commission Boat Ramp, Cedar Island Ferry Landing. Parking available.
- Cedar Island National Wildlife Refuge Boat Ramp, end of Lola Road just outside of Cedar Island. Small boats only. Parking available.

- Cedar Island National Wildlife Refuge Boat Ramp, N.C. Highway 12 (on the southern end of the high-rise bridge make a right on the first paved road). Parking available.
- Morris Marina Kabin Kamps and Ferry Service Boat Ramp, Atlantic. Parking available. Fee charged.
- Wildlife Resources Commission Ramp, west end of Harkers Island, on the mainland side (Straits) of the Harkers Island Bridge. Parking available.
- Curtis Perry Park, Taylor's Creek, east end of Front Street, Beaufort. Parking available.

When landing at Cape Lookout National Seashore, be aware that most facilities will not permit you to dock for longer than fifteen minutes. You can unload passengers and gear, and then you must move away from the dock to anchor. The exception is Haulover Dock at Portsmouth Village, where visitors can dock for up to two hours while they tour the village.

Landing facilities include:

- Wallace Dock, inlet/ocean dock on northern tip of Portsmouth Village, Mile 0
- Haulover Dock, sound dock on northwest corner of Portsmouth Village, mile 0
- Long Point Ferry Landing, soundside of North Core Banks, mile 16
- NPS Dock or Great Island Ferry Landing, soundside of South Core Banks, Miles 29–30
- Ferry Landing, soundside of South Core Banks at Cape Lookout Lighthouse, Mile 41
- NPS Dock, soundside on west end of Shackleford Banks.

Sailing

Lookout Bight is a blow-boater's dream. Formed by the hook of Cape Lookout and Power Squadron Spit, it is a deep-water safe harbor snuggled between South Core Banks and Shackleford Banks. The surrounding land blocks the wind from every direction, making it a safe anchorage in any weather. For centuries ships have come into Lookout Bight to wait out bad weather. Sailors with a dinghy can easily get to shore to visit the lighthouse complex or go shelling or fishing on beaches. Barden Inlet runs right into Lookout Bight, connecting it with the inner sounds. But this inlet is shallow, only about 5 feet, so boats with a draft of more than 4½ feet should not use

The Visitor's Center on Harkers Island has a soundside beach that's perfect for launching small sailboats.

it. It's best to use Beaufort Inlet if coming from the mainland or Intracoastal Waterway.

The nearby town of Beaufort is a sailing haven. Hundreds of large sailboats enter the area via the Intracoastal Waterway or Beaufort Inlet and dock or anchor in Taylor's Creek, right at the Beaufort waterfront.

The shallowness of the Core and Back Sounds is perfect for sailing in small catamarans and sailboats. If you tip over, you can usually stand in the sound to flip the boat back over. The sound is wide and spacious, so you can easily sail around all afternoon. Just remember that wind is capricious here, often shifting directions and gaining or losing strength. This may affect your abilities to return to your launch site. Always be sure to bring flotation devices with you and keep them where you can reach them easily.

If you're bringing your own boat and want to launch here, see the Launching Sites section earlier in this chapter. One of the most popular launch sites is at the Cape Lookout National Seashore Visitor Center on Harkers Island. A sandy sound beach makes the perfect site.

Paddling

Exploring Cape Lookout National Seashore by kayak or canoe is a great way to see the islands and challenge your navigational and maneuvering skills. The Pamlico, Core, and Back Sounds and the Atlantic Ocean provide exceptional paddling opportunities. You can paddle the open water between the mainland and the islands, explore the marsh or spoil islands that dot the sounds, paddle through estuaries teeming with sea life, stop and fish in a soundside honey hole, cross tricky currents in channels and inlets, ride waves in the Atlantic surf, or paddle between the seashore's attractions.

The three islands of Cape Lookout National Seashore form a barrier from the strong breaking waves of the Atlantic Ocean. The waters on the backside of the islands—the sounds—are much calmer than the ocean. Waves in the sounds are wind-driven and not subject to open swells. However, this does not mean that paddling in the open sounds is entirely safe. The Cape Lookout National Seashore area is not for novice paddlers. Tidal currents and winds can make it difficult to paddle across. Novices should practice elsewhere before paddling long distances here.

Maps and charts are a necessity. Get a good chart book of the North Carolina coast to assist you in navigating the sounds, which are quite shallow in many areas.

The elements that most affect paddlers are wind and sun. Wind may switch direction or build up during the day, so it's important to listen to weather reports. You might want to consider bringing a weather radio.

Respect your limits as a paddler and if you are a beginner, stay within sight of land, in case bad weather brews or winds build. Remember, too, that the sun reflects off the water, making your skin more susceptible to burning. Wear sunscreen, a hat, and lightweight long-sleeved clothing if possible.

Paddlers should think long and hard about attempting to cross open water if winds or rain are forecasted. Do not attempt the crossing if you are not sure how long it will be before weather conditions worsen. Winds can blow up out of nowhere or switch direction rapidly, making the paddle extremely exhausting and dangerous. If you're stuck on an island, wait it out or call a ferry service and try to beg a ride back to the mainland.

A good safety measure is to file a float plan before you leave for your trip. Always file such a plan with a friend or relative who likes you enough to worry if you don't return on time. A good idea is to file a float plan with the National Park Service. You can do this by stopping in at the Harkers Island Visitor Center; faxing a copy to (252) 728–2160, Attn: Interp. Division; or by e-mailing a copy to Calo_Information@nps.gov. Include departure date, put-in location, route, any stopover or sleepover points, and estimated time of return. If the park service needs to search for you on these remote islands, a float plan will be a great help.

Summer is great for paddling around Cape Lookout National Seashore. The wind often picks up as the day goes on, so it's good to go out in the morning when the wind is likely to be lighter and the sun less intense. Fall is also a wonderful season for paddling here. The temperatures are mild and the water is warm. Winter and early spring are generally cold and windy in the seashore, but they still are good times to paddle the area. Dress accordingly, and you'll have a fine time exploring on your own.

You must carry everything you will need with you, as there are no stores or vending machines on the islands. Always bring water, food, sunscreen, insect repellent, chart books, and appropriate clothing. All trash must be carried out of the islands. Be sure to wear a flotation device (PFD), or at least have one on board. That's the law in North Carolina, even for kayaks and canoes. Safety equipment and things you should consider bringing on an extended trip include a compass, first-aid kit, cell phone or VHF radio, spare paddle, tow rope, whistle, flashlight, GPS, sponge or bilge pump, spray skirt, towel, and sunglasses.

Paddlers have to make a decision about where to put in. If you put in on the mainland, you'll have an open-water paddle ahead of you to reach the islands of Cape Lookout National Seashore. The distance between the islands and the mainland, or other islands, ranges from 1 to 5 miles. Assess your paddling skills and check weather reports before attempting to make an

Paddling is an enjoyable way to explore the soundside of Cape Lookout National Seashore. NORTH CAROLINA DIVISION OF TOURISM, FILM AND SPORTS DEVELOPMENT

open-water crossing. The other option is to take your kayak with you on a ferry ride to the island. Some ferry companies can accommodate you and your kayak (see the list of ferries in the Things to Know chapter). You can launch wherever you want to on the islands.

Launching and Paddling Sites

Places to launch when paddling to Cape Lookout National Seashore include:

- Ocracoke Island Public Boat Ramp, next to NPS Visitor Center. Parking available.
- Wildlife Resources Commission Boat Ramp, Cedar Island Ferry Landing. Parking available.
- Cedar Island National Wildlife Refuge Boat Ramp, end of Lola Road just outside of Cedar Island.
- Morris Marina Kabin Kamps and Ferry Service Boat Ramp, Atlantic. Parking available.
- Cape Lookout National Seashore Visitor Center, east end of Harkers Island on the sound beach. Parking available.

- Wildlife Resources Commission Ramp, west end of Harkers Island, on the mainland side (Straits) of the Harkers Island Bridge. Parking available.
- Grayden Paul Jaycee Town Park, Front Street, Beaufort. Parking available.

If you're wondering where to paddle, the best source is the *Guide to Sea Kayaking in North Carolina* by Pam Malec (Globe Pequot Press, 2001). This book outlines thirty-five trips along the North Carolina coast, three of them to Cape Lookout National Seashore. The trips are very detailed, and the guide is easy to use.

One of the more popular trips for experienced paddlers includes crossing Ocracoke Inlet to get from Ocracoke Island to Portsmouth Village. This is a 4-mile paddle across strong inlet currents, so paddlers need to be skilled. If you paddle over from the town of Atlantic, you will have about a 2-mile trip to reach the lower portion of North Core Banks and the cabin areas. Another popular paddle is from the Harkers Island Visitor Center to Cape Lookout or Shackleford Banks. Depending on where you land, the trip over can be from 3 to 4 miles. Shackleford Banks is also accessed from Beaufort, a paddle of about 4.5 miles. All of these trips are extremely demanding open-water trips affected by weather, tides, winds, and currents. Only attempt these trips if you are an experienced sea kayaker.

Kayak Rentals

Ride the Wind Surf Shop
N.C. Highway 12, Ocracoke Village
(252) 928–6311
www.surfocracoke.com
Rentals for trips to Portsmouth for extremely experienced paddlers only

Core Sound Kayaks & Touring Co.
1545 Harkers Island Road, Straits
(252) 728–2330
www.clis.com/chadstsnc
Rentals for trips to Cape Lookout and guided tours at Cape Lookout

AB Kayaks
326 Front Street, Beaufort
(252) 728–6330, (877) KAYAK NC (529–2562)
www.abkayaks.com
Rentals and tours of Shackleford Banks and Core Banks

Camping and Cabins

At night Cape Lookout National Seashore is one of the darkest places you will ever be. With no artificial lights for miles around, you'll be awed by the blackness of the sky and how long it's been since you've seen that many stars. At night even the sea is black, with the white foam of the breakers glowing in the light from the heavens.

What will you do at night? Maybe you'll sit on the beach by the light of a campfire, stargazing for distant constellations. Maybe the kids will chase ghost crabs along the beach, searching them out with a flashlight. Maybe you'll stand in the black surf, hoping for a monster drum to tug at your line. Maybe you'll hang out around a camp stove with old friends, telling long-forgotten fish stories. Maybe you'll fall in with the cycle of the day and retire early, listening to the waves crashing on the shore as you fall asleep.

One thing's for certain: You'll be up at the crack of dawn, awakened by the sun rising over the Atlantic Ocean. With a breath of sea wind and a kiss of salt on your face, you'll be refreshed and ready to face a day of activity in the great outdoors.

If you plan to spend the night, or several nights, on Cape Lookout National Seashore, you have two options—primitive camping or renting a cabin. Camping is allowed on all three islands of the national seashore. The cabins are pretty much in the middle of nowhere on North and South Core Banks, miles from the areas of highest visitation—Portsmouth Village—and the lighthouse area. The cabins are managed by park concessionaires and must be reserved and paid for before you get to the island.

Primitive Camping

There are no designated campgrounds or developed camping facilities at Cape Lookout National Seashore. Basically you find any spot you like (with a few restrictions) and claim it as your own. This is true primitive, or as they call it in the mountains, backcountry camping. You bring everything you need with you.

Pack everything in your four-wheel drive and ferry over to Cape Lookout for the time of your life.

Campers have the usual options for getting to the islands: passenger ferry, vehicle ferry, or private boat. Camper-style vehicles are allowed on the islands, though there are no paved roads so they must be four-wheel drive. Once you get to the islands, you can venture as far into the coastal wilderness as you'd like. You can sleep in your vehicle or just use it to hold all your stuff while you sleep in a tent.

Backpacking is a great way to see the islands. You can hike as far as you want in one day, spend the night in your tent, and get up and hike again the next. You can walk along the beach or on the four-wheel-drive trails on North and South Core Banks. Almost all hiking will be in soft sand, so be sure to bring sturdy walking shoes or hiking boots. If you have only a weekend, you may want to backpack on Shackleford Banks, which is only 9 miles long. You could hike the entire island in two days, seeing the wild horses, the beach, the maritime forest, and the soundside tidal flats during your hike. South Core Banks is 24 miles long and North Core Banks is 18 miles long, so it's more difficult to see them in their entirety on foot. Remember that inlets open and close regularly on North Core Banks, which can affect your plans to travel the entire island (it may be two or three islands when you're there).

Camping is not allowed in the following areas:

- Within 100 yards of any cabin or house
- Portsmouth Village
- Cape Lookout Lighthouse area
- Cape Lookout Coast Guard Station
- Privately leased property
- Harkers Island Visitor Center site
- Turtle- or bird-closure areas
- Long-term parking areas

Fees: It's free to camp at Cape Lookout National Seashore, but you will have to pay the ferry operator unless you boat over on your own.

Permits: Campers are required to obtain a free permit. These are available through Harkers Island Visitor Center, Portsmouth Village, Cape Lookout Lighthouse Visitor Center, Rudy Austin's Ferry Service from Ocracoke, Morris Marina Ferry Service, Alger Willis Ferry Service, or the Crystal Coast Visitor Center in Morehead City. The Cape Lookout location is a self-registration site where you drop your permit in a box. At Portsmouth Village you may have to hunt down a ranger or volunteer to get the permit. Camping is allowed for fourteen consecutive days.

Facilities: There are minimal facilities for campers. On North Core Banks, there are compost toilets at Portsmouth Village (Mile 1) and hot showers and rest rooms at the Long Point cabin area (Miles 16–17). On South Core Banks, there are hot showers and rest rooms at the Great Island cabin area (Miles 29–30) and composting toilets at Cape Point (Mile 44). On Shackleford there are composting toilets on the west end.

Tips: Beach camping is much different than mainland or mountain camping for two main reasons: sand and lack of shade. Plan accordingly and follow these tips:

- When choosing a location, keep the tides in mind. Extreme highs and lows occur at certain times of the year. Some land areas that are exposed at low tide may flood with water at high tide. Know where the high-tide line is before you set up camp on the beach.
- In warmer months, the beach is the best location for camping because it does not have as many bugs.
- Bring longer tent stakes, at least a foot or more in length. Regular tent stakes, especially those skinny metal spindles that come with most tents,

do not anchor in the sand. You might need a small hammer to set the long stakes.

- Tents outfitted for strong winds are highly recommended. Make sure to secure all flaps and tarps, even if it's not windy when you are setting up.
- Prepare for insects. Mosquitoes, biting flies, gnats, ticks, and chiggers plague the seashore in the warmer months, usually from May through October but sometimes longer. Make sure your tent or camper has mosquito netting or screens. Bring insect repellent.
- Fires are allowed below the high tide line on the ocean only. Driftwood and downed wood are the only materials that may be collected for burning. This wood is limited in supply, so you may want to bring a camp stove.
- Bring food and water, as there is no food or fresh water available on the islands. If you plan to camp for a long time, the park may be able to store water for you. Call the visitor center.
- Secure your food tightly to keep it out of reach of raccoons and scavenging birds. If you are using a cooler, wrap it with bungee cords. Keep the food in your car or tent during the day. At night, do not keep food in the tent. Raccoons can get into anything and can easily chew their way into a tent. Do not leave food, trash, or bait lying around in the open, as it will attract wildlife. By all means, never feed a seagull. Once it figures out that you are a food source, it will never leave you alone.
- Dispose of human waste properly to avoid pollution and the spreading of disease. Use a small shovel or trowel to dig a cathole about 6 to 8 inches deep and 4 to 6 inches in diameter. Dig the hole above the high-tide line but away from any area where people are likely to walk or camp. And cover it up.
- Plan for changes in weather. Storms brew quickly and winds switch and pick up often. Be prepared. Bring a battery-powered weather radio if possible. In the event of an approaching hurricane, park rangers will evacuate the islands.
- Pets must be on a 6-foot leash at all times.

Renting a Cabin

On North Core Banks and South Core Banks, there are a number of cabins available for rent through private concessionaires. You must make cabin reservations ahead of time, well in advance in fall and spring.

Morris Marina Kabin Kamps and Ferry Service
Location: 1000 Morris Marina Road (off U.S. Highway 70), Atlantic
North Core Banks
Information: (252) 225–4261; www.portsmouthisland.com

Morris Marina's Kabin Kamps are on North Core Banks, also known as Portsmouth Island, between Miles 16 and 17. This is known as the Long Point cabin area, about a mile north of Old Drum Inlet and 16 or so miles from Portsmouth Village.

Morris has twelve condo cabins and eight Octa-Structure cabins that sleep up to six people in three sets of bunk beds. The condo cabins have gas cooking stoves, kitchen counters and sinks, generators, ceiling fans, lights, heaters, hot water, complete bathrooms, and rocking chairs on the front porch. The Octa-Structures have gas cooking stoves, kitchen counters and sinks, gas heaters, gas lights, hot water, and complete bathrooms. All water in all the cabins is potable. Renters need to bring sheets, pillows, blankets, towels, coolers to keep food cold, all cooking utensils, pots and pans, and tableware. All of the cabins are on the ocean beach, with their front porches facing the sea.

A caretaker is on-site to assist with accommodations, provide information, and to obtain emergency medical services. This person maintains contact with the mainland, so you can get weather reports or emergency messages. Renters can put in an order for ice, bait, groceries, etc. and their supplies are delivered the next day. Gas for vehicles is sold on the island and cannot be transported on the ferry. Hot showers and rest rooms are on-site for area primitive-style campers.

Cabin reservations should be made well in advance. Anglers often book a year ahead for the fall fishing season. Cabins are rented on a per-night basis. Condo cabins cost $110 per night, and Octa-Structures $100 per night. They are available from early March through the second week in December.

Morris Marina offers ferry service to the islands for both passengers and vehicles. The ferries run at 7:00 and 11:00 A.M. and 3:00 P.M. The ferry drops visitors off at a landing right at the cabins. Reservations must be made in advance for the ferry, especially if you plan to bring a vehicle over.

Morris Marina Bar and Grill,, right on the water at the ferry dock, is a great place to fuel up with a big meal before or after visiting the remote North Core Banks.

Alger G. Willis Fishing Camps and Ferry Service
Location: Willis Road (off U.S. Highway 70), Davis
South Core Banks
Information: (252) 729–2791; www.drumwagon.com/awfc

Alger Willis Fishing Camps are on South Core Banks, at Miles 29–30, opposite the town of Davis on the mainland. The cabins are about 6 miles from New Drum Inlet, about 12 miles from the Cape Lookout Lighthouse, and about 15 miles from Cape Point. This is called the Great Island cabin area, a narrow stretch of island from which the sound and the ocean are both visible.

There are twenty-five units, varying in sizes that sleep from four to twelve people. All cabins are wired for generators, but you must bring your own if you want electricity. Cabins are equipped with tables and chairs, gas stoves, kitchen counters, potable-water sinks, mattresses, bunk beds, toilets, and hot-water showers. Renters should bring cooking utensils, food, coolers, dishes, bed linens, blankets, pillows, lanterns, and heaters.

A caretaker is on-site to handle trash, sell gas for vehicles, offer information, maintain contact with the mainland, and help out in emergencies. Gas, block ice, bag ice, and bait are sold, and campers can buy these items even if they are not staying at the cabins. A bathhouse with hot showers and toilets is available, and campers not staying at the cabins can use it.

All cabins are rented on a per-night basis. The price ranges from $65 to $150 a night, depending on the size, plus county and state taxes. Ferry fees for passengers and vehicles are extra. Fall is by far the busiest season due to the outstanding fishing. Some anglers reserve up to a year in advance for the cabins in the fall. The cabins and ferry operate from the latter part of March through December.

Fishing

Surf fishing is legendary at North and South Core Banks. Every spring and fall hordes of anglers junket to Cape Lookout National Seashore with vehicles, gear, friends, and high hopes in tow. In these seasons, fishing is more than a sport, it's an event and a celebration.

Surf fishing may reign supreme at Cape Lookout National Seashore, but inshore fishing in the waters around the seashore is widely renowned as well. Guides in the nearby communities take trips to the inshore waters regularly, and anyone with a boat or a set of waders can fish the sound shores of the seashore. Cape Lookout National Seashore does not have any facilities offering offshore trips, but nearby Morehead City and Atlantic Beach do. Even though going offshore is not technically fishing at Cape Lookout National Seashore, it's such a popular form of fishing in the area that it deserves space in this chapter.

The Cape Lookout waters are in a transition zone between the Mid-Atlantic and South Atlantic Bights, so they can have warm-water or cold-water fish depending on how far south the cold currents run or how far north the warm currents run. In the transition zone, the currents stir up nutrient-rich sediment from the sea bottom and the cold and warm currents collide. This creates some of the richest waters on the East Coast. Cold-water fish like bluefish and striped bass are caught off these shores along with warm-water fish like king and Spanish mackerel and tarpon.

A license is not required for saltwater fishing in the sounds or Atlantic Ocean, unless you are using commercial gear. However, the state of North Carolina regulates fishing with laws regarding size limits, bag limits (numbers of fish caught in a day), and seasons. It is up to the individual anglers to be informed about size and bag limits *before* they go fishing. Limit sheets are available at local tackle shops, on-line at www.ncdmf.net or by calling the North Carolina Division of Marine Fisheries at (800) 682–2632.

Marine patrol officers with the Division of Marine Fisheries make regular inspections for illegal catches. They are allowed to stop you on the water

Surf fishing is not a sport, it's an addiction. NORTH CAROLINA DIVISION OF TOURISM, FILM AND SPORTS DEVELOPMENT

or to approach you on the beach to have a look in your cooler. Possession of undersize or oversize fish or too many of a species is grounds for a stiff fine. Besides, the regulations are for the good of fishing, to help declining fish species build back up so that people will be fishing on the North Carolina coast for generations.

For more information about fishing in Cape Lookout National Seashore or along the Carolina coast, an excellent resource is the book *Coastal Fishing in the Carolinas from Surf, Pier, and Jetty* by Robert J. Goldstein (see the bibliography). Make sure you get the third edition, which was updated in 2000. Another great book for surf anglers is Joe Malat's *Surf Fishing* (see www.joe malat.com to order).

Surf Fishing

North and South Core Banks have a legendary following of surf anglers. Before these islands became part of the Cape Lookout National Seashore, they were primarily the fishing and hunting grounds for generations of eastern North Carolina families. Some people have been coming here for up to fifty years, and now their sons and daughters and grandchildren come with them.

It's not just good fishing that draws anglers here in droves. Anglers who fish here usually develop a fervent passion for the seclusion of the islands.

Cape Hatteras fishing is rumored to be slightly better, but what could be better than a beach with no electric lights, no highway, no minigolf, no hordes of people? Cape Lookout National Seashore fishing is rugged, rustic, and absolutely delicious for those who crave isolation. The effort and expense required to get to Cape Lookout ensure that only serious outdoorsmen/women go there. Everyone on the island is usually of a like mind. The regular fishermen and women who return year after year form tight cliques and are understandably close-mouthed about their little slices of heaven.

Surf anglers tend to congregate in a few main areas, but there are nearly 50 miles of the Core Banks to fish. With a vehicle you can get just about anywhere you want to go. The north end of Portsmouth Island at Ocracoke Inlet is one popular place to surf fish. The cabin areas are obvious locations for angling as well. Both sides of New Drum Inlet are places where you'll see a lot of anglers, as is Cape Point, on the south end of South Core Banks. The hook at Cape Point, known as Power Squadron Spit, is a good spot for fishing in the deep waters of Lookout Bight. The shores along the inlets are excellent surf fishing spots because of all the baitfish moving through in the current.

In the fall, and again in the spring, the predominant catch is red drum. Of all the fish caught in the surf around Cape Lookout National Seashore, anglers get most excited about red drum. Also known as the channel bass or redfish, red drum is the North Carolina state fish. Huge red drum are caught in the surf around Cape Lookout from mid-September through December

Generations of North Carolina families come to the Outer Banks to fish.
NORTH CAROLINA DIVISION OF TOURISM, FILM AND SPORTS DEVELOPMENT

and again from April through June. It doesn't take a genius to figure out how Old and New Drum Inlets got their names.

Bluefish are caught in the surf from April through November, especially at South Core Banks and Cape Point in the area of the Cape Lookout Shoals. Striped bass winter off the beaches from December through March, but unfortunately at that time the ferries do not take vehicles to the island and the cabins are not open. Surf fishing has to be done by campers on foot. Or you can boat over or hire an inshore guide to take you just off the beach to catch the stripers.

Besides these three "biggies," there's a mixed bag of fish to be caught in the surf. Depending on the time of year, you might catch pompano, spot, sea mullet, flounder, Spanish mackerel, or a gray or speckled trout. New Drum Inlet is said to be one of the top flounder-catching locations in the state.

Most surf anglers stay at the cabins at Miles 16–17 on North Core Banks and Miles 29–30 on South Core Banks (see our Camping and Cabins chapter). The cabin areas have from twenty to twenty-five units, each sleeping from four to twelve people, and the cabins are booked solid from September through November and are usually booked from March through May. If you're planning to come in spring or fall, reserve early. The cabins are closed from mid-December through March. Other anglers camp on the beach in tents or bring over four-wheel-drive camper-style vehicles.

Cape Point, at Mile 44, is often the most crowded fishing area. If you want to bring a vehicle there, you have to ferry to the Great Island cabin area (Miles 29–30) and drive down to Cape Point (about 15 miles) on the beach or an interior four-wheel-drive trail.

When surf fishing at Cape Lookout National Seashore, remember to bring everything you'll need. If you're staying at the cabins, the caretakers can sell you supplies like ice, bait, gas, and water, and Alger Willis Fishing Camps even makes supply runs to the mainland for its customers.

Inshore Fishing

Fishing is fantastic in the Pamlico, Core, and Back Sounds. If you have your own boat and a reliable chart book, you can explore these sounds on your own. But if you have no idea where to start in these massive, shallow sounds, it's best to hire a guide. There are numerous guide services operating out of Ocracoke, Harkers Island, Beaufort, Atlantic Beach, and Morehead City that run regular trips to the waters around Cape Lookout National Seashore.

Inshore fishing yields a great variety of fish, challenges anglers' skills, is less expensive, and generally provides a relaxing day on the water. "Inshore" in the guide means the waters of the sounds, the inlets, and the ocean up to about 12 miles offshore. Wading in the marsh, dangling a line from a structure, or fishing from small boats, even canoes or kayaks, is considered inshore fishing. It can be fly-fishing, light-tackle casting, bottom fishing, wreck fishing, structure fishing, and trolling. Saltwater fly-fishing is renowned off Cape Lookout National Seashore.

When inshore fishing, anglers look for structural or geographical formations. Fish gather around inlets, jetties, channel markers, buoys, artificial reefs, wrecks, islands, marsh points, sandbars, and shoals. Man-made structures in the water provide a surface that attracts algae, sponges, barnacles, mussels, crabs, snails, and all kinds of sea creatures. These in turn attract hungry fish. Other fish hang out next to inlets or sloughs, where they can feed on baitfish that drift by in the current.

North Carolina has an artificial reef program that provides structures to support its fisheries. Concrete, steel, boats, and even old train cars are sunk on the sound or ocean floor to attract fish. For information and locations, see www.ncdmf.net or use a nautical chart. Wreck and reef fishing in this area is best from May through November, with catches like cobia, king mackerel, Spanish mackerel, barracuda, bonita, grouper, and sharks.

Depending on the time of year you're fishing inshore, you might catch albacore, flounder, speckled trout, bluefish, Spanish mackerel, or drum. Red drum are abundant in the sound throughout the year. An experienced guide with a shallow-draft boat can take anglers into the shallow marsh waters to find these fish. Interestingly, tarpon are caught in the Pamlico Sound in the summer, when the sound waters heat up to over 80 degrees.

Some of the most talked-about inshore fishing around Cape Lookout National Seashore is for false albacore in October and November. Fly anglers from all over the United States (and even some from foreign countries), including former President George Bush, return to the area every year to fish for the biggest false albacore found anywhere in the world. All of the local inshore guides get so booked up that guides "from off" come in to take up the slack. The fish hang around in Lookout Bight, an ideal fishing ground because it is protected in all weather.

The local marinas and tackle shops book charters and/or recommend guides for fishing in the Cape Lookout area.

Marinas

Harkers Island Fishing Center
Island Road, Harkers Island
(252) 728–3907
www.harkersmarina.com

Barbour's Harbor Marina
1390 Island Road, Harkers Island
(252) 728–6181
www.sanddollarferry.com

Calico Jack's Marina
Island Road, Harkers Island
(252) 728–3575
www.capelookoutferry.com

Tackle Shops

Cruise Mart 2 Red & White
814 South Seashore Drive, off U.S. Highway 70, Atlantic
(252) 225–0191

Harkers Island Tackle Co.
989 Island Road, Harkers Island
(252) 728–3016
www.harkersislandtackle.com

East'ard Variety Store
1344 Island Road, Harkers Island
(252) 728–7149

EJW Outdoors
2204 Arendell Street, Morehead City
(252) 247–4725

Pete's Tackle Shop
1704 Arendell Street, Morehead City
(252) 726–8644

Cape Lookout Fly Shop
601-H Atlantic Beach Causeway, Atlantic Beach
(252) 240–1427
www.captjoes.com

Offshore Charter Fishing

Like the Cape Hatteras area, the central coast area enjoys a healthy offshore fishery. Giant bluefin tuna are caught in December and January, and the rest of the year there are catches of yellowfin tuna, wahoo, dolphin, blue marlin, sailfish, and white marlin. Morehead City and Atlantic Beach are the area hubs of offshore sportfishing. Numerous boats make the trek to the Gulf Stream daily. Beaufort Inlets offer access to the fishing grounds of the Gulf Stream.

Offshore fishing near Cape Lookout National Seashore is accessible out of nearby Morehead City and Atlantic Beach. NORTH CAROLINA DIVISION OF TOURISM, FILM AND SPORTS DEVELOPMENT

Chartering a boat for an offshore fishing trip is an expensive endeavor. All charters are full-day and can take up to six people. Expect to pay up to $1,000 for a full-day offshore charter, plus you need to tip the boat's mate at least 15 to 20 percent of the price of the boat. It's worth the money, though, to go out on a deep-sea fishing trip, and you could split the cost with the others on board. Trips typically leave about 6:00 A.M. and return in the later afternoon, about 4:00 P.M.

When you charter the boat, the captain and mate will supply all the tackle and bait you'll need for the day. The captain will take you to the best places to fish, and the mate will help everyone, even children or disabled people. In other words, you don't have to be a world-class sportsman to catch the fish. Most of the time the boat will be trolling for fish, but often you will cast to the fish as well. Fly anglers are welcome on board, but you should let the captain know if you plan to fly-fish. You will need to bring food, drinks, sunscreen, sunglasses, and extra clothes. Offshore trips leave early in the morning, usually before sunrise, and return in the late afternoon.

Offshore fishing is great fun unless you get seasick. You can take an over-the-counter motion sickness remedy the night before and in the morning, and you can also try a topical patch. Greasy food, alcohol, and dehydration make seasickness worse. Eat lightly, drink water, and stay in the fresh air on deck if you feel sick.

If you don't want to go offshore fishing, but you want to see the catches, go to the Morehead City boat docks in the afternoon between 3:30 and 5:30 P.M. You'll be able to see the fish being unloaded from the boats when they come in.

Offshore charter boats in Morehead City are not organized under one central booking agency. Ask around on the docks when you get there or call a local tackle shop for a recommendation. You can also do a search on the Web for North Carolina offshore fishing, or call the Crystal Coast Visitor Center at (800) SUNNY NC or (252) 726–8148. The Atlantic Beach marinas listed below book offshore charters.

Capt. Stacy Fishing Center
Atlantic Beach Causeway, Atlantic Beach
(252) 247–7501, (800) 533–9417
www.captstacy.com

Seawater Marina
400 Atlantic Beach Causeway, Atlantic Beach
(252) 726–1637

Hiking

Walking and hiking here is like making a pilgrimage to solitude; the farther you get from the ferry landings, the more serene the island gets. The landscape is stark and the atmosphere is rugged, and anyone who appreciates the outdoors will find it inviting. Hiking the islands allows you the chance to see wildlife, birdlife, and sealife and to get a better understanding of barrier island ecology. When you get tired, pitch a tent and sleep on the beach, right next to the ocean.

Fifty-six miles of pristine ocean beach await you, though those miles are broken up by inlets. There are 24 miles of South Core Banks, 18 miles of North Core Banks, 9 miles of Shackleford Banks and, if you can get there, 4 miles of Middle Core Bank between Old Drum and New Drum Inlets. Unless you have a boat or kayak, it is not possible to get to one of these islands from the other, although some ferry operators will shuttle passengers between the southern portion of South Core Banks and Shackleford Banks. Usually you have to go back to the mainland and take a ferry to the next island of choice.

It is not always possible to walk the entire length of North Core Banks because of inlets. At this writing, because of a tropical storm, two new inlets had broken through at miles 2 and 7, making it impossible to cross those areas at high tides. At extreme low tides they were passable. These inlets were expected to close within a few months; however, anything could happen before you get here. Ask at the visitor center or ask a ranger about the possibility of walking the entire island.

If you just want to hike around for the day, head to the Cape Lookout Lighthouse, the Cape Village area, and Cape Point. It's about 2 miles from the lighthouse to Cape Point. On North Core Banks, most visitors go to Portsmouth Village and then out to the beach, a distance of about 1.5 miles. On Shackleford Banks, you can walk as far as you'd like on the east or west end and look for wild horses or search the beach for shells. Superb shelling is probably the primary reason walkers and hikers come to Cape Lookout National Seashore.

The Visitor Center on Harkers Island has a spacious picnic area, and the lighthouse is visible across the water.

The interior four-wheel-drive trails are good places to hike, though they aren't as scenic as the beach. The trails run almost the entire length of South Core Banks and about half the length of North Core Banks, plus there are offshoots to get you to the beach, the cabin areas, and the lighthouse and surrounding village. See the Off-Road Driving Map for an overview of the interior trails. There are no interior trails on Shackleford Banks, but you can walk the paths that the horses have made.

Hiking a great distance here is a formidable task because of sand and the lack of shade and facilities. But it's worth it for the chance to experience the wild beauty of these lands. You'll find shells, like sand dollars, scotch bonnets, and whelks, because no one is there to pick them up. You'll encounter shorebirds and wildlife, and you'll see parts of the island that most visitors never see. Bring insect repellent, a hat to shade your skin from the sun, sturdy shoes, food, and water. Water will be the bulkiest item you'll have to carry, but bring plenty of it because it is not available on the islands. Hot showers and rest rooms are located at Miles 16–17 on North Core Banks and Miles 29–30 on South Core Banks.

Off-Roading

Here is your chance to take that SUV off-road. But remember, you're driving in a fragile ecosystem, not a racetrack. Stay within the boundaries of the four-wheel-drive trails and beach and don't trample all over dunes and vegetation or closed areas.

Trucks, campers, SUVs, and ATVs are allowed on North and South Core Banks but not on Shackleford Banks. Motorcycles and dirt bikes are not allowed anywhere in the seashore. Vehicles and ATVs are ferried over from the mainland to the Long Point area at Mile 16 on North Core Banks or the Great Island area at Mile 30 on South Core Banks.

A network of four-wheel-drive sand trails winds around the ferry docks and cabins and connects to unpaved interior trails, which connect to numerous beach-access points. The interior trails or "back roads" run about 8 miles on North Core Banks and most of the length of South Core Banks, and there are offshoots to get you to other parts of the island. Using these roads helps protect the ecosystems of the islands so that vehicles aren't driving over dunes and vegetation. Legal trails are marked with JEEP signs, while illegal trails are marked with a jeep with a red slash through it. Beach ramps are well marked with RAMP signs. See the Off-Road Driving Map for an overview of the interior trails. If a section of beach is impassable due to high tide, back up and retrace your route to a ramp and take the interior trail. Do not drive over the dunes.

You can also drive along the beach in any areas that aren't closed in nesting seasons. Do not even think of taking a non-four-wheel-drive vehicle to the islands. Getting stuck is an expensive nightmare. Parking areas are well marked. Mile markers are placed in one-mile increments along Core Banks. Portsmouth Village is at Mile 1; Cape Point is at Mile 44.

It is advisable to lower the air pressure in your tires for beach driving. Air is available for refilling tires at the ferry docks on the mainland. Gas is sold at the ferry landing and cabin areas on North (Mile 16) and South Core Banks (Mile 30).

Cape Lookout National Seashore Off-Road Vehicle Routes

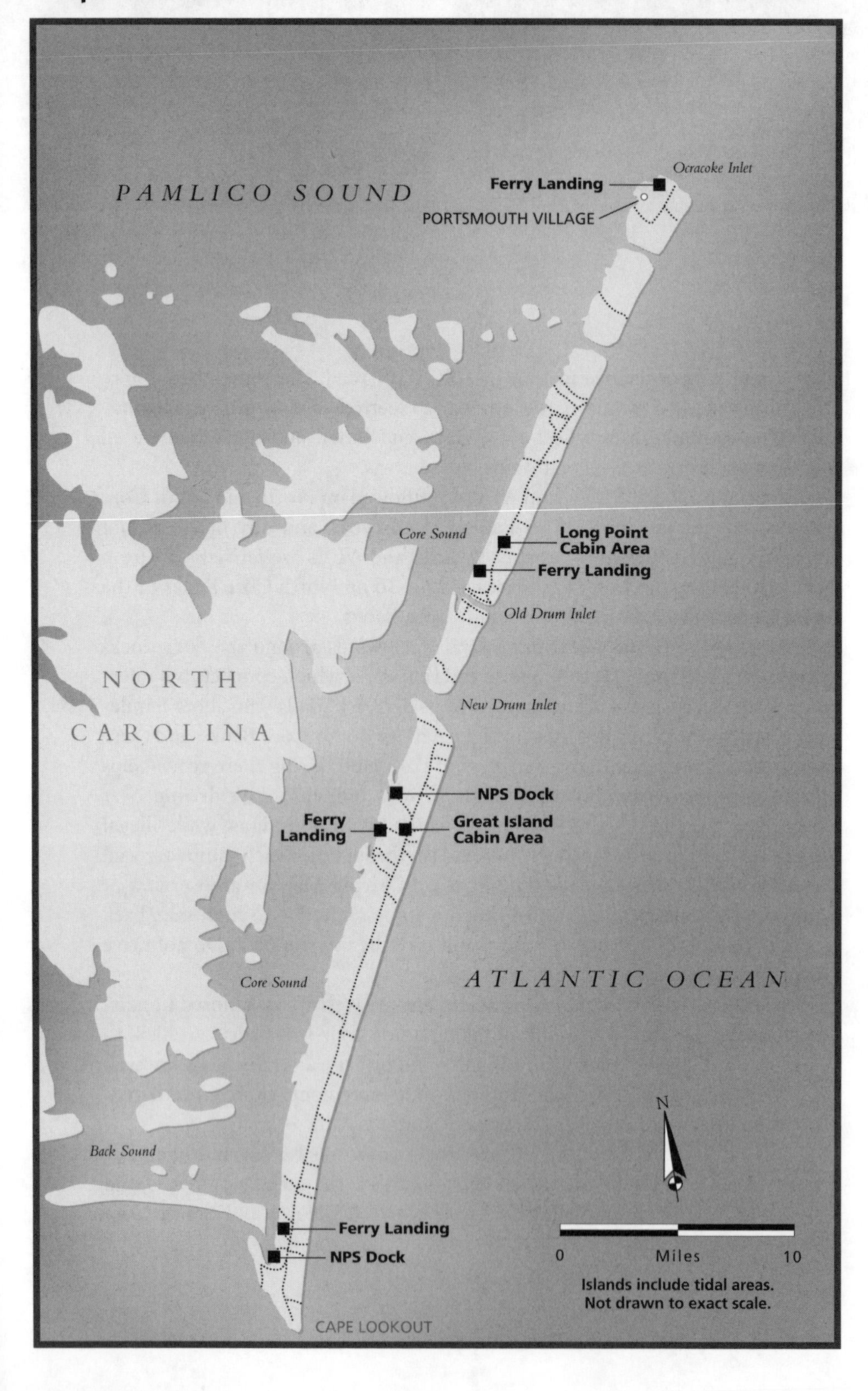

For off-road driving tips and NPS beach driving rules, see The Basics chapter at the beginning of this book.

Vehicle Parking

The National Park Service allows vehicles to remain unattended on North and South Core Banks between March and December 31. This is ideal for anglers and campers who return often. The marked parking areas are often filled with rusty beach buggies plus campers and trucks outfitted with all the gear needed for life in the beach wilderness. Permits are required for vehicles that will be unattended for more than twenty-four hours. Vehicles must be parked in one of three designated parking areas at Long Point, Great Island, or Cape Lookout. A fee of $10 per week, or portion of a week, is charged per vehicle for storage. Permits and parking decals are issued at Cape Lookout National Seashore Headquarters on Harkers Island during business hours Monday through Friday. No cash is accepted, so you must pay by check or money order. You can also get permits and decals through the mail (131 Charles Street, Harkers Island, NC 28531). All vehicles must be removed from the island by December 31, though the ferry services—the only way to get your vehicle off the island—often stop running earlier in the month.

Scuba Diving

Everything from German U-boats to freighters and tankers to steamships have sunk at Cape Lookout Shoals—a dangerously shallow area considered a part of North Carolina's infamous Graveyard of the Atlantic—so wreck diving is incredible here. Though the wrecks aren't considered a part of Cape Lookout National Seashore, they're so close that you wouldn't want to miss them if you're a diver.

Diving is a year-round activity here, thanks to the warm waters of the Gulf Stream, which is about 40 miles offshore. Summer is the best month for diving, with water temperatures averaging in the 80s and with visibility from 75 to 150 feet. Of course, the closer you dive to shore, the less visibility there is. Tropical fish can be seen on the wrecks from June through September.

The most popular wreck in this area is the *U-352*, a German submarine in 115 feet of water, so you must be a very experienced diver. On May 9, 1942, the sub tried to attack the U.S. Coast Guard cutter *Icarus*, but its torpedo exploded prematurely, revealing the sub and starting a battle between the two ships. Thirteen German sailors lost their lives in the battle. The outer hull has rusted away, but the pressure hull remains intact and the hatches are open.

The tanker *Papoose* is another interesting wreck at Cape Lookout Shoals. It was sunk during World War II by the German *U-124* on March 18, 1942. Amazingly, the crew of the *Papoose* survived, rowing to shore in the light of the fire of another burning ship. The wreck lies upside down in 130 feet of clear, warm water. Her large keel rises to within 85 feet of the surface. Olympus Dive Center reports that in recent years schools of Atlantic sand tiger sharks have been present on this wreck year-round.

The *Neaco* is considered one of the best dives in North Carolina. It's a tanker that was sunk off Cape Lookout by the German submarine *U-124* on March 23, 1942. The tanker was split in two sections by the attack; the stern is the most popular diving area. The wreck, at 140 feet deep and far offshore, is for experienced divers only. It's covered with coral, sponges, and anemones and is surrounded by fish.

There are many more wrecks to see in the Cape Lookout area, some in shallow water and accessible to novice, certified divers. For instance, the *Theodore Parker*, a World War II liberty ship, is in 30 to 55 feet of water, only a mile and a half off the beach. She is an artificial reef, meaning that after a useful life she was sunk on purpose to provide fish habitat. Indeed, a variety of fish live around this wreck. Another easy dive is the *Indra*, between 35 and 75 feet deep and close to shore.

If you're really into diving, get a copy of *Shipwrecks, Diving the Graveyard of the Atlantic*, by Roderick M. Farb (Menasha Ridge Press, 1991). The Web sites for the companies listed below have a wealth of information about the local dive sites.

Discovery Diving Company
414 Orange Street, Beaufort
(252) 728–2265
www.discoverydiving.com

Olympus Dive Center
713 Shepard Street, Morehead City
(252) 726–9432
www.olympusdiving.com

Surfing

Surfing is a favorite sport all along the North Carolina coast. If the conditions are right for the beach you're on—if there's an onshore swell and an offshore wind—you'll be able to ride a wave. Cape Lookout may not have the notoriety of Cape Hatteras, but it's a worthy surf destination nonetheless. If you make the extra effort to get here under these conditions, you'll be rewarded.

The Cape Lookout area across from the lighthouse and the west end of Shackleford are the most popular surfing destinations at Cape Lookout National Seashore, mainly because they are the easiest places to get to from the mainland. It is the rare bird that makes a trip to Portsmouth Island or the north end of South Core Banks specifically for surfing.

The Core Banks are the only east-facing beaches in the central coast area, so when swells are coming in from the east or southeast and the wind is from a westward direction, it is the place to go to catch the waves. You can anchor your boat in the sound in front of the lighthouse and use the boardwalk to access the ocean beach.

Shackleford Banks faces due south and is good for surfing on south swells and north winds. The beaches of Bogue Banks face the same direction and are much easier to get to, so most people just paddle out there. But if you're looking for privacy and you have boat access to the islands, the west end of Shackleford is a good spot.

There are no ocean piers at the national seashore to form good wave breaks, but shipwrecks and submerged debris form good sandbars, hence breaks. Remember, sandbars are constantly shifting, so wave breaks are constantly shifting.

As with everywhere on the East Coast, east and south swells are most prevalent from June through November, during hurricane season. But surfing is a year-round sport in this area. The water is warmest from May through October, but with a good wetsuit you can get in any time of year.

Getting there when the conditions are right is the biggest issue for surfers

Searching for a break.

at Cape Lookout National Seashore. Boat travel is never quick and it requires a little planning, especially if you're taking a ferry. Watch the *Weather Channel* for conditions and check the Web for a report. You might be able to get a report from one of the local surf shops. If conditions are lining up to be favorable, make a plan. Most people who surf at the Cape Lookout or Shackleford go over in their own boats. If you're taking a ferry to the islands, you won't be able to get there until the first ferry runs, usually 9:00 A.M. (See the Things to Know chapter for a list of ferry operators.)

For surfboard rentals, contact:

Action Surf Shop
5116 U.S. Highway 70, Morehead City
(252) 240–1818

Bert's Surf Shop
N.C. Highway 58, MM 2, Atlantic Beach
(252) 726–730

Other Adventures

Cape Lookout National Seashore Summer Programs

Every summer rangers at Cape Lookout National Seashore offer a variety of family-oriented nature and cultural programs that help visitors better understand their surroundings while they're here. The programs are held at the Harkers Island Visitor Center, the Cape Lookout Lighthouse, the dock at the west end of Shackleford Banks, or at the North Carolina Maritime Museum in Beaufort.

At the lighthouse keepers' quarters, you might encounter a program on Lighthouse Lore or Discovering the Cape Lookout National Seashore. At the Maritime Museum, a slide show all about the seashore is the offering. (This is a great way to entice you over to the islands.) At the Harkers Island Visitor Center, you can take in a video presentation or a stargazing program or request another program of your choice. The programs are short, ranging from fifteen minutes up to an hour long. Other programs may be available when you are visiting. Stop by or call the visitor center to see which programs are being held while you're here. Some programs are handicapped-accessible. The best way to find out what programs are being offered is to pick up a copy of the seashore's newspaper, which is available at local visitor centers.

On Shackleford Banks you can take a horse-watching tour with Ranger Sue Stuska. Visitors will do well to take the tour with Dr. Stuska, who is the park biologist in charge of the horses and is extremely knowledgeable about the wild Shackleford herd. On Wednesdays in the summer, from 9:00 A.M. until 2:00 P.M., Stuska leads visitors all over the west end of the island in search of the horses, all the while teaching about their habits and the island environment. You must make advance reservations for this tour offered monthly during the summer; call (252) 728–2250.

A special seashore program for kids is the Junior Ranger Program. Anyone between the ages of six and thirteen can earn a Junior Ranger patch at Cape Lookout National Seashore by going to programs and completing a

Discover Cape Lookout National Seashore on a guided tour.

booklet. Rangers at the Harkers Island Visitor Center or the Cape Lookout Lighthouse Keepers' Quarters can give you information about this program.

Environmental Education

Those who want to know more about the fascinating ecology and geology of barrier island ecosystems have several opportunities for education. For intensive educational workshops there are two on-site learning centers with accommodations on the southern end of South Core Banks near Cape Lookout—the Cape Lookout Environmental Education Center and the Cape Lookout Studies Program. For shorter learning sessions combined with fun, there are kayak and boating ecotours.

The **Cape Lookout Environmental Education Center** (CLEEC) is a National Park Service–sanctioned, on-site learning center that offers summer camps for children, educational programs for school groups, and weekend programs for families and adults. The focus of CLEEC is the ecology and geology of barrier islands. Its on-island headquarters and lodgings are in a legendary soundside location of Cape Village, in what was Les and Sally Moore's General Store in the 1960s. CLEEC took over and renovated the buildings in 1995 and began offering environmental education programs in 1999. Weeklong summer camps, offered to rising fourth graders through high school students, include habitat exploration, hiking, sea turtle patrol, interaction with biologists and marine scientists, astronomy, and exploration, plus arts and crafts, swimming, kayaking, and games. CLEEC can also arrange special programs for school groups. Family camps and weekend programs are held in the spring and fall and can include topics such as birding or alternative sources of energy. CLEEC offers on-island accommodations and meals, all for a very reasonable price. To contact them write to: CLEEC, P. O. Box 19286, Greensboro, NC 27419; call (336) 292–0774; or visit www.cleec.org.

The **Cape Lookout Studies Program,** managed by the North Carolina Maritime Museum, offers environmentally minded groups and families a way to stay at Cape Lookout while learning more about the ecology and geology of the island. The program utilizes the museum's field station—the 1917 Coast Guard Station at Cape Village on South Core Banks. The museum offers the historic building to groups that set up programs on environmental education, research, or conservation. Groups that use the building set up their own programs based on their interests and find an appropriate instructor to assist the museum's field staff. (The museum staff can assist in finding the instructor and setting up the program.) Participants then pay a per-night fee for use of the building and instruction. Most often the facility is used for teacher workshops, retreats, science classes, environmental groups, summer camps, families, and scout troops. Examples of program topics include bottle-nosed dolphins, sea turtle conservation, marine field research, ecokayaking, barrier island ecology, photography, and birding. Groups interested in using the facility must submit an application with a detailed agenda and instructor that complies with the goals of the program. For information write to North Carolina Maritime Museum, Attn. Cape Lookout Studies Program, 315 Front Street, Beaufort, NC 28516; call (252) 504–2452; or visit www.capelookoutstudies.org.

The **North Carolina Maritime Museum** at 315 Front Street in Beaufort also offers dozens of scheduled programs for those who want to learn more about the cultural and natural history of the area. Many of the programs deal with topics relating to Cape Lookout National Seashore. At the museum you can see slide shows, talk to local authors, and listen to lectures on a variety of topics. It also offers hiking trips to various local islands (including Shackleford and South Core Banks), sailing lessons, photo expeditions, boatbuilding workshops, sound-seining programs, and much more. For a listing, call the museum at (252) 728–7317 or visit its Web site at www.ah.dcr.state.nc.us/sections/maritime/programs/programs.htm.

Capt. Andy's Water Tours, departing from the Morehead City waterfront, is a touristy-looking tour boat that offers quality marine education field trips. Capt. Andy's hands-on, feet-wet field trips are led by biologists and focus on teaching visitors about the ecology and geology basics of Shackleford Banks. Participants do things like capture crustaceans, rake for clams, find the wild horses, hike through the island ecosystems, look for shells, compare ocean and sound life, and learn about the formation of barrier islands. Capt. Andy's also leads dolphin-watch trips that focus on education about dolphin behavior. For information call (252) 728–3988 or visit www.captandy.com.

Good Fortune Charters offers coastal ecology sails to Cape Lookout National Seashore. The *Good Fortune* is a 41-foot custom ketch, and her captain, Ron White, is a marine biologist and dive instructor. White's sails include snorkeling, shelling, dolphin-watching, and birding for up to six people. Contact him at (252) 241–6866 or (252) 247–3860 or visit his Web site at www.nccoast.com/goodfortune.htm.

Hunting

Hunting is permitted on all the islands in Cape Lookout National Seashore. The primary hunting done here is for waterfowl, but pheasant and small mammals like raccoons are also available. All hunting must be consistent with state and federal regulations, and all hunters must have legal state and federal hunting licenses. Waterfowl hunters need a North Carolina hunting license with a waterfowl privilege and a Federal Duck Stamp. Landbird and mammal hunters do not need a park permit, but waterfowl hunters must apply for a permit to build a temporary blind. Up to 140 duck blind permits are issued by the park staff every year. Anyone who wishes to construct a blind must show up on a certain day at the Harkers Island Visitor Center to register and receive a location and permit number. All blinds must be temporary and removed within thirty days of the end of the season.

The seashore has established safety zones that are closed to hunting. Hunting is not allowed within 200 yards of any campsite or structure, including all buildings, docks, and storage sheds. Loaded weapons are not allowed in any of these closed areas. During boat or ferry transportation to the islands or vehicle transportation on the islands, weapons must be broken down and unloaded. Target practice and dog training are not permitted on the islands. Dogs are allowed to be off their leashes in the act of hunting and at no other time.

For information on state hunting regulations, contact the North Carolina Wildlife Resources Commission at (800) 675–0263 or www.ncwildlife.org. For information about hunting at Cape Lookout National Seashore, contact a ranger at (252) 728–2250.

Windsurfing/Kiteboarding

If you have your own equipment, you can windsurf or kite around Cape Lookout National Seashore, but no outfitter rents equipment or organizes trips at the seashore. Experienced sailors and kiters head to Shell Point on the east end of Harkers Island to get their wind fixes. Windsurfing and kiting are at their best here on northeast winds. Shell Point is the location of the Cape Lookout National Seashore Visitor Center, so there is plenty of parking. There is also a great sound beach that's perfect for launching. The sound is wide and shallow here and there is little boat traffic, so it's perfect for a day on the water. There are picnic facilities on-site as well.

Local Attractions

Portsmouth Village
North Core Banks, Mile 1

North Core Banks is often called Portsmouth Island after the village on its northern tip, Portsmouth Village. Meticulously maintained and preserved, historic Portsmouth Village is unoccupied, achingly devoid of the people who once belonged there. Its buildings—lifesaving station, schoolhouse, post office, church, and homes—are empty, their people driven out by the wrath of storms and a depressed seafaring economy. It is a rare place frozen in time, untouched by the commercialism of the modern era.

When the National Park Service established Cape Lookout National Seashore in 1976, they decided to keep and preserve the buildings of Portsmouth Village, which is on the National Register of Historic Places. The last two living residents of the village, two elderly women, had reluctantly moved away in 1971, leaving Portsmouth to weekend fishermen, campers, and explorers. The National Park Service restored many of the buildings and preserved them exactly as they were, with the same furnishings in the church, post office, and lifesaving station. They established a visitor center and exhibits in the Dixon/Salter House. Volunteer caretakers live on the island in season to maintain the grounds and buildings and oversee visitation. Some of the homes on the island are leased to individuals in exchange for maintenance and upkeep of the buildings, though no one lives here year-round.

Long ago Portsmouth Village was a thriving port town along the banks of busy Ocracoke Inlet. In 1770 it was the largest settlement on the Outer Banks, bustling to serve the major shipping trade that flowed through Ocracoke Inlet to and from mainland North Carolina. For nearly a century, residents of the town made a living in commerce, serving the shipping industry. Portsmouth was primarily a lightering village, which meant that its residents were responsible for getting heavily laden ships through the inlet by taking off some of their cargo as they approached the inlet and putting it back on

The Portsmouth Island Life Saving Station is perfectly restored.

once the ships were safely through. Portsmouth residents also served as pilots to steer ships through the inlet; ran mercantile stores, restaurants, and hotels; and worked in a hospital for seamen. In its heyday, in the mid-1800s, Portsmouth had more than 500 residents.

Several factors contributed to Portsmouth Village's decline. In 1846 at Hatteras Village and Bodie Island, two, deeper inlets opened, which then steered the shipping industry north. In 1860 many residents fled as Union soldiers marched down the Outer Banks; many of them never returned. After the Civil War most shipping had been diverted to the northern inlets, and the residents turned to fishing. In 1894 the U.S. Life Saving Service established a station at Portsmouth and that provided a few jobs until 1937, when it was decommissioned. As folks moved out of Portsmouth because of its isolation, depressed economy, and the constant threat of storms, no one else moved in. In 1971 there were only three residents left and when one of them died that year, the other two left.

Visiting Portsmouth Village today makes one feel wistful and nostalgic. Preserved as it is, it's so easy to image how wonderful, and yet difficult, it must have been to live on this island outpost. You can enter the 1894 U.S. Life Saving Station, seeing the very bunks the crewmen slept in and climbing to the watch tower to survey the surrounding waters. You can walk past the Life Saving Summer Kitchen, imagining what it must have been like to cook without electricity, refrigeration, or running water. You can enter the 1914 Methodist Church, rebuilt after a 1913 storm demolished both the Methodist and Primitive Baptist Churches. Inside, the church is pristine, and outfitted with pews, hymnals, a piano, and a lectern as if a congregation meets here every Sunday. Today, some people are married in the tiny church. You can peek into the windows of old homes, imagining the people who sat in the chairs and used the things that were left behind. You can enter the old schoolhouse, seeing pictures and report cards and stories of the former students. Visit the 1840 U.S. Post Office in the center of the village, with its general-store counter and rows of mailboxes. The stately, restored Dixon/Salter House welcomes visitors with rest rooms and exhibits about life at Portsmouth Village.

Portsmouth Village also offers opportunities for exploring the outdoors. A 1.2-mile trail leads from the village to the beach. Along the way you'll see the wide marsh flats, a variety of plants, animal tracks, and birds. The beach here is wide and spacious and filled with shells.

Most people visit Portsmouth Village from Ocracoke Island. One ferry service and one tour guide take passengers over from Ocracoke Island (Rudy Austin's Ferry Service and Portsmouth Island ATVs; see the list of ferry operators in the Things to Know chapter). Otherwise you can visit by private boat or kayak. It is sometimes possible to drive from the cabins on the southern end of North Core Banks to Portsmouth, but the route is unreliable as the tidal flats and beach between the two are often flooded at high tide. You may be able to get over on low tide and then wait for another low tide to go back. Depending on the winds and any recent storms, the route may be impassable.

Portsmouth Village has no conveniences and can be a hostile environment on excessively hot, cold, or windy days. Be prepared for unpredictable weather and mosquitoes. Bring your own water (including some for your pets), food, insect repellent, sunscreen, sturdy walking shoes, extra clothing, and camera. Camping is allowed on the island, but not in the village area or within 100 feet of any structure. Obtain a free camping permit at the Portsmouth Village Visitor Center.

Cape Lookout Lighthouse
South Core Banks, Mile 41

Wearing a daymark of black and white diamonds, Cape Lookout Lighthouse stands 163 feet tall on the southern end of South Core Banks. The active beacon warns ships to stay off Lookout Shoals, the site of many shipwrecks and part of the Graveyard of the Atlantic.

The Cape Lookout Lighthouse wears a distinctive black and white diamond daymark.

Congress first authorized a lighthouse for Cape Lookout in 1804, but many years were spent looking for a suitable site. A 107-foot tower was finally constructed and put into service in 1812. It was a wooden building with an interior brick wall and an iron lantern. The wooden exterior was painted with red and white bands. It took thirteen oil lamps and reflectors to produce a light that could be seen 16 miles out to sea. Mariners complained about the tower, as they had about the Cape Hatteras Lighthouse, saying it was too short and the beacon was unreliable.

In 1857 construction began on the second tower, while the original tower remained standing. The new tower, 163 feet tall and left unpainted, was lighted on November 1, 1859 and is still operational today. It was given a first-order Fresnel lens with one oil-burning lamp.

In 1861 a Confederate raiding force damaged the tower and ruined the lens, but it was repaired in 1863. Two years later another group of Confederates dynamited the structure, damaging part of the wooden stairs, which were then replaced with iron stairs. By 1868 the old tower was crumbling. The new lighthouse was painted with its black and white "diagonal checker" pattern in 1873, when it became necessary to give it a daymark to distinguish it from the new lighthouses at Cape Hatteras and Bodie Island. The black diagonal checkers, or diamonds, are aligned north-south, while the white are aligned east-west, which makes the tower look different depending on your point of view.

As a large lighthouse, the Cape Lookout Station had three full-time keepers, including a primary keeper, a first assistant keeper, and a second assistant keeper. The primary keeper occupied one house, while the two assistants shared the double assistant keepers' quarters (this building still stands today). When on duty, the keepers were required to dress in the Lighthouse Service uniform—blue pants, vest, suit jacket, and hat. Their main duty was to fill the lens with oil and light the wick, a trip of 201 steps. Another trip up the stairs was required during the night to refill the oil. During storms and hurricanes, the beacon had to be lighted twenty-four hours a day. Keepers also had to clean and polish the lens, clean the tower windows of salt and ice; maintain the tower, lawn, and houses; paint the lighthouse; and grow and raise their own food.

In 1950 the Cape Lookout Lighthouse was electrified using a generator, so there was no longer a need for an on-site keeper. Today, thanks to an underwater electric cable, it is self-sufficient. The lighthouse has had various flash patterns that helped mariners discern which lighthouse they were approaching. The flash pattern today is one flash of white light every fifteen seconds, and it can be seen 20 miles out to sea.

The Cape Lookout Lighthouse tower is not open for climbing, though the National Park Service is taking it over from the Coast Guard and has long-range plans to open it to the public—someday. The stairs, which were designed for only a few people, will have to be proven safe before the public can climb.

Even though you can't go inside, the lighthouse makes a great photo opportunity and there is much to do around it. In the historic assistant keepers' quarters at the base of the lighthouse is a museum and visitor center that's open from April through November. Exhibits, a bookstore, and rest rooms are located inside. The National Park Service offers special programs here in the summer, and volunteers are on-site to answer questions. Outside, there are boardwalks, picnic facilities, and a great sound beach. The ocean beach is only a couple hundred yards away. Cape Point is about 2 miles to the south, and if you don't want to walk there you can catch a ride on one of the shuttles that park near the lighthouse. The Cape Lookout ferries from Harkers Island drop off passengers at the lighthouse. Remember to bring water and food with you; you will not find any for sale on the island.

Cape Village

South Core Banks, Miles 42–43

Cape Village, south of the lighthouse, is a controversial part of the Cape Lookout National Seashore. It is a loosely defined area with fourteen historic structures, most of which are the getaway camps of local mainland or Harkers Island families. There are no year-round residents on the island today. The structures were established before the national seashore was created. When the NPS took over this land, it became the owner of the camps but agreed to lease them to the private owners for another twenty-five years if the structures were maintained. The leases are expired, but the leaseholders are contesting ownership in court. The National Park Service wants to take over the structures and establish a historic district, but the leaseholders don't want to turn over the property that has been in their families for generations. Who knows where this situation will stand when you visit?

In the meantime you can see the historic structures on a walking or guided driving tour south of the lighthouse. If you're walking, head south of the lighthouse on the interior trail that runs parallel to the ocean, then switch back over toward the sound on the various sand roads. If you want to hear a bit of commentary about the structures, take a guided driving tour with Mule Train Tours or Cape Lookout Tours (see below). The structures are rustic and enchanting, some constructed of shipwreck materials or adorned with colorful buoys. They are simple and efficiently equipped for a life of recreation on the island. You'll notice that pine trees surround the village. The camp owners and a Boy Scout troop planted these trees as a windbreak in the 1970s.

One part of the village is called The Landing, the place where old-timers would anchor their large vessels and come ashore in smaller skiffs or rowboats. The gray two-story structure near The Landing is known as the Barden House, which dates to 1907 when it was primary lightkeeper's quarters of the Cape Lookout Lighthouse. In 1950, when the lighthouse was automated, the Coast Guard sold the building to the Barden family, who relocated it to this point.

Another building in the village is the 1887 Cape Lookout Life Saving Station. This station was built following the wreck of the schooner *Crissie Wright* off Cape Lookout in 1888. There's also the 1917 Coast Guard Station, which replaced the Life Saving Station. The building is now leased by the North Carolina Maritime Museum for the Cape Lookout Studies Program.

For guided tours, contact Cape Lookout Beach Tours at (252) 728–6181, or Mule Train Beach Tours at (252) 504–4121, both on Harkers Island. The tour vehicles are four-wheel-drive trucks with bench seats in the back. Sometimes a trailer is pulled behind the truck to carry more people. Some tour vehicles are shaded. Usually the tour company will conduct an hourlong tour, then drop the tourists off at Cape Point to walk on the beach or look for shells.

Shackleford Banks Wild Horses
Shackleford Banks
www.shacklefordhorses.org

Shackleford Banks is home to a herd of more than a hundred federally protected wild horses, also called Banker ponies. The chestnut and bay horses live an idyllic life, having the 9-mile-long, half-mile wide island all to themselves. It's an amazing sight, in this day and age, to see wild horses, truly free, roaming the dunes, beaches, maritime forest, and marsh flats of an uninhabited, undeveloped coastal island.

Stories abound as to how Spanish-bloodline horses got to Shackleford Banks, but most people believe the horses are the descendants of horses that were brought here during European exploration or that swam ashore during shipwrecks in the sixteenth century.

Geneticists have discovered that the horses have an old variant gene, called Q-ac, which links them to Spanish bloodlines. This makes the wild horses of interest not only to history and animal lovers but also to scientists. Equine geneticists believe it is important to preserve the genetics of this herd. D. I. Rubenstein, Ph.D., chairman of the department of ecology and evolutionary biology at Princeton University, and his graduate students have been studying and documenting the horses and their behavior for more than two decades.

In the summer of 2002 there were 142 horses roaming the island, 122 adults and 20 foals. The adult Shackleford horses range in height from 12 to 13½ hands at the withers (between the neck and back). Some of the horses are bay colored (brown with a black mane and tail), while others are chestnut (reddish brown with the same colored mane and tail). Others have flaxen-blond manes and tails.

With a rigid social behavior pattern, the horses have divided themselves into approximately twenty harems and seven bachelor bands. Harems consist of a dominant adult stallion plus several females and their offspring. When the young colts are about two years old, they are pushed out of the harem. Bachelor bands are groups of young males who have not proven their dominance and therefore do not have female accompaniment. As part of a bachelor band they mature and spar with one another until they are strong

A young bachelor stallion surveys the Shackleford landscape.

enough to challenge stallions and steal mares to start their own harems.

The horses eat grasses, such as Spartina, sea oats, even poison ivy. They drink fresh water from the island's freshwater lens (ground water) and Mullet Pond. The fresh water under the surface of the island often bubbles up in springs, but sometimes the horses have to dig with their hooves to find water.

Each horse's name starts with the same first letter as its mother's name. In recent years, each year's foals have been named in a category, like countries or movie stars. This accounts for horses with names like Judd and DeNiro. The horses rarely live beyond twenty years old.

The National Park Service, in conjunction with the Foundation for Shackleford Horses, manages the herd to keep it natural and wild, with as little human contact as possible. They do not feed, water, medicate, or vaccinate the horses, though they do limit horse reproduction with contraception (given by an immunization dart), and they allow off-island adoption when the herd gets too large for its own good. Horses are chosen for contraception and adoption with the help of the scientists who study the herd.

If you plan to horse-watch, remember these key points:

- The horses are not always in plain view, so you may have to walk quite a way to find them. They are more easily seen on the eastern end of the island where the land is flat, though there are not as many there. Horse-watching is better on the western end, though the land is hilly and the horses may be down in the low swales between the hills. The best way to spot them is to climb the highest hill you can find and look around in every direction. Bring binoculars and good walking shoes. Another way to find the horses is to look for and follow their tracks.

- If you see horses, do not approach too quickly or they will run away. Don't worry about them running off before you get to them. The horses often stay in one place for quite a while, eating, drinking, or resting.
- The horses are wild animals. Though they are used to and unafraid of people, do not try to touch or feed or get too close to them. Getting too close stresses the animals. Feeding can harm them, as they are used to a natural diet of grasses. Also, the horses have a lot more going on than may appear to the casual observer. Two competing males could easily run you over if you happen to be in their way when they decide to spar. Watch from a respectful distance.
- If you want to photograph the horses, bring a zoom lens. A 200m lens will help you stay out of the horses' space.
- Observe how the horses interact. Note stallions and mares and watch their behavioral differences. Notice how, in harems, the mare always decides what to do or where to go while the stallion stays on constant watch to protect his harem. Notice how the bachelor bands of young stallions interact with each other and with the harems.
- Plan for a hostile environment. Always bring water, food, insect repellent, sunscreen, comfortable walking shoes, and appropriate clothing to Shackleford Banks. Composting toilets on the soundside of the west end are the only conveniences on the island. There are interior horse trails on the western end of the island, but they are made of deep sand, which can be very hot in summer. All of the walking on Shackleford is in deep sand, so you'll need comfortable walking shoes, such as boots or running shoes, not flip-flops or sandals.
- If you bring dogs to the island, they must be kept on a leash that is at least 6 feet long.

Park ranger and horse biologist Sue Stuska leads educational horse tours on Shackleford in the summer. Call the Harkers Island Visitor Center for information.

Services and Necessities

Where to Eat on the Mainland

(There are no restaurants, or even vending machines, on the islands of Cape Lookout National Seashore.)

Driftwood Restaurant
N.C. Highway 12, Cedar Island
(252) 225–4861

Morris Marina Bar and Grill
1000 Morris Marina Road, Atlantic
(252) 225–4261

Captain's Choice Restaurant
977 Island Road, Harkers Island
(252) 728–7122

Ruddy Duck Deli and Grill
980 Island Road, Harkers Island
(252) 728–5252

Island Restaurant
1243 Island Road, Harkers Island
(252) 728–2247

Beaufort Grocery Co.
1117 Queen Street, Beaufort
(252) 728–3899

Clawson's 1905 Restaurant
429 Front Street, Beaufort
(252) 728–2133

The Spouter Inn
218 Front Street, Beaufort
(252) 728–5190

Finz Grill of Morehead
105 S. Seventh Avenue,
Morehead City
(252)726–5502

Windansea
708 Evans Street,
Morehead City
(252) 247–3000

Where to Stay on the Mainland

(For cabin rentals on the islands of Cape Lookout National Seashore, see our Camping and Cabins chapter.)

Driftwood Motel, Restaurant and Campground
N.C. Highway 12, Cedar Island
(252) 225–4861
www.clis.com/deg

Harkers Island Fishing Center Motel and Marina
Island Road, Harkers Island
(252) 728–3907
http://harkersmarina.com

Calico Jack's Inn and Marina
Island Road, Harkers Island
(252) 728–3575
www.capelookoutferry.com

Inlet Inn
601 Front Street, Beaufort
(252) 728–3600, (800) 554–5466
www.inlet-inn.com

The Cedars by the Sea
305 Front Street, Beaufort
(252) 728–7036
www.cedarsinn.com

Comfort Inn
3012 Arendell Street, Morehead City
(252) 247–3434, (800) 422–5404
www.moreheadhotels.com

Weekly House Rentals

Cape Lookout Realty
834 Island Road, Harkers Island
(252) 728–2375
www.capelookoutrealty.com

Beaufort Realty
325 Front Street, Beaufort
(252) 728–5462, (800) 548–2961
www.beaufortrlty.com

Grocery and Supply Stores

Island's Choice
158 Ditch Path Road, Cedar Island
(252) 225–0246

Cruise Mart 2 Red & White
814 South Seashore Drive, Atlantic
(252) 225–0191

Grover's Country Store and Deli
U.S. Highway 70 East, Davis
(252) 729–1893

East'ard Variety Store
1344 Island Road, Harkers Island
(252) 728–7149

Food Lion
1901 Live Oak Street, Beaufort
(252) 504–2442

Medical Services

Eastern Carteret Medical Center
U.S. Highway 70, Sea Level
(252) 225–1134

Carteret General Hospital
3500 Arendell Street, Morehead City
(252) 247–1616, (252) 247–1540 (emergency room)

Veterinarians

Carteret Animal Hospital
814 West Beaufort Road, Beaufort
(252) 728–7600

Live Oak Veterinary Hospital
210 Campen Road, Beaufort
(252) 504–2097

Arendell Animal Hospital
213 Commerce Avenue, Morehead City
(252) 726–4998

Nearby Attractions

Cape Lookout National Seashore is close to a number of other attractions of interest.

Core Sound Waterfowl Museum
Island Road, Harkers Island
(252) 728–1500
www.coresound.com

This "working-man's museum" is a gem that pays homage to Harkers Island and Down East traditions. By the time you read this, the museum will have moved from its small house in the village to a massive lodge near the NPS Visitor Center. The people of Harkers Island and Down East have spent years fund-raising and preparing for their island museum to move to the new building in the spring of 2003. The building itself is remarkable for its architecture and the fact that it was built entirely by grassroots efforts. There will be some exhibits in the museum at opening, though it may take a while for the complete masterpiece to come to fruition.

The main focus of the museum is decoy carving, and if you're lucky you might catch a local carver at work on the porch. Sit down in one of the rocking chairs and chat with the carver for a while. You'll learn more about the culture of the island than you ever would anywhere else. Inside, the museum displays decoys from many of the regional greats plus the blue-ribbon pieces from all the past competitions. Other elements of island life are worked into the exhibits: duck hunting, boatbuilding, shrimping, commercial fishing, pony penning, and the like. A traditional boathouse and locally built wooden fishing boat are inside the museum.

Inside the rambling building is a staircase that leads to a tower with views of Core Sound and Cape Lookout National Seashore. The museum gift shop sells decoys, decorative bird carvings, cookbooks, books about the region, stationery, art, and much more, all with a waterfowl or coastal theme.

The Harvey W. Smith Watercraft Center is a standout on the Beaufort waterfront.

Rachel Carson Component of the National Estuarine Research Reserve
Beaufort
(252) 728–2170

This reserve is a series of several estuarine islands, extensive salt marshes, and tidal flats. The site is between the mouths of the Newport and North Rivers, across Taylor's Creek from the Beaufort waterfront. It is named after the naturalist and writer who conducted research here and wrote books that made people aware of the importance of the coastal ecosystems. The locals often refer to the islands as Bird Shoals or Carrot Island, the names they formerly held. The islands are home to feral horses (descendants of domesticated horses) and about 160 bird species. Visitors like to kayak or boat over to the islands from the Beaufort waterfront to explore the landscape and wildlife or swim and sunbathe. You can rent kayaks on the waterfront. Some ferry companies on the Beaufort waterfront will also drop you off on the island. In summer, tours of the island are conducted; call the number above.

North Carolina Maritime Museum
315 Front Street, Beaufort
(252) 728–7317
www.ah.dcr.state.nc.us/sections/maritime/default.htm

North Carolina has a rich maritime history of boatbuilding, piracy, commercial fishing, shipwrecks, and lifesaving. This museum does an outstanding job of teaching about this maritime history as well as the natural history of the North Carolina coast. The 18,000-square-foot center has exhibits on many aspects of maritime and natural history, including displays on shells, fossils, coastal plants and animals, indigenous watercraft, Blackbeard, and shipwreck artifacts. In the Harvey W. Smith Watercraft Center visitors can watch boat restoration or building in progress. In the John S. MacCormack Model Shop, visitors can see model builders constructing scale models of boats and ships. There are also educational programs at the museum. Boat-building classes as well as environmental education field trips and camps are offered. The museum runs the Cape Lookout Studies Program in the old Coast Guard Station at Cape Lookout National Seashore (see the Other Adventures chapter). There's also a Junior Sailing Program and a Summer Science School for kids.

Beaufort Historic Site
100 Block of Turner Street, Beaufort
(252) 728–5225, (800) 575–SITE
www.historicbeaufort.com

The seaside town of Beaufort is quite charming, thanks to a bustling waterfront harbor and a wealth of historic homes and buildings. The town is made for strolling around, browsing in shops, eating in fine restaurants, and visiting historic sites, cemeteries, museums, and art galleries. Ten of the town's historic buildings have been authentically restored to what they were when the town was incorporated in 1723. These are part of the Beaufort Historic Site and include the old courthouse, the old jailhouse, an apothecary and doctor's office, and several private homes. They can be toured for a taste of history. One of the best parts of the Beaufort Historic Site is the Old Burying Ground on Ann Street, a cemetery that dates to 1731. Start your tour of the Beaufort Historic Site at the Safrit Historical Center at 138 Turner Street, where you can get maps and see exhibits and a video presentation. If you want to take a guided walking tour, you can sign up for one here. Guided tours are recommended because of all the stories and history the docents tell.

Fort Macon State Park
N.C. Highway 58, Mile Marker 0, Atlantic Beach
(252) 726–3775

Just across Beaufort Inlet from the west end of Shackleford Banks is Fort Macon State Park, on the easternmost end of Bogue Banks. The location has held several forts that were used in pre-Revolutionary times against the Spanish, in the Revolutionary War, the War of 1812, the Civil War, the Spanish-American War, and World War II. Today the fort is decommissioned and is a state park. You can tour it with a self-guided tour map or with a guide. The fort and a museum are open daily. Re-enactments are sometimes held, as are various talks and programs on the military and war. The rest of the park includes an incredible stretch of beach with amenities like rest rooms, a bathhouse, refreshment stands, picnic facilities, and a nature trail. Shelling is great on this part of the island.

N.C. Aquarium at Pine Knoll Shores
N.C. Highway 58, Mile Marker 7, Pine Knoll Shores
(252) 247–4003
www.ncaquariums.com

Anyone interested in sea life and coastal ecology should visit one of the three North Carolina Aquariums. This one, in Pine Knoll Shores on Bogue Banks, is about fifteen or twenty minutes from Beaufort, a worthy diversion if you have the time. The aquarium displays a variety of fish and sea life in a number of coastal North Carolina habitats, both salt and fresh water. One of the most interesting exhibits is a 12,000-gallon saltwater tank with a shipwreck and the fish that live around it. The hands-on touch tank for kids is also popular. There are indoor and outdoor exhibits plus a nature trail, kids' programs, and environmental education programs.

Annual Events

North Carolina Blackbeard Festival, Morehead City and Beaufort; (252) 808–0440. Annual festival with pirate lore, films, tours, food, family events, and more. Held in May.

Wooden Boat Show, North Carolina Maritime Museum, Beaufort; (252) 728–6894. Largest gathering of wooden watercraft in the Southeast, demonstrations, races, lectures. Held in May.

Beaufort Homes and Gardens Tour, Beaufort; (252) 728–5225. Forty-third annual event in 2003, offering tours of private homes and gardens. Held in June.

North Carolina Seafood Festival, Morehead City; (252) 726–6273. Legendary celebration of seafood prepared a hundred ways, plus music and family entertainment. Held in October.

Core Sound Waterfowl Weekend, Core Sound Waterfowl Museum, Harkers Island; (252) 728–1500. Exhibits, competitions, arts, crafts, food. Held first weekend in December.

Core Sound Decoy Festival, Harkers Island; (252) 726–8367. Carving, painting decoys, exhibits and sales of decoys, loon-calling contest, children's activities, auction. Held first weekend in December.

Bibliography

Alexander, John, and James Lazell. *Ribbon of Sand.* Chapel Hill and London: University of North Carolina Press, 1992 and 2000.

Cape Hatteras National Seashore. *In the Park.* Summer issue, 2002.

Cape Lookout National Seashore. Summer issue, 2002.

Cook, Craig. "A Guide to Diving the Top Five Offshore Wrecks," *The Island Breeze* 12, (August 2002): no. 22–25.

DeBlieu, Jan. *Hatteras Journal.* Winston-Salem, N.C.: John F. Blair, Publisher, 1998.

Fussell, John O. III. *A Birder's Guide to Coastal North Carolina.* Chapel Hill and London: University of North Carolina Press, 1994.

Goldstein, Robert J. *Coastal Fishing in the Carolinas from Surf, Pier, and Jetty*, 3rd ed. Winston-Salem, N.C.: John F. Blair, Publisher, 2000.

Malec, Pam. *Guide to Sea Kayaking in North Carolina.* Guilford, Conn.: The Globe Pequot Press, 2001.

Payne, Roger L. *Place Names of the Outer Banks.* Washington, N.C.: Thomas A. Williams, Publisher, 1985.

Pilkey, Orrin H. Jr., William J. Neal, and Orrin H. Pilkey Sr. *From Currituck to Calabash: Living with North Carolina's Barrier Islands.* Research Triangle Park, N.C.: North Carolina Science and Technology Research Center, 1978.

Schoenbaum, Thomas J. *Islands, Capes, and Sounds.* Winston-Salem, N.C.: John F. Blair, Publisher: 1982.

Schumann, Marguerite. *The Living Land.* Chapel Hill: Dale Press, 1977.

Stick, David. *The Cape Hatteras Seashore.* Charlotte and Santa Barbara: MacNally and Loftin, Publishers, 1964.

———. *Graveyard of the Atlantic.* Chapel Hill: University of North Carolina Press, 1952.

———. *The Outer Banks of North Carolina.* Chapel Hill: University of North Carolina Press, 1958.

Stick, David, ed. *An Outer Banks Reader.* Chapel Hill and London: University of North Carolina Press, 1998.

———. "Cape Hatteras National Seashore." Collection of personal narratives on file with the Outer Banks History Center Manteo, North Carolina, 1987–1997.

Williamson, Sonny. *The Lookout Adventure.* Marshallberg, N.C.: Grandma Publications, 1999.

Index

About the Author

Freelance writer and editor Molly Harrison lives in Nags Head, North Carolina, a mile north of the entrance to Cape Hatteras National Seashore. Her love of the outdoors takes her into the national seashores often, whether it's for camping, fishing, clamming, biking, running, hiking, walking her dog, swimming, searching for shells and sea glass, exploring historic sites, or researching a story. She has written extensively about the history, attractions, activities, people, and stories of the Outer Banks and is the author of the twenty-third edition of *Insiders' Guide to North Carolina's Outer Banks*, the *Manteo Walking Tour and Roanoke Island Guide*, *Corolla Then and Now: A Walking Tour and Guide*, and the forthcoming *It Happened on the Outer Banks.*